Kaandossiwin

Kaandossiwin

How We Come to Know

Kathleen E. Absolon
(Minogiizhigokwe)

Fernwood Publishing • Halifax & Winnipeg

Photos by Kathy Absolon, unless otherwise specified
Editing: Brenda Conroy
Cover design: John van der Woude
Printed and bound in Canada by Hignell Book Printing

Published in Canada by Fernwood Publishing
32 Oceanvista Lane
Black Point, Nova Scotia, B0J 1B0
and 748 Broadway Avenue, Winnipeg, Manitoba, R3G 0X3
www.fernwoodpublishing.ca

Fernwood Publishing Company Limited gratefully acknowledges the financial support of the
Government of Canada through the Canada Book Fund, the Canada Council for the Arts,
the Nova Scotia Department of Tourism and Culture, the Manitoba Department of Culture,
Heritage and Tourism under the Manitoba Publishers Marketing Assistance Program and the
Province of Manitoba, through the Book Publishing Tax Credit, for our publishing program.

Library and Archives Canada Cataloguing in Publication

Absolon, Kathleen E., 1961-
Kaandosswin : how we come to know / Kathleen E. Absolon
(Minogiizhigokwe).

Includes bibliographical references.
ISBN 978-1-55266-440-7

1. Native peoples--Research--Canada--Methodology. 2. Indians
of North America--Research--Methodology. 3. Research--
Methodology. I. Title.

E76.7.A26 2011   305.897'071072   C2011-903222-8

Contents

This book is dedicated to

My Cocomish and Shaumish, who have gone home to the Spirit world. They knew how to search the Anishinaabe way. Their Spirits inspire me to remember who we are, what we know and where we come from. They wanted us to know our identity and language as Anishinaabe and would have wanted these understandings and knowledge passed on.

My children: Amanda (M'skwa jidamookwe), Aki (Giizhigokwe) and Cody (Mshiikenh), who supported my countless hours of searching and writing and whose patience allowed me space to get the job done. I love you all!

My parents, who taught me how to *not* get lost in the bush and for the opportunity to grow up with the space and freedom that living close to the land affords. My sisters (Debbie, Jo-anne and Christine) and brother (Mark), who supported me through tough times.

My partner Hilton, who is always there to dust me off, to help me and to love me. You teach me to walk a little slower, have patience and laugh along the way.

And to all those searchers, gatherers and hunters who are coming along the path. I dedicate this to you. Remember who you are and don't get lost!

Acknowledgements

Chi miigwech Creator for guiding me on this frightful, exciting and learned journey. *Miigwech* for blessing me with the abilities and resources to undertake this search. *Miigwech* for your guidance, love, protection and gifts along the way. *Miigwech* for the dreams, ceremonies, teachers and teachings as I searched and gathered. *Miigwech* for the memories of how to not get lost and for helping me find my way home. This book was a long and challenging process and there are many helpers and supports to thank.

To my eldest *daanis* (daughter), Amanda: I am grateful for her maturity and her own academic goals as she completed an undergraduate degree at Ryerson University and moved on to her graduate studies at York. *Miigwech* for your editorial support and feedback. It was most valuable and appreciated. I love you and am so proud of you and your accomplishments. *Ndaanis* (my daughter) Akiesha and *ngwis* (my son) Cody witnessed most of my process of gathering and searching. I would like to thank them for being who they are. They would ask me from time to time when would I be done and really inquiring when I would be free. I would show them what I was doing and explain my process. Thank you for asking and for caring enough to see how it was going. I love you both and see how special you both really are. My daughters Amanda and Akiesha assisted me with tedious editorial tasks and I am grateful for their contributions. *Miigwech* to my partner, Wahmahtig for his support, understanding and love. I am truly blessed. *Miigwech* to my mother, who read and affirmed the knowledge, experiences and history presented in this book. *Miigwech* to my father for teaching me to be strong and for the words of support. My brothers and sisters cheered me on and kept me grounded as I was reminded about the importance of our families, children and communities. Ultimately, through our work this is *who* we serve.

Miigwech to my doctoral committee members for their mentorship and support: Dr. Laara Fitznor, Dr. Jean Paul Restoule and Dr. Eileen Antone. *Miigwech* to Laara, who supported me during my doctoral studies and who attended my sessions at the Shawane Dagosiwin Conferences. *Miigwech* to Dr. Angela Miles for all her time and energy in providing feedback, advice and guidance. *Miigwech* for the tea and sandwiches when eating and sharing seemed more appropriate than thesis analysis. *Miigwech* to all of you for the conversations, feasting and learning along the way.

And I am indebted to those who shared with me. I acknowledge those Indigenous re-searchers who left solid footprints and whose path I could follow because of their work. I also acknowledge the people who participated in this search and who generously shared their knowledge and wisdom with me. And congratulations to those that completed their doctoral theses! I hope that this book is what you too can feel proud of. I thoroughly enjoyed our conversations and felt supported and inspired in my journey. It's an amazing circle. I am privileged to be a part of it.

I also acknowledge those helpers along the way whose support helped me complete this: Denise, Brock, Jean, Bill and Tina. My team at Wilfrid Laurier University in the Faculty of Social Work, Aboriginal Field of Study supported me to work on this project. *Miigwech* to my team: Mac, Dorothy, Laura, Diana and Charisse. *Miigwech* to Wayne and Brenda and the team at Fernwood for all your support for how I write and who I write for. I felt accompanied by many people, Spirits and sacred beings who walked and carried me on this incredible journey of learning and sharing.

Finally, we never really walk alone and there are many other teachers, Elders, friends and community members who walk with me and who have supported my journey. *Miigwech* to my community, Flying Post First Nation for all their support. *Miigwech* to my many Anishinaabe, brothers and sisters across Turtle Island (Edna M. and Kathy B. of Earth Medicine, Brenda C., Rejean P., Carrie T., Bob A., Shelley C., Shelley S., Violet C., Susan D. and Gale C.). *Miigwech* for placing me in your prayers and for the long distance phone calls and support. *Miigwech* for encouraging me to persevere and persist on a journey that can, at times, feels lonely and alienating. You know who you are and because of your heartened support I continued.

Preface

Boozhoo nindiwaynimaaginidok. Chi miigwechiwendam noongiizhgad. (Greetings to all my relations. I am grateful today.) My fingers slowly strike the keyboard and I feel uncertain about how to begin to explain my intentions for this book. An internal hurdle creeps in. One of my grade school report cards stated: "Kathy is a pleasant girl but should not expect to be successful." That report card exposes the working place I was *supposed* to occupy in society. Today, I feel empowered and triumphant that I, that "supposedly unsuccessful" Indian child, would be publishing a book on Indigenous ways of coming to know. I want other Indigenous peoples to see and know that who we are, what we know and where we come from matters. I want them to see possibilities. "Kaandossiwin, how we come to know" exemplifies one possibility.

Many people encouraged me to publish my doctoral thesis because we need more books that validate Indigenous ways of searching for knowledge. The scary thing is that how we come to know is living and fluid, not concrete and fixed like typeset words. I trust that this book is part of a larger process where Indigenous searchers are articulating the spaces where voices and knowing reside but were never allowed to be heard. Until exposure to knowledge occurs, you don't know what you don't know. This book is important because colonizing knowledges have attempted to silence Indigenous ways of coming to know and have fabricated false notions that Indigenous methodologies do not exist. I contest those notions in this book. Creating space on how we come to know is what this book is about. *Kaandossiwin* is an Anishinaabe word that describes a process of how we come to know, a process of acquiring knowledge. It is a living word. This book is about *kaandossiwin* and speaks to journeys of learning, being and doing. I present Indigenous ways of searching (research methodologies) and share some of the diverse and varied ways that conscious Indigenous re-searchers are conducting research within the academy. My commitment is to honour Indigenous re-searchers, knowledge and ways of producing knowledge.

I am now presenting this book as an offering, much like an offering of a blueberry pie after the searching, gathering and sorting is done. This offering is to those who themselves are knowledge seekers and those who are searching for ways of knowing that wholistically include the spirit, heart, mind and body. My blueberry pie is now ready to share. As an avid berry picker myself, I know that I have spent months contemplating and preparing to search. Searching for the best berries, the mothership of berries, takes preparation, perseverance and patience. Travelling and searching for blueberries is very much like re-search. Searching the land for berries is hard work and picking

I am an avid berry picker and I search for the bluest berries

the berries is even harder. After gathering baskets and baskets of the bluest berries, I sorted them, organized them and prepared them for jam, pies, tarts and sauce so that I could share my harvest with others. This book is a culmination of my search for knowledge on how we come to know. This is my blueberry pie offering. I hope you enjoy it!

Chapter One

Preparing to Search

Boozhoo G-chi'manidoo...
Minogiizhigokwe n'dizhnikas...
Waabshishii n'dodem...
Niizhoo midewiwin
Anishinaabekwe n'dow
Kakatush Ziibiing Flying Post n'doonjiba
(Minogiizhigokwe)

Indigenous re-search is often guided by the knowledge found within.
Aboriginal epistemology (the ways of knowing our reality) honours our inner
being as the place where Spirit lives, our dreams reside and our heart beats.
Indigenous peoples have processes in place to tap into this inner space and
to make the unknown — known (Ermine 1995). This is a key Indigenous
methodological principle (Rigney 1999). Indigenous re-search methodology has been a process for me, whereby I make the invisible — visible.
Colonization has attempted to make our realities invisible and has tried to
turn us into the disappearing race. Alongside other Indigenous re-searchers,
I contest the notion that we are a vanquished race or remnants of the past.
This re-search and my work as a community helper have further convinced
me that our role and responsibility rests in sustaining a valid, visible and
thriving existence for our peoples in the present and future. We exist and
we are here. Our knowledge is valid, real and concrete. I do not make comparisons with eurowestern methods of searching. There is no need to. There
are many pathways to knowledge. My hope is that this book will contribute
to establishing the visibility and knowledge of Indigenous methodologies in
search for knowledge in the academy and elsewhere.

Kaandossiwin, How We Come to Know results from a search for Indigenous
methodologies by graduate Indigenous re-searchers in the academy. It
describes the diverse and varied ways and experiences of Indigenous academic re-searchers employing their worldviews. Actively engaging Indigenous
worldviews in methodology has also been called Indigenist re-search (Rigney
1999; Smith 2005). This is a search for Indigenous ways of coming to know
in the academy, and the harvest of this search is wholistically presented as
a petal flower with roots (worldview), centre flower (self), leaves (journey),
stem (analytical backbone) and petals (methods). Petal flowers are as varied
as Indigenous re-search methodologies; thus the type of flower is undefined.

Soon after beginning this project I realized that the re-searchers' experiences were as important as the methodologies they used and that the two were interdependent. Thus, I also explore the environmental context that influences Indigenous searchers' ability or inability to employ Indigenous ways of searching.

This book is a result of a search into eleven selected theses by Indigenous graduate re-searchers in adult education, social work, Indigenous studies and sociology; conversations with Indigenous re-searchers in the academy; and a learning circle of Indigenous re-searchers. It is not exhaustive by any means but rather provides a general sense of Indigenous re-search methodologies used by graduate Indigenous re-searchers. Graduate theses provided a ready source of information about the context of Indigenous re-search projects in terms of the use of Indigenous re-search methodologies and student experiences of Indigenous re-search in the academy. Their successful completion evidences an acceptance within the academy and establishes precedence of the application and legitimacy of Indigenous knowledge and methodologies.

Locating My Self in My Search

I begin by locating my self because positionality, storying and re-storing ourselves come first (Absolon and Willett 2005; Graveline 2004; Lather 1991; Sinclair 2003; Weber-Pillwax 2001; Wilson 2003). Where I come from you are either White or Métis or Native. People know who I am. I am one of the daughters of Jennie (nee Cryer) and David Absolon. When my mother married my father, she became dismembered and lost her Indian status. Earlier, from the ages of six to thirteen, she also became dismembered from her family and community when she was forced to attend Chapleau St. John's Anglican Residential School. My maternal grandparents were Lizzie (nee Pigeon) and Shannon Cryer from Shawmere Lake, Ontario — they were both Anishinaabe and are now in the Spirit world. Our ancestors lived and travelled up and down the Groundhog and Nat Rivers in Northern Ontario. My paternal grandparents were Kathleen (nee Woodcock) and Jack Absolon, and they had always lived in England. They too are in the Spirit world. My dad came to Canada at age twenty-one and met my mother at a dance in Winnipeg. They have been married for fifty-four years now. My blend is of both the Anishinaabe and english nations, and I belong to Flying Post First Nation. Flying Post First Nation has a land base on the Groundhog and Nat Rivers. I belong to the Three Fires Society Midewiwin Lodge. I am of the Marten Clan and also a close relation to the Bear Clan people.

I grew up at Cranberry Lake, Ontario, which is a Canadian National Railway (CNR) signal posting. Cranberry Lake is located between Sudbury and Parry Sound. The passing trains used to make our living room lamps shake.

Today, trains chugging along the tracks send off a sound that is comforting to me. I remember counting the boxcars as they rumbled past our house. We lived so close to the tracks that I felt the earth tremble as the train passed "Here comes a train," we would yell, and I often raised my arms, tilted at the elbow, with my hand in a fist gesturing for the train conductor to blow the horn. Holy smokes, that horn was loud, yet hearing it evoked a big smile and wave, and I'd run off feeling good that the conductor understood and waved back.

This photo shows me sitting with my mother, Jennie Absolon (nee Cryer), and my father, David Absolon. Their loving blend makes me who I am today. (Photo by Hilton King)

Cranberry Lake is in the bush; not in a town or a reserve. I lived among the trees, swamps, lakes, bulrushes, bears, snakes and wildflowers. My socialization was dominated with bush immersion, which, as you will see, plays a central role in who I am and how I search for knowledge.

I went to elementary school in a small town called Britt and then to high school in Parry Sound. Making long bus commutes were our daily reality. There were no Indigenous teachers or curriculum at my schools. My education was filled with racist representations of Indigenous people, and I vividly remember shrinking in my chair while the teacher rambled on about Indian savages and how uncivilized we were. I remember being unfairly treated by teachers, and in grade four was tossed across the classroom (with my desk being tossed too) because a White girl said I stole her book. I wasn't asked, just tossed across the room. I really disliked going to that school.

When I was small, I asked my mom what type of Indian we were. She said, "We are Ojibwa Indians." And I asked her if that was good. She said yes and that there were a lot of Ojibwa Indians here and that our nation was a big one. I felt so proud to hear that and to know that I belonged to a strong nation. School never taught me that. The friends that I have are lifelong, people who have known me since elementary school. That is quite a privilege today. Most of my friends were other Anishinaabe girls, and we hung out with one another at school. After-school socializing was not an option for my siblings and me because the bus dropped us off at the highway and we returned to our home at the CNR posting. Our after-school play was to venture into the bush and build forts and tarzan swings and explore. I

My Cocomish, Elizabeth Cryer (nee Pigeon), and my Shaumish, Shannon Cryer, wanted us to know who we are. They are both in the Spirit World.

come from a humble place without malls, movie theatres, restaurants and commercial outlets. That solid bush kid who loved the land, lakes and trees is still within me in my very different context today.

I want my words to reflect my way of thinking, being and doing, and it's difficult at times to balance what I think I'm supposed to write with my sense of self, so I get knotted up inside. I began to connect my aching back with my own history and the reasons why this book feels important. Yes, there are bunched up knots in my personal and political history, and I thought about the years of suppression of my cultural identity and traditions. The body ache is connected to other aches that are exposed through this book. I too have felt dismembered from my grandparents, Cocomish and Shaumish, and from the members of my own community. The aches and pains of being dismembered as a people and being severed from our families of origin, as was the case in my family with residential schools and the reservation system, runs deep. I missed having aunts, uncles, grandparents and cousins around me. We were severed from them and their ability to transfer their knowledge to us. I thought about my grandparents, their lives and what they would have wanted us to know. I want my children to know something about being Anishinaabe. I want them to know about their Anishinaabe culture, and I feel that is what my grandparents would have wanted us to pass on.

To remember who we are and where we come from as Anishinaabe is an act of resistance against being dismembered.

Shaumish (my grandfather) walked on the land searching for food. As he walked he talked to the Spirits of the land. He saw the ancestors and acknowledged their presence in his life. He journeyed the rivers and lakes in Northern Ontario, fishing, trapping and hunting. Shaumish was a proud Anishinaabe *nini* (Ojibwa man) who must have felt so angered and disempowered by the forced removal of his children to residential schools. It was my shaumish, in my dreams, who ushered me to the doorway of our traditional lodge. It was he who told me, in a dream, to tune into my own journey with the Spirits. It was my shaumish who showed me the path. He was a strong man, yet his life was disrespected and he was treated like an insignificant stupid Indian. What must he have thought or felt? I don't have the answers; I can only speculate what he must have gone through, and my speculations probably don't do justice to his truth. My *Shaumish* was a very smart man though.

My grandmother, we called her Cocomish, worked hard and only took small breaks in her day. Her cabin was small and I loved her old jam cupboard where she made dumplings and rabbit stew. A trapper's wife works hard to keep wood chopped, the cabin warm and food bubbling on the old cooking stove. Silence was her friend and she would sit looking out her cabin window twiddling her thumbs, seemingly lost in her thoughts. She seemed so calm. Her energy was soothing, but her dark brown eyes reflected a pain that I will never completely comprehend. What must she have felt when her children were removed from her arms and sent to the residential school? My mother told me that she remembers her mother and father standing outside of the residential school gates. My mother was crying. She wanted to go with her parents, but wasn't allowed. Cocomish must have been in such anguish to have to leave her children there. I loved how my Cocomish was and felt safe with her. When my grandparents returned to the Spirit world, in my grief I knew that our loss would never be fully acknowledged or understood. Now, my Cocomish holds me when I feel lonely and uncertain in this world. She comes to me and cuddles me in her arms telling me that I am not alone. In doing so, she gives me love and support to continue on my path even though, at times, it feels too difficult. Both Cocomish and Shaumish have travelled with me during the most difficult journeys I have taken. Their pain is also my pain.

I grew up in the bush, so in a literal sense there were no fences in my world. There were no neighbours' fences or boundaries other than natural ones. My siblings and I wandered where we wanted and did what we wanted. There were no critical or judging gazes watching us. Because even our parents were out of sight most of the time, we grew up without "shoulds" or "codes of conduct" and without feelings of inferiority, condemnation or ridicule. Trees don't dictate how you should be; they just let you be. The same goes for the creeks, lakes, rocks and animals. Well, the animals want to be respected, as does all of Creation, and so if you move around Creation in a manner that demonstrates respect for other life forms, you will be okay. I grew up knowing that the Spirits were all around me, and when I walked into the bush, I talked to the Spirits of the trees, plants, creatures and I felt safe. I somehow knew that they would not hurt me and that if harm was coming my way the trees would protect me. Sometimes I would imagine a wolf creeping up on me and the trees would swipe it away and scare it off and I wouldn't know a thing. I felt safeguarded by the trees and for this I was thankful. It was my immersion with the land that taught me to trust the life that the land had to offer. I knew that our life came from the land and that this was the knowledge that my grandparents and mother had. Ever since I can remember I've known that the land has educated and sustained our people. There has never been a time when I have forgotten my or my peoples' relationship to the land. My family knows that I love being on the land and have always made time for this.

When I need to find ways to balance the demands of contemporary stressors, like work and more complex lifestyles, I return to the land. I love to be where the earth touches my feet, the trees are visible and I can see the water. These do not exist in the hallways of academia. Am I getting lost? I remembered that this book is for my grandparents: Cocomish and Shaumish. Sometimes the reasons we end up doing what we do are simple, yet the journey is infinite, without a beginning or an ending, just phases in between. My maternal grandparents are central to my search. Cocomish and Shaumish had the knowledge, the language, the traditions and the life on the land. They knew about searching for knowledge and knew how to do it. Both were fluent Anishinaabe speakers, and both had survived and lived in balance with the land. They had what many of us are now searching for, and their life was disregarded and torn apart. I wondered why their presence in my life felt so strong. My doctoral research, I realized, was a means to what they really want me to do: to join other Indigenous voices and carry our knowledge forward. Searching for information and knowledge is not new to us. Indigenous knowledge should never have been eradicated, dismissed, omitted, exploited or abused. My grandparents want me to continue to be Anishinaabe *kwe* and to help Anishinaabe people regain their rightful place within humanity. Acknowledging the source of my ache soothes it and I continue.

I know I am here to leave Anishinaabe footprints so others don't get lost or forget who we are. I also know I am not a novice to searching and learning. All my life I have been searching: for those cultural mirrors, for like-minded

Spirits, for kindness in the world, for a sense of belonging, for acceptance and for knowledge. Oh how thirsty I was to learn about what happened to our people. It was like I was born into a time where the cyclone had hit and the people were still walking around in states of trauma. No one could explain to me what happened. No one could connect the dots between my personal chaos and the political, institutional and cultural attacks against Indigenous peoples in Canada. No one could explain because everyone was reeling from the colonial aftermath. It wasn't until I was in my early twenties that I began to meet other Anishinaabe people who were involved in our cultural ways. It was only then that I slowly started to see what it was that my grandparents would have wanted me to know. It was then that I started to realize the beauty of being Anishinaabe and the richness of our culture. Coupled with my relationship to the land and love for the Creator, being reintroduced to the Anishinaabe teachings and traditions helped me understand the nature of my existence on this earthwalk.

Growing up immersed in the bush was a gift, and because of that strong foundation I resisted being fenced into eurowestern ways of knowing, being and doing. From the land I came to understand and know what freedom really feels like, and now I want to tell my stories in my way, even if it means using my authentically Anishinaabe english voice and grammar. I was raised by an Ojibway/Anishinaabe mother whose first language was Anishinaabemowin and who was forced to learn english. Anishinaabemowin is grammatically different than english. I speak from an Anishinaabe worldview, but in english. That is who I am. I write from a place, in a way that says I am Anishinaabe and I am also english. I now restore myself by re-storying myself into my doctoral journey on how we search for knowledge.

Decolonizing and Indigenizing My Re-search

My own experiences as an Anishinaabe *kwe* and an Indigenous searcher led me in the creation of this book. Experiences, thoughts and feelings about who I am are a result of cultural, political, social and spiritual effects in my life. I have been socialized in a dominant culture and in Anishinaabe culture and have been thinking about decolonization for many years. Like Indigenous Australian scholar Lester Rigney (1999: 116), my lived experiences enable me to "speak on the basis of these experiences and [they] are powerful instruments by which to measure the equality and social justice of society." I have always identified as an Anishinaabe person, and my first experiences with racism were because I am visibly Ojibwa, with brown skin, dark eyes and hair. I was treated poorly by teachers in my school and teased by White kids in the schoolyard. These were mainly felt and lived experiences without much reflection, analysis or critique. My Spirit and heart always felt Anishinaabe, but my political and social awakening as an Anishinaabe person happened when I was about twenty-four years old. I began to be introduced to cultural teachings, gatherings and Aboriginal cultural leaders and critical thinkers. Through my conversations with Aboriginal leaders I began to develop a historical, race, gendered and colonial consciousness about who I was and am as an Aboriginal person. Additionally, the beauty of my culture, its teachings and life philosophies led me on a healing journey out of internalized inferiority.

Like all the re-searchers recognized in this project, the politics of decolonization and indigenizing is a conscious and necessary part of the journey. "You don't know what you don't know" is a phrase I find myself repeating over and over. What I mean is that colonization has attempted to eradicate every aspect of who we are. Colonizing knowledge dominates, ignorance prevails, and we internalize how and who the colonizers want us to be. Seeking my own truth meant opening up all aspects of my being to seeing what I missed and acknowledging that "I don't know what I don't know." So I had to deal with my own ignorance about who I am and I had to learn to see what was rendered invisible, which was our whole way of life as Anishinaabek. For me, indigenizing has involved rediscovering and nurturing my Anishinaabe Spirit, healing my Anishinaabe heart, decolonizing my mind and creating a critical action plan in my own life. Decolonization and indigenizing my life includes learning and practising my culture; learning my language; speaking my language; fighting ethnocentrism in education, research and writing; battling institutional racism; and the list goes on. Decolonization and indigenizing is about both knowing and having a critical consciousness about our cultural history.

When I was a graduate student it was important and possible to tackle decolonization in Indigenous re-search methodology. The work of Linda Tuhiwai Smith (1999) inspired me to further study Aboriginal ways of searching and has provided a foundational basis for my work. Decolonizing is arduous work and full of contradictions. At a personal level decolonization means examining the inherent conflicts within myself: I am Anishinaabe and english. I am decolonizing in a colonial education system and am doing so in english, the colonizers' language. I seek to advance Indigenous knowledge systems in a mainstream education system. Doing a research project on Indigenous re-search methodology is an act of decolonization as I claim my own Aboriginality and Indigenous knowledge. For example, I now see that Indigenous ways of searching were taught to me a long time ago and those teachings occurred in the bush. Indigenous searchers, like myself, experience frustration, anger, oppression and conflict within the academy when attempts to indigenize our research, methodologies and learning are met with antagonism and resistance by the gatekeepers of colonizing forms of knowledge production. Indigenous methodologies are often not perceived as valid forms of knowledge production within western science, and therefore not taken seriously. This needs to change. Additionally, as a community practitioner I have coordinated community-based research projects with several First Nations communities. Although the context of each is different, these research projects began with similar methodologies before developing into processes with their own life. Each community in its distinctness ended up gaining knowledge in different ways. In keeping with Aboriginal principles, worldviews and values, each community's reality was respected and each community's ownership of their research process was honoured. As a community-based researcher, I have witnessed the fear and suspicion Aboriginal people have about research, especially when carried out by academic researchers. Also, I have seen community-based researchers embrace research as a community development tool once they learned about and saw the value of research for themselves. When First Nations create research methods that are in accordance with their own priorities, philosophies and traditions, they are using Indigenous methodologies and research practices. Voyeurism, outsider interpretation, objectification of culture and reductionist analysis become non-issues when the research is owned and controlled by respectful Aboriginal researchers.

I have journeyed with fear, ignorance, suspicion and trepidation about research. I have also journeyed toward developing critical analysis, personal groundedness and courage about re-search. After all, my main goal in my education and re-search is to empower, privilege and elevate Aboriginal knowledge, epistemologies, paradigms, philosophies, practices and methods. We have for too long relied on the outsiders' interpretation of our reality. We have the knowledge and the methodological processes. My aim here is to explore these and articulate how they may be developed and honoured in mainstream academic contexts. My travels in the bush guide this journey.

Language and Terminology

In this work I use both intellect and heart to understand and cleanse a painful and empowering history and reality. I have journeyed into text written by Aboriginal and non-Aboriginal writers, fiction and non-fiction and academic and narrative. In work by Aboriginal authors I have found wisdom, understanding, comfort, solace and healing. I chose to write from a combined and intertwined place that acknowledges all aspects of my Aboriginality today. In my articulations, I sought more colourful ways to make the pages sing those songs that can invoke Spirit and heart into our work. I tried to break the monotony of the written text by using voice, photography, poetry, stories and visual aids. Using narrative, story, prose and slang, I include myself in the terminology and refer to Aboriginal people as "our" or "my" people. I do this to make my allegiances visible and myself accountable for my own writing. I want the reader to know that an Aboriginal woman, an *Anishinaabe* kwe, is authoring this book and text. I want the reader to see a whole picture. I acknowledge that I am the artist painting myself in the picture. My voice is present and my experiences are not neutral.

My language and terminology warrants clarification. First and foremost I write as an Anishinaabe person. However, the scope of my search goes beyond Anishinaabe to include other Aboriginal nations within Canada. For variety, I use the terms Aboriginal and Indigenous interchangeably. Indigenous is frequently used in a global context but is also nationally applied. "Aboriginal" is the legal term in Canada that includes First Nations, Inuit and Métis peoples. The term that feels most accurate is Anishinaabe, which roughly translates to mean "the people." I also use the plural Anishinaabek to refer to Aboriginal peoples.

I use the Ojibwa language, Anishinaabemowin, because I am Anishinaabe and this is my mother tongue. Sometimes I conjure up words and use english words in atypical ways. How can I explain this? Sometimes english in its grammatically correct form does not convey or enact my intentions, and I must apply english words in new ways to help the reader view through a different lens. For example, earlier I used the word dismember to evoke an image and meaning of a forced disconnection. And then I used the term remember to evoke memory and reconnection.

The term "research" has a lot of colonial baggage attached to it. In most Indigenous communities, research is a bad word (Smith 1999). It conjures up suspicion and distrust. As an Indigenous knowledge seeker I have struggled with this term. While writing this book I sought to identify or create other terms that reflect Indigenous processes of knowledge seeking and production. I journeyed into my experiences and remembered, for example, that Indigenous peoples search for knowledge, food and medicines. We gather berries, plants and herbs and we hunt moose, deer, geese and ducks. We also trap rabbits, beavers and muskrats. We harvest food and medicines from the forest and earth, and the knowledge of how to do these things has been developed, shared and passed down from generation to generation. Terms that reflect Indigenous ways of collecting and finding out are searching, harvesting, picking, gathering, hunting and trapping. Within this book I commonly use the words search and gather in lieu of research. I now hyphenate re-search, meaning to look again. To search again from our own location and to search again using our own ways as Anishinaabek is Indigenous re-search. It is the process of how we come to know. The focus, topic and questions surrounding the re-search are relative to Indigenous peoples' realities. The research is by nature related to Indigenous peoples' contexts: historical, political, legal, economical, geographical, cultural, spiritual, environmental and experiential. Indigenist re-search promotes Indigenous knowledge and methods. As we re-search, we re-write and we re-story ourselves.

Making meaning is what we do with knowledge, and when we gather berries we make meaning of those berries by making jam or pies and then we share all that we have gathered with the people. In lieu of "data analysis," I use the term "making meaning" to refer to the process of sorting the information and interpreting from all that was gathered and harvested. I use the terms "methodology" and "conscious Indigenous scholars" throughout this book. "Methodologies" refers to a series of methods that are used in searching for knowledge. "Methodologies" address the how, who, where, what and when of Indigenous re-search. It is pervasive and inclusive of a wholistic process.

Indigenous re-searchers are by definition Indigenous people who engage in searches for knowledge, also known as research. Indigenous could mean Aboriginal, First Nations, Native, Indian, Inuit or Métis. They are identified as such by their genealogy, nation, family and community. The term "conscious Indigenous scholars" refers to those Indigenous searchers who are aware of our cultural and colonial history and who are on a path of intentionally learning, recovering and reclaiming their Indigeneity.

Indigenous re-search methodologies are those re-search methods, practices and approaches that are guided by Indigenous worldviews, beliefs, values, principles, processes and contexts. Indigenous methodologies are wholistic, relational, interrelational and interdependent with Indigenous philosophies, beliefs and ways of life. The methods are determined by understanding the nature of our existence, of how we come to know, of how knowledge is produced and of where knowledge comes from. Methods or ways of coming to know stem from understanding natural laws. Indigenous peoples still carry this knowledge close to the heart and Spirit. Indigenous ways of knowing, being and doing are connected to the nature of our existence, just as eurowestern researchers are guided by colonialist beliefs and values, even though they claim, sometimes vehemently, that they are "value neutral"!

I must also comment on what this book is not. It is not a formula or prescription for Indigenous methodologies. This book is not about Indigenous methodologies globally and must not be construed to be a general representation of all Indigenous methodologies. It is not exhaustive. It does not address methodologies that are employed informally at the community level or within commissioned searches such as the Royal Commission on Aboriginal Peoples, although such work would be worth undertaking.

This book emerged from a focus on Indigenous graduate researchers' implementation of Indigenous methodologies in academic research contexts. The aim is to validate and make Indigenous methodologies a solid methodological choice. Any shortcomings in the articulation of such methodologies are mine alone.

Chapter Two

Indigenous Re-Search

... Miigwech Cocomish, miinwa Shaumish...
Miigwech nsitam miinwa kaandaassiwin
Miigwech minobaamaadsiwin
Niin bemoose miinwa niin ndanewaad kaandossiwin
Miigwech wedookwishin G'chi Manidoo...
(Minogiizhigokwe)

Indigenous Peoples' Cultural History and Research

> Aboriginal people have inherited from earlier ages a mission to explore and seek metaphysical knowledge. We know that this quest for knowledge took place along various avenues. Mythology, ritual, and ceremonies, the medicine wheel, nature, and language all reveal vestiges of grand discoveries and communion with the universe within...mamatowisowin is the capacity to connect to the life force that makes anything and everything possible. (Ermine 1995: 110)

Knowledge quests and knowledge searchers are all around us. Indigenous peoples have always had means of seeking and accessing knowledge Yet, Indigenous searchers are usually caught in the context of colonial theories and methodologies. We tend to spend a lot of time there while compromising the development of our own knowledge. This book positions Indigenous knowledge up front and centre. Far too often, as Indigenous people, we are negotiating the sensitive area of research as both researched and researcher. While Indigenous peoples are the most studied ethnic group in the world (Rigney 1999; Smith 1999), the study of the "other" is not something we are preoccupied with. In Aboriginal culture "one does not tell or inquire about matters that do not directly concern one" (Allen 1998: 56). Devon Mihesuah explains:

> While non-Indian historians and some Indians have made careers out of speaking for tribes and interpreting culture besides the one to which they belong, many Indians will not write about tribes other than their own, even if they have insights into those cultures. When it comes to speculating on Others' motivations and world-views, many Indians are simply uncomfortable and won't do it. (1998a: 12)

We do however have a history of studying the earth, animals, plants and beings (human and others) that we interact with and relate to. Traditionally, research has been conducted to seek, counsel and consult; to learn about medicines, plants and animals; to scout and scan the land; to educate and pass on knowledge; and to inquire into cosmology. The seeking of knowledge has been usually solution-focused and often has had an underlying purpose of survival. Searching for knowledge was congruent with the principles, philosophies, customs, traditions, worldview and knowledge of a particular nation (Absolon and Willett 2004; Battiste 2000b; Battiste and Henderson 2000a; Deloria 1996). Today, Indigenous re-searchers are committed to rediscovering that congruency between worldview and methodology (Absolon and Willett 2004; Alfred 2005; Archibald 1997; Sinclair 2003; Wilson 2001).

Oral Traditions and Narrative

my culture has been labeled oral in terms of traditional practice
by western scientists humanists ethnographers and other academic researchers
yet oral does not go far in describing the sense of community
facilitated through gestures eye contact being in good relation with
audience participation breathing the same air walking the earth together
be / com/ ing in the same weather the same wind rain calm snow
sharing locale and to some extent context consensuality commensuality
even being hungry and sad together sharing with ancestors and thenotyetborn
with the plant nations the waters sky and earth sun and moon
powers and spirits and beings of all the directions. (Cole 2000: 53)[1]

In keeping with my Anishinaabe culture, I begin by paying respect to the oral traditions and knowledge that I was raised with and that guide Aboriginal methodologies of searching. Vine Deloria (1996: 36) explains that oral tradition is the "non-western, tribal equivalent of science," where Indigenous experiences and knowledge are passed from generation to generation and where that knowledge explains the nature of the physical, emotional, mental and spiritual worlds of the people. Other Indigenous scholars today also assert the legitimacy of beginning with our experiences and cultural orientations, which is seen as integral to the resurgence of Indigenous knowledge (Archibald 2008; Cardinal 2001; Cole 2006; Deloria 1996; Hampton 1995b; Weber-Pillwax 2001). Oral cultures are still reliant on the environment and exist in relation to Creation. Deloria supports the application of oral traditions in my search for Indigenous knowledge when he emphasizes the importance of the scout — the one who searches for food, the better trail to take, the best place to lodge, etc. Scout were revered by their tribes. Deloria states: "Indians know that human beings must participate in events, not isolate themselves from occurrences in the physical world. Indians thus obtain information from birds, animals, rivers and mountains, which is inaccessible to modern science" (40). Lewis Cardinal (2001) further explains that it is our experiences in the bush that best teach us about our relationship to the land and animals, and thus our relationship to our research ideas. Deloria goes on to state:

> Essentially, I am saying that Indigenous re-search methods and methodologies are as old as our ceremonies and our nations. They are with us and have always been with us. Our Indigenous cultures are rich with ways of gathering, discovering, and uncovering knowledge. They are as near as our dreams and as close as our relationships. (182)

I return to the bush because that is where my first teachings about searching began. The animals, the earth and Creation are the original teachers of the Anishinaabek. As an Anishinaabe *kwe*, my search for knowledge and life began at home in the bush, where I was taught to fish, hunt, trap and go berry picking. Searching is so intrinsic to living in the bush that we can connect this tradition to our contemporary search for knowledge. The ethics of our search are instilled in the land, and I agree with Peter Cole (2000, 2006) on Indigenous ethics when he states that we learned to give thanks and express our intentions, actions and feelings for what we needed and took from the earth. Indigenous ethics are implied in life itself and exercised through the teachings. If we needed the bark from a tree, expressing thanks, intentions and actions would precede the taking. Thus, the origins of any feast, basket, lodge or canoe would have been honoured and a consciousness of its Spirit respected.

When going on a search, negotiating the bush requires an understanding of the laws of nature. These laws are non-negotiable, meaning we must be prepared. Also, when going on a spiritual search for guidance and knowledge, we need to follow a process. Searching the land, in sacred spaces or human spaces, is guided by the nature of how we exist. In retrospect, I realize certain principles and philosophies guided my searches for life, berries, fiddleheads, mushrooms or fish. *Preparation* is essential to any search: bring *semaa* (tobacco), be of a good heart and mind, think about your route, wear the proper clothing, gather your tools, bring food and water and plan for the unexpected. Announce yourself and your intentions; share this with others. In our search for berries we *started with our own knowledge*. Know where to begin looking and know how to find your path. Thus, in my search for principles of Indigenous methodologies, I begin with my own knowledge of searching in the bush. I was taught to *attune* to the land and what the animals were doing. *Announcing my intentions* to the land or warning the creatures of my presence was a central philosophy that *respected* the animals and our *relationship* to Creation. I learned to offer a prayer with *semaa* to acknowledge the Spirits of the land. I learned to *watch* the animals and birds, particularly the bears. Bears love blueberries too. Walking the land and negotiating the elements of the bush called for another principle: *do not get lost.* As a young child, I learned to *identify landmarks* from which I could locate my position and from where I would retrace my steps. Sometimes I used markers along the way in the form of rocks, broken twigs or flag tape to identify the path I had taken and to guide me safely home. Trees, rivers, creeks and landscapes also were important in finding my way. Markers were essential because after a while the bush begins to all look the same. You might think you know where you came from — and some very knowledgeable people do, such as my mother and grandparents — but I am not as skilled and require physical markers to guide my path home. *Listening and walking carefully* were other principles central to my search. My eyes *watch*ed for animals and obstacles and helped me to retain balance in my steps. I listened for animals to ensure that I wouldn't startle a bear. I used a stick to shake the lower juniper bushes or bang on the rocks to warn snakes or other small creatures of my presence. In practising these principles I learnt about *demonstrating respect* for the land and its inhabitants. In my search I might not find what I sought, but that did not mean giving up; it just meant I would need to try another day. Thus I learned about *persevering.* I learned to walk through the bush *patiently*, knowing that my search would take time. Sometimes I would find an abundance of berries and would pick for hours, reaping the gifts of Creation. For that, I was always grateful: *gratitude* is another principle. On other occasions, I would find other medicines and foods. Sometimes, I would just find myself and would spend the day in the bush with Creation. Always, searching in the bush was guided by principles, and it felt good to come home with baskets full of berries and a *sense of connection, understanding and knowing.*

Indigenous cultural histories are rich and have been passed from one generation to the next since time immemorial. Our lived experiences are records of these histories. Cultural histories speak about the cosmology of the universe and our location in it. Such histories have been carried on from generation to generation via oral traditions of storytelling, ceremony, songs, teachings, ritual and sharing. Each nation retained, recorded and recounted its own cultural histories. These histories were/are relevant and meaningful to the lives, culture and survival of each Indigenous nation. Intertwined in histories were methodologies from which purpose and meaning were actualized. The "hows" to life's questions and quests were pivotal to seeking answers. These "hows" are central to Aboriginal methodologies as Indigenous re-searchers claim and articulate what is Aboriginal in our research practices and processes. Linda Tuhiwai Smith explains what this means for Indigenous peoples today:

Every issue has been approached by Indigenous peoples with a view of *re*writing and *re*righting our position in history. Indigenous peoples want to tell our own stories, write our own versions in our own ways, for our own purposes. It is not simply about giving an oral account or a genealogical naming of the land and the events which raged over it, but a very powerful need to give testimony to and restore a spirit, to bring back into existence a world fragmented and dying…Franz Fanon called for the Indigenous intellectual and artist to create a new literature…to write, theorize and research as Indigenous scholars. (1999: 28–29, italics in original)

As Indigenous scholars, we are challenged to take back control and change the way research is conducted within our communities, peoples and cultures. We are being given the task to re-write and re-right our own realities and truths (see also Hart 2009). An acknowledgement of Indigenous re-search methods in communities and research contexts is pivotal to this task. If we intend to theorize and research as Indigenous scholars, then we must identify what that means and how that happens.

Many Indigenous scholars have documented the colonizing role of re-search (Colorado and Collins 1987; Hampton 1995a, 1995b; Gilchrist 1997; Bishop 1998b; Rigney 1999; Smith 1999; Battiste and Henderson 2000b; Cajete 1994, 2000; Sinclair 2003; Absolon and Willett 2004; Kovach 2009; and Hart 2009). These scholars provide critiques of the eurocentric, hegemonic and artificial contexts in which Aboriginal people have been forced to exist. Shawn Wilson (2003) links the colonists' agenda for imperialistic control over the land and resources to the lack of development of Indigenous re-search paradigms. This agenda played a major role in establishing and maintaining Indigenous people as the researched and not the researcher. Critical Indigenous scholars, today, contend that Indigenous discourse must be understood in the context of racism and colonialism. For example, Lenore Stiffarm suggests that measuring Aboriginal knowledges against western criteria is academic racism and colonialism:

> Aboriginal knowledge was invalidated by Western ways of knowing. This unconscious, subconscious and conscious means of invalidating Aboriginal knowledge served to perpetrate a superior/inferior relationship around knowledge and how this knowledge is passed on. Systemic racism was clearly perpetrated in this way. (1998: xi)

The legacy of colonizing knowledge has created a disconnection of people from their traditional teachings, people, family, community, spiritual leaders, medicine people, land and so on. The oppressive silencing of Aboriginal knowledges has perpetrated oppression and threatens the ultimate extinction of cultures whose epistemologies, philosophies, worldviews and theories have sustained both the earth and its inhabitants for centuries.

Indigenous Science and Knowledge

> Indigenous knowledge is the property of those individuals, their communities and their Nations. It is inappropriate for outside researchers to document such knowledge for the sole purpose of thesis, dissertations and academic advancement. (Leanne[2])

Undeniably, the waning of traditional science among Indigenous peoples was not voluntary or spontaneous. It was caused by the historical denial, degradation and even destruction of "traditional Elders, keepers of knowledge [who] were deliberately murdered" (Colorado 1988: 51). Sacred birch bark scrolls, knowledge bundles and ceremonial objects were confiscated, destroyed and outlawed. Traditional science was replaced with belief systems based on western scientific thought, which "created the illusion that western science is THE Universal Truth with THE true methods. As a result, since the invasion of the Americas, the science that has studied Native life has been Western science" (50–51, uppercase in original). Truth was then explained within european paradigms. Pam Colorado led Indigenous critiques of western science colonialism as "intellectual imperialism" and called for the strengthening of "traditional Native science and to block further penetration of traditional Native science by Western science" (50). In the 1960s, the first generation of Indigenous scholars and activists in the academy applied sociocultural models of social science research using history as a methodological tool and addressing historical, economic and political issues. The voices of Indigenous peoples and Indigenous re-searchers began to re-emerge and call into question western theoretical models. Whisperings in the wind carried forward notions that Indigenous peoples might have a science of their own (Colorado and Collins 1987). And so, along with feminist and critical scholars, Indigenous scholars criticized the limitations of western science and actively advanced methodologies which embraced our own historical, social, political, economic, spiritual and cultural realities (Absolon and Willett 2004; Archibald 2008; Bishop 1998b; Cole 2006; Colorado 1988; Deloria 1996; Duran and Duran 2000; Fitznor 2002; Graveline 1998, 2000; Kenny 2000; Kovach 2005, 2009; Little Bear 2000; McPherson and Rabb 2001, 2003; Martin-Hill 2008; Thomas 2005; Wilson 2008). Jefferson Faye, an Indigenous science educator, describes his experience teaching Native science to his students:

> I have to speak the "captor's language." I offer students a history of Western science from a Cartesian view, talk about the separa-

tion of humankind and nature, discuss mechanistic models of the world and the death of the Earth (including the evolution of the engineering mentality), and describe what it is like to work at a software firm. We talk about Darwinism natural selection, Newtonian physics, Einsteinian relativity, and quantum mechanics… And when I have done all that, I drop the bomb on them: stepping into my own mukluks, I tell them that all these things they believe to be TRUE are culturally constructed, that the science they have been taught to revere is only one worldview, and that incontrovertibility of scientific proof is a fallacy. Then I tell them about Native sciences, about the living Earth, and about the prevalence of spirits everywhere. (2001: 271)

Faye confronts the notion of an absolute truth — asserting that truth is a construction of those in positions of power over knowledge — and makes a trail for Indigenous worldviews as another form of truth. He does not negate the existence of other models of explanation but opens up science to include an Indigenous worldview.

Shawn Wilson (2003, 2008) identifies the development of Indigenous re-search paradigms on a continuum of four stages. The first finds Indigenous re-searchers working solely from a western paradigm, with few Indigenous people present in academia. The second and third stages move toward integration of western and Indigenous paradigms, with the third illustrating a stronger thrust toward decolonization. The fourth, and most recent stage has Indigenous re-searchers illuminating their own worldview using Indigenous paradigms. As an Indigenous searcher, my focus is on these recent developments. Indigenous paradigms are increasingly receiving recognition and respect as Indigenous scholars re-search and teach from their own distinct stance. Indigenous paradigms enable Indigenous re-searchers to talk back and assume control of our own search for knowledge (Calliou 2001; Hart 2009; Talbot 2002). When we indigenize or Aboriginalize (Fitznor 2002) research, Indigenous worldviews and perspectives are affirmed (Cardinal 2001; Simpson 2001; Sinclair 2003; Steinhauser 2002). Indigenous critiques are vital to create space for Indigenous paradigms and methodologies in Indigenous searches to emerge.

As western scientific research methodologies get taken to task by Indigenous re-searchers and critical non-Indigenous re-searchers, allied methodologies emerge and are guided by emancipatory, liberatory, anticolonial and anti-racist principles. Common experiences of oppression link us as positivist research was connected to class and gender oppression. Allies emerged and laid to rest claims to be value-neutral. Anticolonial, critical, feminist, multicultural and Indigenous critiques have introduced new and relevant theories and epistemologies of research to include socio-political and historically critical perspectives. Narrative, lived experience and phenomenological methodologies have supported our goals of establishing an Indigenous voice in the research story. Methodologies such as action-based research, participatory action research and community-based strategies have gained validity among critical Indigenous re-searchers (Day, Blue and Peake Raymond 1998; Nabigon, Hagey, Webster and MacKay 1998; Sinclair 2003; St. Denis 1992; Stringer 1999; Voyageur 2003). Community-based research methodologies are being employed by Aboriginal re-searchers as they often fit with community goals such as capacity building, education and community ownership (McPherson and Rabb 2001, 2003; Menzies 2004; Simpson 2001; Sinclair 2003; Smith 1999; Talbot 2002). Raven Sinclair acknowledges the burgeoning new body of knowledge coming out of the Indigenous scholars movement to "explore the theoretical intersections of Indigenous ontology and epistemology with research methodologies in an attempt to create research that is useful for the people and respects Indigenous ways of knowing in research" (2003: 120). These critiques are consistent with stage three of Wilson's (2003) model. He states that you can try to deconstruct or decolonize a western research methodology, but it is still a western paradigm and inseparable from the originating paradigm. To indigenize is to position your Indigenous worldview as the centre. I see an important distinction here between having an Indigenous perspective within a western research paradigm and doing re-search methodologies within an Indigenous world-view/paradigm. Nevertheless, some qualitative research methodologies are compatible with Indigenous paradigms. For instance, methodologies such as talking circles can be akin to focus groups, storytelling is related to personal narrative, and participatory action research is an empowering methodology that facilitates Indigenous peoples' ownership, control and access to the re-search process. In reclaiming our forms of knowledge production, we need to look at our own understandings of existence and the nature of knowledge and ethics (ontology, epistemology, methodology and axiology) as a starting point. Indigenous paradigms are fundamentally different, in that they are built on the

> fundamental belief that knowledge is relational. Knowledge is shared with all of Creation. It is not just interpersonal relationships, just with the research subjects I may be working with, but it is in relationship with all of Creation. It is with the cosmos, it is with the animals, with the plants, with the earth that we share this knowledge. It goes beyond the idea of individual knowledge to the concept of relational knowledge. (Wilson 2001: 176–77)

The concept "we are all related" informs the wholistic and relational nature of Indigenous methodologies. Indigenous thought and knowledge guides how we search for knowledge — a search that considers reciprocity and interdependence.

Indigenous knowledge is as old as life. Indigenous re-search can now be guided by a re-emergence and assertion of Indigenous knowledge. You will see the depth and breadth of such knowledge reflected by Indigenous searchers throughout this book in our stories and narratives. Here, I pause to stress the significance and extent of Indigenous knowledge within Indigenous re-searchers' consciousness. Indigenous knowledge is knowledge that is wholistically derived from Spirit, heart, mind and body. Indigenous forms of knowledge production accept intuitive knowledge and metaphysical and unconscious realms as possible channels to knowing (Colorado 1988; Deloria 2002; Little Bear 2000).

Many Indigenous searchers from diverse nations share common principles regarding Indigenous worldviews.[3] It is a given, for instance, that Indigenous worldviews are wholistic and relational. "Most Aboriginal worldviews and languages are formulated by experiencing an ecosystem" (Henderson 2000a: 259). Indigenous worldviews teach people to see themselves humbly within a larger web or circle of life. This web contains our relationships to one another and to all of Creation. Indigenous knowledge lives in the animals, birds, land, plants, trees and Creation. Relationships among family and kinship systems exist within human, spiritual, plant and animal realms. Indigenous knowledge systems consider all directions of life: east, south, west, north and beneath, above and ground levels. Life is considered sacred and all life forms are considered to have a Spirit. We manifest this knowledge in our humility in offering thanks for life and in seeking life's direction.

Knowledge for Indigenous peoples exists in the heart and Spirit too. Indigenous knowledge comes from ancestral teachings that are spiritual and sacred in origin (Ermine 1995). It exists in our visions, dreams, ceremonies, songs, dances and prayers. It is not knowledge that comes solely from books but is lived, experiential and enacted knowledge. It is cyclical and circular and follows the natural laws of Creation. Indigenous knowledge is earth-centered, with ecology-based philosophies derived out of respect for the harmony and balance within all living beings of Creation. Indigenous knowledge occupies itself with the past, present and future. The past guides our present, and in our present we must consider the generations to come. Our ancestors have used their knowledge to respect the laws of Creation, while subsisting on the land, since our earthwalk began. Thus, research that is derived from Indigenous knowledge certainly entails methodologies that demonstrate respect and reverence within these understandings. Indigenous re-search is about being human and calls all human beings to wake from the colonial trance and rejoin the web of life.

My Own Search: A Journey of Making Meaning

G-chi' manidoo, what is it that you ask of me?

Chi-Miigwech for helping me on my search
Help me to listen with an open mind
And to see with an open heart
Help me to recognize the leadership and wisdom of those before me
And to honour the knowledge of those today and those of the past
Give me the landmarks so that I can remember my own path for those to come
Help me to not get lost on this search
And to gather with humility and integrity
Zhiway miishnaun G-chi' Manidoo...
Chi'miigwech G'chi'Manido for your guidance
(Minogiizhigokwe)

My own search involved a process of preparing, searching and making meaning.

Preparing: The Purpose of My Search
I have always known that there are Indigenous ways of searching for knowledge; I just didn't have a path to communicate this. I do now! The purpose of my search was to make what we know visible by identifying what Indigenous methodologies graduate Indigenous re-searchers are using and how they are employing those methodologies within the academy. I want to provide other Indigenous re-searchers with methodological options based in Indigenous worldviews. I chose graduate research theses because they would articulate their methodologies and demonstrate the varied ways that Indigenous re-searchers are searching in the academy. Like searching for berries, I searched in fields that I was familiar with, which was primarily the social sciences. Searching for these would enable me to reveal and empower Indigenous methodologies and worldviews within re-search contexts.

Searching: How I Searched and What I Did
My gathering process was eclectic, flexible and organic. A multi-method approach best suited the wholism of Indigenous culture (Denzin and Lincoln 2003; Sinclair 2003) and provided rich berries in my search. My search combined the following:

1. a review of selected Indigenous graduate theses;
2. individual conversations with Indigenous searchers; and
3. a group learning circle with Indigenous searchers.

I choose theses by and conversations with Indigenous peoples who were conscious of their own locations: culturally, colonially and politically. I choose theses whose methodologies explicitly revealed an Indigenous consciousness and worldview. I brought to this task my own experiences as an Indigenous re-searcher and much prior reading and study. The first element of my search involved identifying Indigenous graduate re-search projects and re-searchers within the academy in Canada. Before selecting the theses and researchers, I had done a lot of work and reading on Indigenous knowledge and worldview in my life, teaching, research and course work. I came to the search with my own Indigenous knowledge and understandings. My existing relationships and knowledge of the circle of Indigenous searchers within the Canadian academy allowed me access to people I already had a relationship with and whose research I was aware of. This harvest presents a synthesis of my experiences, the literature and all the berries I gathered during my search.

I cite the written and spoken words of the graduate re-searchers differently than the literature citations. I use only the first names of participants for their written and spoken words. In the written thesis work of participants I cite the year to distinguish the thesis from their spoken voice. In this manner I create space for all the re-searchers to have a central place and voice herein.

Making Meaning: Reading the Landscape of Indigenous Searches
Making meaning implies the process of interpreting and finding meaning in all the berries I gathered. It is also known in its western form as data analysis. Surprisingly, reading other Indigenous theses was delightful. First of all, I thought they would be dry and boring, filled with academic jargon. I wasn't looking forward to reading them at all. Yet, I was searching to see what the landscape looked like. Some theses I couldn't put down because they were so articulate, meaningful and relevant. Some theses were narratives filled with personal stories of the re-search journey. They helped me demystify my own doctoral search. It was as if I was being mentored and shown how to proceed with my search through the thesis projects. One of my fears of writing was that my writing wouldn't be academic enough, in the western sense. That fear evaporated while reading other Indigenous theses. The most amazing and captivating dissertations were written in very accessible and personal styles. The searchers wove themselves into their projects. Each dissertation was unique and taught me about Indigenous methodology. Reading them excited me and gave me hope that we are making legitimate space for Indigenous methodologies in academic re-search. I encourage others to read projects by Indigenous searchers for they will nurture and nourish you on your search.

Having Conversations
Having conversations meant travelling over the land to meet people in spaces that we both agreed upon. Searching for Indigenous scholars to converse with led to the bluest of blue blueberry patches. While travelling

and having conversations about how we search for knowledge I met with leading Indigenous scholars and we shared and wove our stories together. My baskets of knowledge were full and I felt content with this harvest. After gathering berries I now had to make meaning of it all. Making meaning of the conversations refers to analyzing them and turning berries into jam or pie or sauce (Marsden 2005). After all the searching, gathering and making meaning I present this book as my giveaway. To see the details of how I made meaning, go to the Theses Canada web portal to view my full dissertation.

Prayer and dreaming were sources of support, guidance and direction during the phase of analysis and making meaning of the conversations. During this phase I was preoccupied with how I would sort, and more importantly, represent all the information I had gathered. I dreamt of a petal flower, which I use later, where I present the bounty of my harvest.

I felt a strong need to embody the process of working with all the knowledge and information I gathered. Making pies after all is very hands on and creative. So one day, I stopped typing at my computer, got up and started working with textiles and tapestry. Eber Hampton (1995b), in his thesis process, identified his need to set his research aside and return to it to redo the analytic process. Stepping back for a while provided time and space to mentally, emotionally, spiritually and physically breathe, contemplate and reflect on the process. I needed to embody the knowledge that I was working with and do something physical and manual. I chose textiles because I can sew and bead and enjoy creating. From my dream I fashioned a tapestry representation. I pulled out ribbons and assorted materials. After experimenting with a variety of designs I chose black cloth as a background, to represent space. A bright red circle surrounds the sunflowers, creating a wholistic framework.

In the centre sits a red circle with a deer hide medicine wheel, representing self and central tendencies. Outside the red circle, sunflowers situated in the four directions represent and reinforce the wholistic nature of Indigenous methodologies. All the sunflower appliqués are accompanied with words identifying Indigenous methodological tendencies in search for knowledge. Making meaning involved prayer, dreaming, visual arts and tapestry. Creating this tapestry took me on a journey from my head to my heart and Spirit. It removed me from cerebral analysis and brought me to another level, where I was able to wholistically conceptualize what I had gathered. In creating the tapestry, I thought about what I had learnt and what I needed to represent. I thought about my dreams and honoured them. I thought about the people I talked to and whose work I read. As I sewed and embroidered, I embodied my search in the tapestry. I didn't plan on it then, but the tapestry became the focal point of sharing in the learning circle.

Tapestry of Indigenous Methodology

The Learning Circle as Giving Back

The learning circle is a small group format where the process benefits those who participate in the exchange and sharing of ideas and experiences. The intention of the learning circle was to provide an opportunity for Aboriginal re-searchers/participants to dialogue and share their re-search methodologies and the ways they bring their worldviews into their re-search within the academy. I prayed for direction, somehow trusted the universe, and along came an opportunity. I responded to a call for proposals for the Shawane Dagosiwin Indigenous re-search conference in Winnipeg, Manitoba.[4] The committee welcomed my proposal. At the conference, my session (the learning circle) was open to Indigenous re-searchers wanting to share about Indigenous methodologies.

At the time of the learning circle, I knew that my basket was full and that I did not need to gather anymore. Sharing what I was learning from my search, as a way of giving back and reciprocating other searchers' generosity, became my goal. I invited people to share their ideas, comments and thoughts on Indigenous methodologies in search for knowledge. Mainly, the sharing within the circle validated the information I had already gathered.

Many circle attendees expressed that talking about Indigenous methodologies validated possibilities and gave them hope for how they search for knowledge. The learning circle was a small example of a need for Indigenous searchers to gather and share their experiences, challenges and accomplish-

Shawane Dagosiwin learning circle, Winnipeg, June 2006

ments. I offered strawberries as a token of my gratitude to the universe and to each person for listening, sharing and attending this learning circle.

These theses, conversations and gatherings are processes within a larger continuum of conversations and work being done among Indigenous researchers. Those I had the privilege of learning from and speaking with are searchers in the academy who are actively engaged in decolonization and liberation of Indigenous peoples. While in the academy, we all struggle to learn, grow, read, search and write from our own cultural, political, spiritual and personal locations. Contributing to the collective good of Indigenous well-being and humanity seems to be a shared goal of Indigenous searchers. The next part is my giveaway of what I found on my search for knowledge.

Notes

1. The unusual line breaks and capitalization in Peter's quotes duplicate the original text.
2. Voices from the conversations are cited with the first name only
3. Absolon 1993; Allen 1986; Battiste and Henderson 2000b; Benton-Banai 1988; Brant Castellano 2000; Cajete 2000; Colorado 1988; Fitznor 2002; Graveline 2000; Gunn Allen 1991; Hart 2002; Henderson 2000a; Holmes 2000; Kovach 2005; Martin 2002; Nabigon 2006; Thomas 2005.
4. Shawane Dagosiwin translates to mean being respectful, caring and passionate about Aboriginal research. This conference was held from May 31 to June 2, 2006.

Chapter Three

Introducing the Re-Searchers and Their Searches

I wish to honour the Indigenous re-search and re-searchers that were the sources of my berry picking and information. All of the graduate theses I studied achieved precedent-setting recognition of Indigenous worldviews and methodologies in re-search in their respective academic institutions. Many of the re-searchers have gone on to publish their dissertations (Archibald 2008; Cole 2006; Kovach 2009; Martin-Hill 2008; Wilson 2008), just as I also am publishing my re-search. My work profiles significant tendencies, and it honours Indigenous ways of knowing, being and doing in relation to how we come to know. I also honour the re-searchers' earned title of Dr. because the environments within which they searched were hostile and harsh. Despite oppressive climates these searchers and their methodologies survived, much like we as peoples have. Interestingly, in addition to sharing a buffet of methodologies, this book profiles the stories of those who chose academic channels of education and re-search and how they negotiated and survived their complex research journeys. I am grateful to these scholars for their sharing and their contribution to the field of Indigenous methodologies in search for knowledge.

Indigenous Re-Searchers' Theses

Dr. Jo-ann Archibald (Jo-ann)
"Coyote Learns to Make a Storybasket: The Place of First Nations Stories in Education" (1997)
Dr. Jo-ann Archibald works in Aboriginal education and completed her doctoral dissertation at Simon Fraser University. Jo-ann Archibald is from the Sto:lo Nation, British Columbia, and identifies as the River People of the Fraser Valley. I included Jo-ann's dissertation because it speaks to the journey of learning through an emphasis on "cultural learning processes." Jo-ann learned about the process of First Nations storytelling and worked with many Elders on her doctoral journey. The methodology employed is storytelling, called "storywork," and utilizes Indigenous principles to establish a Sto:lo and Coast Salish framework, which become strands of the cedar basket, the ultimate framework for storywork. Jo-ann sets forth methodologies that honour oral traditions and stories.

Dr. Peter Joseph Cole (Peter)
"First Peoples Knowings as Legitimate Discourse in Education:
Coming Home to the Village" (2000)

Dr. Peter Cole completed his doctoral dissertation at Simon Fraser University in the Faculty of Education. Peter is of the N'Quat'qua Nation of British Columbia. He centrally positions Indigenous knowledge. For example, the means of transportation of the dissertation besides language is a canoe, and Peter writes about the canoe journey as the vehicle for his search. His text is a combination of poetic, dramatic and storytelling voices — a rhetorical strategy to better reflect the orality of Peter's and other First Nations cultures. Throughout, he interrogates, from an Indigenous standpoint, the ethics of research and problematizes western academics' claim to know "other" cultures by means of western methods of research.

Dr. Lauri Gilchrist (Lauri)
"Kapîtipis ê-pimohteyahk: Aboriginal Street Youth in Vancouver, Winnipeg, and Montreal" (1995)

Dr. Lauri Gilchrist completed her doctoral dissertation at the University of British Columbia in the Faculty of Education. Lauri is Cree from Flying Dust First Nation, Saskatchewan. I chose this unpublished dissertation because it is steeped in a critique, through the lens of an Indigenous scholar, of the "social science research industry." She tells the stories and experiences of Aboriginal street youth and provides an in-depth look at nine Aboriginal youth living on streets in major Canadian cities. Integrated into the stories of the youth are Lauri's stories and reactions to what she discovers. This personal investment in our research is very evident in Indigenous peoples' searches. Lauri's approach is inextricably linked to who we are, our lived experiences and the need to contribute to changing our location from object of study to active re-searchers.

Dr. Dawn J. Hill (Dawn H)
"Lubicon Lake Nation: Spirit of Resistance" (1995)

Dr. Dawn Hill completed her dissertation at McMaster University in the Faculty of Native Studies. Dawn is from the Mohawk nation. Dawn's inspiring dissertation is written with heart and for an Indigenous audience. It explores the way Indigenous re-searchers, like Dawn, bring a new voice and perspective to research. This was validating of my own re-search and methodological considerations. Dawn wrote about developing a context that is relevant to the Lubicon Lake Nation, herself and the social sciences. She shares her experiences as a Mohawk woman working in Lubicon territory. Dawn identifies and articulates her methodology with personal narrative and storytelling, and her process as an Indigenous re-searcher is eloquently captured. Her methodology provides the Lubicon Lake men and women an opportunity to tell their stories in their way and through their own processes.

Dr. Leanne Simpson (Leanne)
"The Construction of Traditional Ecological Knowledge: Issues, Implications and Insights" (1999)

Dr. Leanne Simpson completed her doctoral dissertation at the University of Manitoba in the Department of Sociology. Leanne is of Anishinaabe and Scottish ancestry and has grown up, like many of us, off reserve. Her Anishinaabe name is Betahsemoakae (Walking Towards Woman) and she has roots in Alderville First Nation. The goal of Leanne's dissertation was to examine the concept of traditional ecological knowledge (TEK) from Aboriginal and non-Aboriginal perspectives using Anishinaabe methods of inquiry, such as learning by doing, dreaming, ceremonies, storytelling and self-knowledge. One of the first things she does is situate herself in relation to her research. She focuses on Indigenous voices highlighting that it is the Aboriginal peoples who have firsthand experience of traditional ecological knowledge and Indigenous ways of searching for knowledge. In these ways, Leanne's dissertation, is steeped in Indigenous ways of coming to know.

Dr. Winona Stevenson (now Wheeler) (Winona)
"Decolonizing Tribal Histories" (2000)

Dr. Winona Wheeler completed her doctoral dissertation at the University of California in the Department of Ethnic Studies. Winona is a Cree woman from Manitoba. She stated that she is a student of Cree history and struggles to balance Cree identity with Irish blood; urban and bush lifestyles; english and Cree language; written and oral cultures and being a Cree woman and an academic. She asserts that Indigenous intellectual traditions provide the form and framework required for the development of Indigenous models and methods in research. Throughout her dissertation, she positions Indigenous knowledge as a basis to develop Indigenous scholarship and methodologies. Like other conscious Indigenous scholars, she critiques colonialism and internalized colonialism. The framework and foundation of this thesis is based on *nehiyawiwihtamawakans*, Cree teachings, which come from many sources. Doing oral history the Cree way, Winona states, is as much about social relations as acquiring information. And her research project demonstrates that the dynamics of her methodology are steeped in Indigenous knowledge.

Theses and Conversations

Willie Ermine (Willie)
"A Critical Examination of the Ethics in Research Involving Indigenous Peoples" (2000)
Willie completed his master's thesis in the Faculty of Education at the University of Saskatchewan. Willie's research critiques applications of western social science doctrines on Indigenous peoples. Further, he examines the ethics of western research involving Indigenous peoples and uncovers the discursive strategies that impede Indigenous peoples' empowerment. Willie writes about the possibility of configuring new models of research and knowledge production at the location where two worlds (Indigenous and non-Indigenous) intersect and create an overlapping space for innovative, cross-cultural and respectful modes of inquiry; a space he calls an "ethical space." The community context of Indigenous knowledge production is pivotal to ethical research involving Indigenous peoples.

Willie Ermine

Our conversational context: Willie is from the Prince Albert area and was in Regina for a meeting. Before I began, I offered Willie *semaa* (tobacco) and a small gift to give thanks for his sharing. Our discussion was thought provoking, and he validated what I already felt about working for and with the community. He affirmed the need to remain aware of where our knowledge goes when it enters the academy and to be critical of this process. He emphasized that we need to be careful what knowledge we bring into the academy, because our communities need our knowledge. I left this meeting wanting to make sure that I am cautious about what I chose to include in my work so as to not create that "super highway" to our traditional knowledge. Willie said that the processes I undergo are essential to my search for knowledge. Focus on my own process! I was thankful to have such a stimulating and challenging discussion.

*Dr. Laara Fitznor / Missisak
(Laara / Missisak)*
"Aboriginal Educators'
Stories: Rekindling Aboriginal
Worldviews" (2002)

Dr. Laara Fitznor completed her dissertation at the Ontario Institute for Studies in Education, University of Toronto. Laara is Naheyow ikswew — a Cree woman from Manitoba. Laara describes the meanings attached to the experiences of members of the Aboriginal Teachers Circle (ATC). Laara's dissertation searches for congruent methodologies and asserts Indigenous worldview and methodologies. She problematizes eurowestern research hegemony and, in doing so, calls for Aboriginal researchers to look at our own

Laara (Missisak) Fitznor

issues using Indigenous methods and processes. This down-to-earth dissertation is written for an Indigenous audience.

Our conversational context: I travelled to Winnipeg to meet with Missisak at her home. Her english name is Laara, but I acknowledge her Cree name and use that because it means horsefly and is significant to who she is. During our conversation we sat in her living room and drank tea. Missisak talked about how she struggled with searching for methods that fit within her worldview. She is adamant about advancing Indigenous perspectives and methods in all areas of teaching and researching within the academy. Missisak shares her knowledge through stories of her experiences and uses circle processes.

Dr. Michael Hart (Michael)
"An Ethnographic Study of Sharing Circles as a Culturally
Appropriate Approach With Aboriginal People" (1997)

Dr. Michael Hart completed his master's thesis at the University of Manitoba and successfully defended his doctoral thesis there too. Michael is a Cree man from Northern Manitoba and has a big heart in his work with Elders and with his traditions. Michael studied sharing circles as a culturally appropriate method of practice at a time when Indigenous people were unsure what traditions were okay to research. His research follows ethnographic research methodology, yet is strongly informed by his own Aboriginal perspective in terms of subjective voice, voice of the participants, protocols and ceremony surrounding his research. Michael's important thesis evidences the changes that are occurring as Indigenous scholars forge pathways of research within the academy.

Our conversational context: I have known Michael for many years in the field of Aboriginal social work. I travelled to Winnipeg to meet with him. I had food to offer, *semaa* and a small gift for his sharing. When we spoke, Michael was working on his doctoral research, interviewing

Michael Hart

Cree Elders and Cree social workers who incorporate their own ways of helping and identifying what knowledge is useful for social workers. We talked about the push we receive from non-Indigenous academics to do our research in areas that they are interested in, such as comparing their theories and practices to Indigenous ones. We talked about barriers we deal with, the double knowledge set we work with and our frustrations with the academy. Interweaving who we are into our research is a strong theme in our continuing conversations, and the learning doesn't really end.

Patricia McGuire /
Kiskshekabayquek (Patricia /
Kiskshekabayquek)
"Worldviews in Transition: The
Changing Nature of the Lake
Nipigon Anishinabek Metis"
(2003)
Patricia completed her master's thesis in the Department of Sociology at Lakehead University. Patricia is also known as Kiskshekabayquek, the woman who stands in the snow whirlwind. She is from Northwestern Ontario. Pat's thesis is a narrative that portrays the life teachings and stories of one Anishinaabek Métis

Patricia McGuire

Elder, her father. Patricia's research is based on a request that her father made of her in 1987 to finish his story for him, their family and their community. The thesis has a framework that is based on lived experiences, values, ethics and community knowledge of the Anishinaabek Métis. She depicts her father's life stories through a culturally mediated framework. Patricia's reliance and commitment to her worldview and the Anishinaabe knowledge that guided her process provides a strong model for the derivation of Indigenous knowledge.

Our Conversational Context: I travelled to Saskatoon and met with Kishebabayquek at her home. I offered her *semaa* and a gift and she offered me tea. It was good to have an opportunity to talk with Kishebabyquek as we are both Anishinaabe *kwe* (Ojibway women). Our meeting was a welcome reconnecting of kin. At that time Kishebabayquek was working on her doctoral research with family, community and traditional knowledges.

Dr. Dawn Marsden (Dawn M)
"Indigenous Holistic Theory for Health: Enhancing Traditional-Based Indigenous Health Services in Vancouver" (2005)

Dr. Dawn Marsden
(Photo by Dawn Marsden)

Dr. Dawn Marsden completed her doctoral dissertation at the University of British Columbia. Dawn is Anishinaabe *kwe* from the Mississaugas of Scugog Island First Nation. Dawn's research project and the methodologies she employed evidence an Indigenous worldview. Dawn writes about her re-search being grounded in the land and about her methodology as "getting grounded." For her, location is important and she first shares a story of her childhood name. "Hawk eye," and then addresses the relevance of her life to the research she is doing. Personal life history and lived experiences often form the basis of our research as Indigenous people, and Dawn's dissertation clearly illustrates that relationship. Central to her research is an assertion of Indigenous rights to traditional-based Indigenous health practices, such as culturally appropriate health services and an assertion of Indigenous knowledge and methods within the research process. In her dissertation, Dawn develops the Wampum Research Model.

Our conversational context: Through a conversation with another Anishinaabe sister, I was informed that Dawn had finished her Ph.D. The moccasin telegraph is a strong phenomenon in Indian country, and as I already knew Dawn, I connected with her by email and phone, and she agreed to have a telephone conversation about her search for knowledge. My conversation with Dawn was exquisite. She shared details of her Wampum Research Model and touched on many issues of Indigenous methodologies, such as translating Indigenous concepts and languages into english and the challenges and potholes inherent in that process. Dawn talked about how her search facilitated remembering what she already knew and where she was from. I shared with her my thoughts on remembering too. Her search also became a process of "learning about self." This conversation reminded me that much of what we do as Indigenous searchers relates back to the basic search for self.

Conversations Only

At the time of the conversations all but Dr. Hampton were in the process of their doctoral research, about which they shared their methodologies and experiences. Through our conversations we shared ideas and visions and discussed the ideals versus the actualities of their written graduate work.

Dr. Eber Hampton (Eber)

I met Eber in his office at the University of Regina. He has been in the field of education in the Canadian context for the past twenty-five years, and it was really good to have the opportunity to talk with him. When I asked him about including a photo he smiled but respectfully declined. Eber researches in Aboriginal education and has a keen interest in Indigenous re-search. I felt privileged to meet with Eber. I offered him *semaa* and we acknowledged the role of the Spirit in our work. He often paused and talked thoughtfully during our discussion. He shared a few stories and laughed easily. He talked about the role of prayer in his work. He shared a prayer he said while doing his research that I really liked: "Help me so that I can be of help." I actually wrote that prayer down and stuck it on my desk. He reminded me to tell stories of my life, experiences, physical process and the aches and pains we go through in our journey. Eber emphasized "audience" and who we write for and encouraged us to write for our people.

Dr. Maggie Kovach (Maggie)

I met Maggie at her home in Regina, where we had tea and snacks. It was a beautiful day. I felt excited to meet with Maggie because I knew that we shared research interests and that her dissertation was similar to mine. When we spoke, Maggie was working on her doctoral studies at the University of Victoria and has since successfully defended her re-search. Her topic was Indigenous re-search methodologies, specifically a Cree/Saulteaux

Dr. Maggie Kovach

methodology. I am very proud of Maggie and the work she has contributed. I presented Maggie with *semaa* and a small gift and expressed my gratitude that she took the time to share her ideas with me. Maggie's research is about hearing other people's stories about research and capturing the journey that Indigenous ways of knowing took her on. Our mutual and like-minded interest in the topic led to a dynamic and validating discussion. Her entire energy shifted and lifted when she talked about how coming home was so much a necessary part of her research process.

Maggie shared her process of coming home and the emergence of her journey as a major role in her methodological process. She talked with endearment of the open landscapes and big sky. She generously shared her dreams, particularly a significant one of a pearl necklace. We talked about how creating space to be ourselves is essential for learning and searching. The space is where we can feel, think and be with our truth. Our search for knowledge, Maggie said, is a portal or a doorway to self discovery and recovering our Indigeneity. These doorways can lead us on journeys we never anticipated or help quench our thirst for answers, direction, history and knowledge. She asserts that Indigenous methodologies must become a viable methodological choice for Indigenous re-searchers.

Dr. Raven Sinclair (Raven)

Raven is a Cree educator, re-searcher and writer in Saskatchewan. She completed her doctorate at the University of Calgary and is in the field of social work. Her doctoral research was focused on the experiences of Indigenous people who were transracially adopted. Raven has also searched how Indigenous re-searchers operationalize their worldviews in their research (Sinclair 2003).

Driving from Regina to Saskatoon on a fresh morning gave me some space to reflect. I met Raven at her home. She decided it was better to meet at her office, so we got ourselves coffee and I followed Raven's car to her workplace. Raven began our conversation by talking about

Dr. Raven Sinclair (Photo by Raven Sinclair)

remembering her worldview and becoming reacculturated into Indigenous community connections after being transracially adopted and living in a predominantly White westernized world. Raven too searched for methodologies or elements of methodologies that could fit within her own work, and it was only when she became exposed to Indigenous scholars and researchers that she begin to understand what she needed to do. Raven also talked about her need to contribute her "voice to the increasing and growing discourse that is Indigenous, which articulates to the world that we always had a way of being in the world that was extremely intelligent, because we operated on certain principles that result in balance and harmony." Her passion is to contribute to the reassertion, remembering and recreation of an Indigenous discourse. Raven's energy fired up when we started talking about issues of concreteness, objectivity and eclectic facets of Indigenous methodologies. This started a "myth busting" conversation. Like other Indigenous searchers, Raven is a myth buster! Raven saw her doctoral search as a process, a spiritual journey, and uses her intuition, ceremony and prayer to stay attuned to the Spirit and the heart, because that is where the process resides.

Chapter Four

Wholistic Worldviews and Methodologies

G'chi-Manidoo… where am I searching?
I walk through academic corridors
Searching for a route, a path, where is it?…
I don't recognize the landmarks… I jump through hoops…
I search for others… where are they?
Where are the other?… they must be here somewhere…
ohh here are some relatives… I recognize them…
I am not alone… Phew… Sigh… Breath…
I was worried… others have been here too… I am not lost
Miigwech for helping me find the others
Miigwech for the courage and re-searching of my relatives
(Minogiizhigokwe)

We must stand on our merits and not countenance anything less than full acceptance in the academy. Compromising who we are, what we know and where we come from is unacceptable. We are not alternative. One of the researchers described her methods as "alternative information-gathering." I wondered about that description, knowing this searcher fought and struggled in the academy, and concluded that when we describe our methodologies as "alternative," we consent to becoming "other." Being othered or alternative depends on whose turf it is. If it's not your turf then I guess you're the other. We must own our own turf within Indigenous search agendas. If the methods are Indigenous, within an Indigenous context and for Indigenous purposes, then it is normal and the mainstay of knowledge collection. The sooner the academy recognizes the existence and vitality of Indigenous methodologies, the closer the academy comes to creating a welcoming environment for Indigenous scholars, who can then focus their energy on all areas of Indigenous knowledge production.

My aim is to present the methodologies Indigenous graduate searchers employ and their experiences of conducting Indigenous re-search in the academy. This book illustrates Indigenous searchers who are searching from their worldview in their re-search. I want to convey to other Indigenous searchers that you don't have to turn yourself inside out to do work that is of you and about you. Our own knowledge and methodologies are there and can be applied to the work we are doing in the academy. The Indigenous re-searchers in this book are evidence of this. This chapter presents the harvest of my search within a framework of a petal flower. Each element of the petal flower is connected and interrelated to the whole of the flower and ought not to be interpreted in absence of its wholistic context. Likewise, the elements of Indigenous worldviews and methodologies are wholistic, relational and interdependent.

> I entered the dream world...
> wandering and wondering...
> searching, hunting, looking...
> "use me"... a small voice beckoned... "you can use me"
> (Minogiizhigokwe)

The methodologies, ideas, concepts and issues that are discussed herein represent concrete, multi-layered, dynamic, multi-dimensional and wholistic ways of searching for knowledge. Prescriptions or formulas for Indigenous methodologies do not exist. Many people are curious about Indigenous knowledge and ceremonies, but I am certain that it is Indigenous people that need to reclaim that pathway first. I have been cautioned to write primarily for the Indigenous audience, which is where my commitment lies. My intention is not to create pathways to sacred knowledges, but to provide support and information from which Indigenous scholars will benefit.

When I was finished gathering, my basket was overflowing. I offered my *semaa* and prayed for guidance on how I could make meaning and best represent all that I had learned. A gift of a dream was sent to me — I dreamt of a petal flower. It could have been any species of petal flower, which I believe best represents the open space Indigenous methodologies require. The dream was so vivid that as soon as I awoke, I drew out the petal flower and identified its components in relation to Indigenous methodologies. Upon reflection, it was the components and not the specific flower that was significant to my work. All elements of the petal flower are essential to crafting a wholistic framework for Indigenous methodologies. Roots represent worldviews, the centre is the self, the leaves are the journey, the stem is the backbone and the petals represent all the diverse methodologies I was learning about. Standing back from the drawing, I realized that my framework was congruent with an earth-centred worldview, and the petal flower became the wholistic representation of Indigenous methodologies.

Flowers are indigenous to the land, and petal flowers are a natural part of the Earth's beauty. Although there are many petal flowers, the ones that come to mind are wild daisies, roses, strawberries and sunflowers. I humbly borrow the petal flower as a metaphor to help summarize and create a framework for this harvest. The ecology and survival of the flower is dependent, like humans, on its environment: the earth, sun, water and air. It goes through various life cycles according to the seasons. Maintaining a balanced life and living in accordance with natural and spiritual laws ensure its survival.

Indigenous methodologies are similar in that they call for the recognition and understanding of the natural and spiritual laws that govern their existence and survival. The flower is rooted in the earth, yet is moved by the wind and rain. It is an exquisite example of how something so concrete can be flexible and fluid at the same time. Beauty is a gift the flower brings and its scent can invoke reactions at the sensual, physical, emotional, mental and physical levels. People have harvested and grown flowers for their medicinal, culinary, aromatic and beautiful properties. They have healed and soothed hearts, wounds, Spirits and minds

I dreamt of a petal flower. "Use me"...a small voice beckoned... "you can use me."

and built relationships. The gift of my dream comes fuller each time I reflect about the teachings embedded in the petal flowers.

Similarly, Leroy Little Bear uses the metaphor of four flower petals to symbolize strength, sharing, honesty and kindness in kinship relations. He states: "The function of Aboriginal values is to maintain the relationships that hold Creation together. If Creation manifests itself in terms of cyclical patterns and repetitions, then the maintenance and renewal of those patterns is all-important" (2000: 81). Like Little Bear, I bring in the petal flower to connect Indigenous searchers, Indigenous re-search and Indigenous methodologies in search for knowledge with all of Creation. In summary, the petal flower is significant in a number of ways:

- all its components are interrelated and interdependent;
- it is earth centred and harmoniously exists in relationship with Creation;
- it is cyclical and changes from season to season;
- the environment it lives in impacts its life; and
- it has a Spirit and a life.

The petal flower framework acknowledges and validates Indigenous leadership and scholarship displayed within a climate that is often foreign, alienating and marginalizing.

I identified some common tendencies in all of the theses I examined and conversations I had with the re-searchers. It is these collectively identified tendencies that I present as parts of wholistic Indigenous methodologies in search for knowledge. I submit the petal flower as their framework integrated with common tendencies:

1. The roots are the grounding for Indigenous methods. Although they are not visible, the life and presence of the flower depends on the strength of its roots. All of the methodologies were rooted and informed in varying degrees by Indigenous paradigms and worldviews. Indigenous re-search is a search for congruency with the re-searcher's own worldview.

2. The centre of the flower represents self and self in relation to the re-search. Indigenous methodologies are just as much about who is doing the searching as the how of the search. It reflects the paradigms and worldviews of its roots, and its health mirrors the ability of the whole to support it. The roots send core nutrients throughout the plant that enable the Indigenous self in the search to flourish. Situating self in the search seemed essential to the purpose and nature of the search and appeared to be directly related to improving social, environmental, political and educational conditions for Indigenous peoples. Indigenous re-search has meaning because of who we are as Indigenous peoples and our accountability and responsibility to our ancestors, family, community, Creation and the Creator. Self is central to Indigenous re-search methodologies, and Indigenous re-searchers recalled memories, motives, personal responsibility and their need for congruency in the search process. Each researcher in this book located themselves in terms of nation, culture, land, historical and personal experiences.

3. The leaves enable photosynthesis of knowledge: transformative journeys. The leaves embody the journey of the self through the research process. Indigenous re-searchers are also on a journey of learning who they are and what they know. Indigenous re-search encompasses multiple journeys. The leaves are interdependent with the environment, receiving their nutrition from the sun and roots. The leaves are connected via the stem to the ways Indigenous searchers navigate academic channels.

4. The stem represents the methodological backbone and connector between all parts of the whole. The backbone of Indigenous re-search comprises a critique of colonialism, imperialism and eurowestern research on Aboriginal peoples. A critical consciousness among the re-searchers expresses a commitment to "rewriting and re-righting" our histories, experiences and realities. The stem/critical consciousness is what holds it all together. It is the connecting pathway between the

The Petal Flower

Wholistic framework for
Indigenous methodologies
in search for knowledge

1. Roots
Foundational elements

2. Flower Centre
Self as central to the search

3. Leaves
The journey, process, transformation

4. Stem
Methdological backbone and supports

5. Petals
Diverse ways of search for knowledge

6. Environment
Academic context

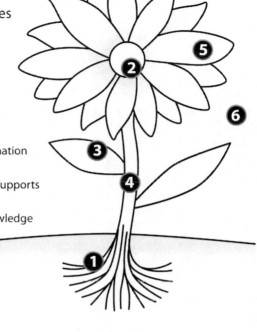

K. Absolon, 2007

paradigms, researcher, process, academia and methodologies. Critical Indigenous re-search agendas are actualized because of the strengths, supports, skills and roles of Indigenous scholars.

5.   The petals represent the diversity of Indigenous re-search methodologies. The methodologies that are operationalized and manifested are those that have been grounded in the roots and journeyed through the self, the research process and the academy to a methodological research enactment. The diverse and varied methodologies then, in essence, become the sum of all their parts. Many Indigenous searchers acknowledged the "Spirit" of and in our work by adhering to the relative protocols. Indigenous language, culture and traditions and the personal challenges were inherent in relearning and integrating our ways into our research.

6.   The environmental context of the petal flower influences the life of Indigenous methodologies in the academy and affects Indigenous re-searchers who are trying to advance their theories and methods. It affects the degree to which Indigenous re-searchers feel able to remain congruent in their searches. In many cases, the environment can be intolerant, harsh, chilly and antagonistic toward Indigenous re-search and methodologies. A cross pollination of Indigenous paradigms and

western paradigms can germinate unfamiliar species, which creates uncertainty and unfamiliarity. The re-searchers shared their experiences and strategies for employing Indigenous re-search in the academy.

All these aspects are interrelated and interdependent. The roots, for example, are aspects of the self, are linked to the re-search journey and determine our role as a searcher. Principles of Indigenous methodologies involve being critically conscious and diverse and seeing your search as a process, but the various aspects of Indigenous methodologies are not exclusive of one another. They are given here in separate sections in an attempt to organize and present them as clearly as possible. Each is connected to the whole petal flower, which represents the essential wholism of Indigenous worldview, knowledge and methodologies. The wholistic nature of Indigenous methodologies is what distinguishes them from non-Indigenous methodologies. The whole package is necessary to understand each of their parts and their distinctness.

Chapter Five

The Roots: Paradigms, Worldviews and Principles

Paradigms and Worldviews

The roots provide grounding to the search. Indigenous methodologies in the academy are shaped by Indigenous paradigms, worldviews and principles. Russel Bishop explains:

> What is of crucial importance is that reciprocity in Indigenous re-search is not just a political understanding, never an individual act, nor a matter of refining and/or challenging the paradigms within which researchers work. It is the very world-view within which the researcher becomes immersed that holds the key to knowing. (1998b: 208)

The roots establish the foundation and support the methodological process of searching and gathering. Although not usually visible, they are essential and are manifested in actions, behaviours, ethics and methods. We cannot talk about Indigenous methodologies without acknowledging the worldviews they come from and the paradigms and principles they rest on. Paradigms are frameworks, perspectives or models from which we see, interpret and understand the world. A paradigm is influenced by culture, socialization and experiences. Our understandings about the nature of our existence and our reality and how we come to know about our existence and reality make up a paradigm. The morals and ethics that guide us are also a part of our paradigm. Academics tend to use words like ontology, epistemology, methodology and axiology. I find them confusing and would rather speak without the jargon. I wonder what words in Anishinaabe would mean our understanding of our existence and how we come to know about our reality and existence? Paradigms are the understandings that ground us in the world, and our knowing, being and doing are guided by these. There can be many paradigms, and paradigms can shift. As our awareness, understanding and knowledge change, so can our paradigms. These understandings have a direct influence on how we search for knowledge, on our research, methodology, data analysis, dissemination of results and so on. This does not mean that the perspectives and rules are fixed or that we must adhere to seemingly correct methods, because paradigm shifts occur, particularly in relation to social research (Jupp 2006) and in relation to Indigenous search paradigms

The Roots

The arrows depict the foundational basis that the roots provide to the centre (self), the leaves (journey), the stem (strength) and the petals (methodologies).

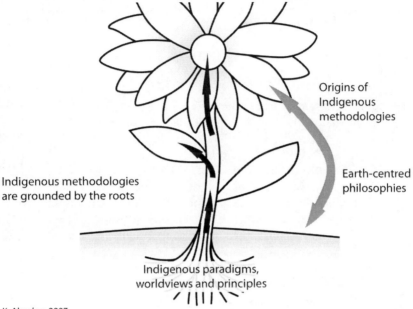

Origins of
Indigenous
methodologies

Earth-centred
philosophies

Indigenous methodologies
are grounded by the roots

Indigenous paradigms,
worldviews and principles

K. Absolon, 2007

(Wilson 2001, 2008; Hart 2009; Kovach 2009). Indigenous paradigms/ways of understanding our existence, how we come to know about that existence and what we think about our existence are the roots of Indigenous methodologies in re-search. Articulating an Indigenous paradigm set the foundation for many of the re-searchers' work. Talking about her own doctoral research, Dawn H asserts that Indigenous perspectives and paradigms enhance research validity and credibility:

> The main objective of this research is to establish the Lubicon's voice and spirit of resistance. I refuse to justify or reduce their experiences, to academic rhetoric... By using the Indigenous perspective, we can better comprehend the cultural richness, depth, and strength of the Lubicon people.

In the academy, Indigenous paradigms are slowly making their presence known, and awareness of their existence is spreading. This awareness is creating paradigm shifts that change the way we perceive and conduct research in the academy. Shawn Wilson's statement is relevant: "We now need to move beyond an 'Indigenous perspective in research' to researching from an Indigenous paradigm" (2001: 175). What I believe he means is that, rather than adding Indigenous perspectives to eurowestern theories and methods, we need to ground our research frameworks and methods in Indigenous ways of knowing, being and doing. This means more than just adding perspective. It is a grounding stance, rooted within an Indigenous understanding of the nature of our existence, how we know and how this understanding affects our realities and searches for knowledge.

Indigenous paradigms (and worldviews and principles) are liberatory, emancipatory and critical. An Indigenous paradigm factors in a historical, colonial and power analysis (Rigney 1999), which gives it its critical contours. It infers that our emancipation as Indigenous people is not freely supported by the colonial state, because it means a loss of colonial power and, historically, this has never happened willingly. Michael (1997) explains that, currently, Indigenous paradigms combine knowing cultural history, colonial history and future aspirations:

> Aboriginal science has its own preferential perspectives, goals, and processes to acquiring knowledge. In order to overcome the historical oppression of Aboriginal peoples in relation to research and to bring to the forefront Aboriginal knowledge, research approaches need to respect the worldviews of Aboriginal peoples.

The past, present and future intersect, and much of our research is about searching for truth, freedom, emancipation and ultimately finding our way home. Finding our way home means searching to return to our own roots and to find the dignity and humanity intended by the Creator. Many of us choose emancipation through research and knowledge. We understand that knowledge is power, and our search for knowledge constitutes a search for power. Indigenous re-search is about being personal and political and responsible for creating change. All of the theses and conversations claimed a personal voice and stance about our searches. Patricia (2003) writes about the responsibility we have in representing our stories and that there is power in "being a researcher and in being a writer," where issues of power and authority evoke a responsibility to family, community and ancestors for truthful representations of the stories and knowledge we gather. Winona writes that we don't need to study oppression because we already know oppression. We are already aware of difference, being othered, and with this awareness we weave our stories and identities into the research process to reclaim our power and knowledge.

Indigenous paradigms must reflect Indigenous ways of knowing, being and doing. Laara, in her thesis (2002), asserts Indigenous paradigms when she says:

> We must follow the lead of Aboriginal and Indigenous scholars who dared to trouble western paradigms and assert ours.... Therefore, the methodological approach used in this research is based on the need to give Aboriginal know-

ings and processes a voice by employing methodological frameworks that are mindful of our knowings.

An Indigenous paradigm instigates a paradigm shift in our thinking and approach to Indigenous re-search. This shift moves us from having a "perspective" to researching from an Indigenous worldview. For Leanne (1999), "The true 'paradigm shift' in this research was from externalism to internalism.... The sacred landscape within is as much a part of the 'environment' as the sacred landscape outside of us." In this sense, Indigenous paradigms come from within. Leanne elaborates in her dissertation the nature of an Anishinaabe paradigm:

> The methods I used were Indigenous methods of inquiry. These methods are Indigenous knowledge, and it was not until I realized that Indigenous knowledge is a creative process, that I came to understand this. Because of the nature of Anishinaabe Knowledge, Anishinaabe ways of knowing generate 'results' of a different kind.... These insights represent my understanding as an Aboriginal researcher and they are not necessarily ideas other Aboriginal Peoples share. They represent a snap shot of my own perspective, one truth amongst many.... My purpose is simply to share my story.

Earlier, I illustrated the stages of the development of Indigenous re-search paradigms suggested by Shawn Wilson. In the fourth and fifth stages Indigenous re-searchers would seemingly move toward research originating within Indigenous paradigms. A continuum exists beginning with Indigenous re-searchers integrating "Indigenous perspectives" into existing eurowestern paradigms and moving to purer applications, which, I agree with Willie Ermine, belong in the community and cultural context. Willie,[1] in our conversation, reiterated the power of his worldview very clearly when he shared his ancestry and community roots:

> I'm from a community called Sturgeon Lake. A Cree community. I lived in the community and I grew up in that community. I spent a little while out of the community, so I can say I've lived there most of my life... so that community is my home... it's what I identify with and most of the things that I do are for the community. That is my grounding and I'll always try to speak from that position. Sometimes it's very challenging for me to clearly understand that's where my power source is. I'd like to protect that as much as possible from harm, any kind of harm, or any kind of abuse or anything like that. That's the community I come from.

This worldview illustrates two interdependent elements. It establishes location and a strong connection to territory, nation and community. His worldview is clearly rooted in his ancestral land.

Unanimously, the re-searchers echo that Indigenous worldviews provide a foundation for Indigenous methodologies. A worldview is an intimate belief system that connects Indigenous people to identity, knowledge and practices. Indigenous peoples' worldviews are rooted in ancestral and sacred knowledges passed through oral traditions from one generation to the next. It is how we see the world. It is the inner lens from which we look upon the world. Indigenous peoples' worldviews are rooted in traditions, land, language, relations and culture. Mary Young (2003) argues that our worldview is in our language and to lose the language undermines the worldview of a people. Worldview represents much more than I can outline here, but I want to say that conscious Indigenous searchers acknowledge their worldview as being pivotal to their search for knowledge. Maggie explains that Indigenous methodology is rooted in the re-searcher's worldview:

> If you use an Indigenous methodology, you are, by very essence, incorporating an Indigenous worldview, whether that be Cree or Saulteaux or whatever. You're going to be incorporating an Indigenous epistemology or an Indigenous worldview that will guide your methods. And that's I think where the real power comes in, in terms of Indigenous methodology, because then the research is analyzed through the eyes of an Indigenous perspective.

Worldview profoundly impacts methodology. Worldview directly influences self as re-searcher, self in the re-search process and methodology. Worldview grounds the re-search in process, motive, purpose and roles. It is a source of strength and life. The entire petal flower framework is rooted in Indigenous worldviews. All the re-searchers wrote and spoke about the significance of an Indigenous worldview and paradigm in determining theory, motive, methodology and process. Indigenous methodologies are derived from understanding that we exist in accordance with natural law and spiritual law. For example, I have heard our Elders describe our earthwalk by saying we are spiritual beings having human experiences. I have also been taught that our original teachers are the plants, animals and sacred ones in Creation. Our philosophies are earth-centred, and we originally looked to the animals and earth for our teachings.

Indigenous worldviews have commonalities across Indigenous nations, but there are also variations. For example, Creation stories vary from nation to nation; the Anishinaabe Creation story is different from the Coast Salish Creation story. Our methodologies are relevant to our geography and land base. The animals we revere are different, and our languages are different. However, across the nations, we do share commonalities in that our worldviews are earth-centred philosophies, express strong ties to the land and hold reverence for Spirit and ancestors.

By following the examples of the plants and animals, we remain attuned to the harmony and balance of Creation. The survival of our peoples relied on the kindness, pity and generosity of Creation. Dawn H (1995) illuminates this further:

The Native perspective is undoubtedly a spiritual view of the universe. It includes an understanding that human beings are not endowed with rights to dominate others or destroy that which is around them…. The Native view takes into account the humanization/subjectification of not only people, but animals, plant life, rocks, all of Creation. This is not "mythology," or even religion; it is a way of life, a Native consciousness. The "awareness" is complex in that it not only accounts for this world but acknowledges the guidance of the Spirit world. "Knowing" involves a developed sense which can inform behaviour and influence social action. Dreams, visions, and prophecies still direct and inform Indigenous people in their everyday consciousness. More than that, "knowing" empowers the Indigenous consciousness.

We view our position in Creation with humility and practise reverence to those elements of Creation that gave us life, such as the earth, sun, water and air. The awareness and knowledge we have about ourselves in relation to Creation is integrated into our methodologies as we locate and story ourselves into our search processes. Our worldview/roots are informed by our ancestral lineage, our personal and political history, our cultural make-up, our nations and the sacred laws that govern our care and occupation of Mother Earth. Our location resides in our roots. Maggie, in our conversation elaborated on where her methodology is rooted:

Through this process I've been able to talk to other Indigenous re-searchers, Indigenous people about Indigenous re-search, to hear their stories about what they see matters to them in terms of their methodology. And I've been able to do this coming from not just an Indigenous perspective, per se, but a Cree perspective. Because I really want to — if you want to use the words of the academy, ground it within a Plains Cree epistemology, because that is who I am. I'm part Saulteaux as well. Being Cree I really connect to on a funda-mental basis. And that may be because even when I was a little girl, growing up with my adopted family, we used to have a Cree *moshom* come. A friend of my Dad's. I've had Cree people around me ever since I was a young kid. As kid I have known myself as Cree. So Cree makes sense to me. And so I want to be able to say that I'm looking at this perspective from a Plains Cree perspective, but a Plains Cree perspective that's my own. And my own means that it's also a woman who has a fundamental love for this land from growing up on the Prairies. I have an appreciation for the people of this province, an understanding for their humour, an understanding for just some of the nutti-ness. (laughs) But I love it. And also a woman who was raised bi-culturally. I've been connected with my Indigineity in my family for 20 years. But I was raised in non-Native and I honour that. So I'm going to bring that in as well. And so those things have to come in as who I am as an Indigenous woman and my worldview will entail those things.

Indigenous thought is wholistic in terms of looking to our past to un-derstand our present and to have regard for the future. We acknowledge our relationship to all that is above, beneath and with us. Gratitude for life is encouraged and expressed on a daily basis. We are related to all of Creation: our Mother Earth, Father sky, Grandfather sun and Grandmother moon. Essentially, our knowledge is derived from the realms of the Spirits, humans, animals, plants, sky world and earth elements. In this sense our knowledge is wholistic and creates a wholistic worldview. I spell wholistic with a "w" to denote whole versus hole or holy. Indigenous wholistic theory is the most appropriate to use when doing research with First Nations communities, because "when using non-wholistic theory, difference or reduction tends to be the foci for academic investigation. When using Indigenous wholistic theory, relationship is the key focus for academic investigation" (Dawn M 2005). Colonization, assimilation, oppression and racism have dismembered individuals, families, communities and nations. Wholistic worldviews reconnect and remember us to each other again in process and in practice. Wholistic approaches are inherently inclusive, which fosters and facilitates healing searches and healing relationships.

Dawn further states that Indigenous wholistic theory is a culturally based grand paradigm with complex organisms and interfacing components. It operates with a focus on maintaining equilibrium and harmony within the whole. All the re-searchers in their thesis or conversation, at one point or another, refer to Indigenous wholistic paradigms and concepts shaping their re-search process. Jo-ann (1997), in her dissertation, elaborates:

> The First Nations philosophical concept of wholism often refers to the inter-relatedness between the intellectual, spiritual (metaphysical values and beliefs and the Creator), emotional, and physical (body and behaviour/action) realms to form a whole healthy person. The development of wholism extends to and is mutually influenced by one's family, community, Band and Nation. The image of a circle is used by many First Nations peoples to symbolize wholeness, completeness, and ultimately wellness. The never ending circle also forms concentric circles to show the synergistic influence and responsibility to the generations of Ancestors, the generations of today, and the generations yet to come. The animal/human kingdoms, the elements of Nature/land, and the Spirit World are an integral part of the concentric circles.

Our worldviews are cyclically governed by natural and spiritual laws. Missisak, in our conversation, said the following:

> It's what else is happening around me (referring to life as a single parent and geography) because what I did in my thesis process was so much assisted or guided by my life around me. I'm from the North. You know my background is from the land base. I grew up on the land and I grew up with a lot of understanding of herbal medicines and traditional medicines and grew up with offering tobacco or placing tobacco — we didn't say offering tobacco. That's such a White word. That we placed tobacco and to give thanks for taking what we took. So I grew up with those very basic principles that's imbedded in our language and on the land.

Tobacco/*semaa* is a sacred medicine and is used to recognize Spirit. Our ancestral ties and our spiritual ties are so strong that even if a person has just a drop of Indigenous ancestry, there's still a bloodline and Spirit connection, and that Spirit might find its voice through that person somehow in some way, and so we have to be really careful and respectful of that understanding. Indigenous wholistic thought demonstrates an understanding of our past and our understanding of the Spirit in our present and how we walk in our day-to-day life. Wholistic thought and processes make Indigenous methodologies distinct. According to Indigenous wholistic thought, knowledge can also be internally derived. Willie (1995) acknowledges the "inner" space and "inner" knowing within Aboriginal epistemology, identifying the ways inner knowing is inherent in Aboriginal epistemology:

> Those who seek to understand the reality of existence and harmony with the environment by turning inward have a different, incorporeal knowledge paradigm that might be termed Aboriginal epistemology. Aboriginal people have the responsibility and birthright to take and develop an epistemology congruent with holism and the beneficial transformation of total human knowledge. The way to this affirmation is through our own Aboriginal sources.

At the heart of Indigenous epistemology is spirituality, and as Indigenous peoples we are responsible to validate spiritually derived knowledge and the various forms of evoking this knowledge and not replicate western research paradigms (Peter 2002). I agree with Leanne (1999) when she says, "Aboriginal worldviews and knowledge systems are spiritually based and that much of Indigenous Knowledge is spiritually derived." Spiritually derived knowledge infers that knowledge also comes from dreams, visions, ceremonies and prayer. It is knowledge that we can search for and gather. For example, rituals and ceremonies come from spiritually derived knowledge. Knowledge on healing comes from the Spirit realm. Spiritually guided paradigms call attention to an existing relationship with the Spirit realm, Creation and those "power-helpers" or Spirit helpers who walk with us. Leanne elaborates:

> Spiritually derived knowledge is fully integrated into the consciousness of Anishinaabe People and contemporary Aboriginal People who follow traditional ways, and into Anishinaabe Knowledge.... Given that the idea that knowledge is spiritually derived is so well documented... it is interesting that it is left out of most non-Aboriginal definitions of TEK [traditional ecological knowledge].

Search frameworks have ethical and spiritual considerations and require us to consider the act of research within the guidelines the Creator gave us to honour the knowledge we have (Peter 2000). In our conversation, Raven talked a lot about attending to Spirit and acknowledging the spiritual paradigms and sacred epistemology in Indigenous worldviews:

Well, I think the first thing that comes to mind when I think about Indigenous methodology is attending to Spirit. So attending to the spiritual/sacred episte-mology of an Indigenous worldview, Indigenous ontology, our reality. Because our reality and our ways of knowing inform everything that we do. It informs how I live my daily life, it informs how I conduct myself and my ambitions, how I play it, how I act out those things that I am directed to do or choose to do. So in terms of research, that's the first thing that comes to mind because from that, the framework then is a sacred spiritual one. From that sacred spiritual framework, regardless of whether it's research or anything else, there's certain things that need to be dealt with and those are dealt with through protocol, through cultural protocol. Mine's going to be different from yours, but basically that's the way it plays out. And then, once those things are dealt with, we have freed up energy to move ahead towards our desired goal.

Spirituality is inherent in Indigenous epistemology, which sees everything in relation to Creation and recognizes that all life has Spirit and is sacred. Raven further said:

I think primarily the distinct element is that ontological and epistemological framework from which we derive not only natural law, but certain spiritual law, from which we derive practices and protocols. I mean maybe there's academics out there who say, "Well, that's kind of the way I did it" you know, "I'm Catholic and God says this and God says that. And so when I'm at work I don't fool around with my wife. When I go home, I've got to use birth control." You know? But my experience of growing up with western religion was it was very compartmentalized, that it was relegated to Sunday between 11:00 and about 2:00 and after coffee hour and then the rest of the time was, you know, kind of the rest of your life. This framework isn't compartmentalized, it is the foundation. Yeah, it's the foundation, and what else is unique is that Creator is the protocol. The reason why we engage in protocol, in the knowledge gathering and the ethical reciprocity. That's one of the primary tenets of our ontology. If it takes away from nature, you have to give it back, so that there's a balance. Because the only person that was going to lose out is you, in the long run, we know that.

Many of us argue for methodologies that are grounded within Indigenous intellectual traditions. Dawn H began her dissertation by telling a story about how she found her voice and with her assertion that the voices of Indigenous peoples should not be silenced. She describes her journeys and dreams and addresses her fear of protecting the knowledge by not speaking or writing about it where it could be disrespected. This is a powerful entry into signifi-cant Indigenous ways of knowing and processes of coming into the knowing. Dawn travels and attends ceremonies and talks with Elders — talks about her fears and shares her dreams for guidance.

Native knowledge is alive in practice because of the oral mode of transmission. Indeed, there is an ongoing conversation in which Indigenous peoples have long participated. The experiential nature of Native knowledge fosters a rich and total sense of understanding process…. Once one enters the Indigenous mode of learning it is wholistic and accumulative, not deconstructive.

Dawn adds that our conversations with Spirit are "normal" for Indigenous peoples and that this presents a paradigm shift in how we begin to think about our research and research methodologies:

> The level of assumptions differ from that of "western" assumptions. Indigenous people assume it is a real event to engage in a dialogue with the Spirit world as much as with the physical world. Indigenous people assume it is normal to believe all of Creation has a Spirit and only the Creator can provide the laws we abide by. If we take into consideration Indigenous understanding of knowledge we can begin to fully comprehend Indigenous reality and issues arising from that reality, such as Native history, culture, resistance, spirituality, and so forth. Therefore, we must place our "facts" within a Native context to represent events truthfully. (1995)

Attaining an Indigenous worldview is not a vicarious process; you cannot read about it and then believe it in your mind — you must live it wholistically. An Indigenous worldview is comprised of Spirit, heart, mind and body, and you have to understand the circle, you have to understand what that means and how you do things and how you more or less walk. Our worldview directly corresponds to how we approach our search. For example, Maggie began with a need to root her methodologies in an Indigenous, not a western, worldview:

> Methodology needs to be rooted in your worldview and it's not just about methods, it's about methods and worldview. So I had been going in thinking that, "Okay, well, there's a buffet of western methodologies and I know I want to interview, so I'll just pick something from that buffet that fits," right? "So I'll take maybe a critical perspective or grounded theory where I could work in critical perspective or a feminist perspective or whatever and just kind of fit it in" and then I could do my interviewing, right? And then I realized that it just wasn't fitting. I couldn't figure out how to do that. I was just becoming increasingly frustrated, because no matter which methodology I looked at that was currently available, they weren't really using an Indigenous perspective, per se.

Only after identifying the need for Indigenous perspectives could her organic methodological process emerge. In our conversation she further said:

> And I couldn't find western methodologies that were saying the same things to me. And from my own place, my own history and my own story as an Aboriginal person, I needed — I knew I needed to go back there, I needed to go and link who I am as a person with how I approach this research. And I just couldn't find one that really fit, or one that really was able to connect me as a researcher, as an Indigenous re-searcher, to the Indigenous re-search that I was about to undertake.

Her search ultimately led to going home to her roots, which became central to her methodology. She had to live her methodology. And "coming home" was a blending of search for self, creating space for self and a process and journey of her search for Indigenous methodologies. Our roots as Indigenous people create a unique position from where we search. Being an Indigenous person in a search for knowledge situates me in a place that non-Indigenous people can never occupy. We have inner cultural knowledge and common experiences of colonization and its subsequent impacts on our families, communities and other relations in Creation. Indigenous people can recognize the reality of other Indigenous people (as was the case with Dawn H's search) without having it take years and years to explain and describe.

Principles

Indigenous methods that are rooted in Indigenous worldviews and philosophies promote Indigenous-based ethics and principles in the research process (Archibald 2008; Kovach 2009; Weber-Pillwax 1999; Wilson 2003, 2008). Our principles and ethics as Indigenous people set us apart from western researchers. Ten of the eleven dissertations I examined identified frameworks based within Indigenous philosophies, such as wholism, the seven grandfather teachings and spirituality. Essentially, the worldviews and principles of Indigenous re-search are embedded in the methodologies themselves. These worldviews are also made up of Indigenous principles, such as respect, reciprocity, relevance, humility, gratitude, purpose, truth, kindness, sharing, balance, harmony, love, bravery and wisdom. Jo-ann (1997) identified four principles she gained an appreciation for during her research process:

> (1) respect for each other and for the cultural knowledge; (2) carrying out the roles of teacher and learner in a responsible manner (a serious approach to the work and being mindful of what readers/other learners can comprehend); (3) practicing reciprocity where we gave to the other, thereby continuing the cycle of knowledge from generation to generation; and (4) reverence towards spiritual knowledge and one's spiritual being.

And Peter (2000) acknowledges the intricate relationship between the teachings and ethics in the practice and art of knowing humility and exercising gratitude.

> we learned to take a canoe from a cedar without felling it
> slate for tools profuse with islands
> not just a way of life but life itself
> hunting trails berry trails trading trails
> we assemble bit by bit the canoe giving thanks
> in that urophilosophy calls "conceptual space" t/here
> I speak with the assembled tree nations to a particular tree

asking permission to use part of its clothing its body its spirit
as a vehicle for my journey of words ideas intentions actions feelings
as a companion
paddle paddle paddle swooooooooooossshhh

Indigenous worldviews and knowledge have our codes of conduct and ethics embedded within them. Humility is in the asking for permission and giving thanks for receiving. Laara (2002), in her dissertation, shared her ethics and protocols and the use of tobacco as a sign of gratitude to the Aboriginal people who helped her along her research journey:

> Because I was relying on Aboriginal people to "help" me with this research journey, I decided to use tobacco to demonstrate my gratitude to them. For example, for the purpose of this research project, I asked the participants to give of their experiences, their knowledge, their thoughts, and their commitment to make this thesis a reality. I also informed them that I would provide a copy of my thesis to each person that was involved: a gift to acknowledge their contributions. By understanding the research outcomes, they knew that in giving their time and energy to this project that they are contributing to a body of knowledge that is needed to contribute to the improvement of Aboriginal Peoples. Also, in preparation for the sharing circle I offered tobacco to the Elder as a way of asking him to carry out a certain responsibility.

Michael (1997) used the term "epistemological humility" as he talked about recognizing, through his search, an awareness of the tentative nature of theories:

> In relation to research processes and community participation, I regularly took part and assisted in traditional ceremonies and rituals to support my inward journey. I also tried to follow proper conduct for working with Aboriginal people traditionally. For example, I offered tobacco to the informants to show my respect to them and acknowledge that I was interested in something they had. Another example was that I offered each of them a gift of a wool blanket after they shared their thoughts. These gifts were given in order to follow through with the concepts of mutual support and maintaining harmonious relationships.

Patricia (2003) relied on the ethics that she was taught from her community and, like Willie, asserts the community context as carrying forth our roots:

> The ethics I followed were ones I learned in my community. If the Anishinabek Métis trust that all knowledge derives from the Creator and that it is primarily spiritual in content and essence, then dreams and ceremonies are the way to approach life. When I had dreams of my father giving me advice, I knew that I should continue with this dissertation

Patricia notes the demand placed upon her as a researcher following Anishinaabek ethics:

The Anishinabek and Anishinabek Métis believe that we are put on Earth to live our lives in Menobimadizenwin (life in balance, the Good life, respectful life). I have tried to include these teachings in this book in a contemporary environment. As I prepared to undertake this book, and was thinking about ethics, I realized that Anishinabek ethics are more exacting and demanding than any others that I am aware of. These teachings forced me to look at my self and how I related and interacted with my social world. They did not allow for academic distance. Bravery, wisdom, love, respect, humility, and truth guided this dissertation and contributed to its trustworthiness and validity.

All the re-searchers pursued their search with a goal of acting in accordance with the teachings of *minobimaadiziwin* — to live a good life, in balance and with respect for all of Creation. Patricia used the seven grandfather teachings of the Anishinaabe as an ethical foundation to *minobimaadiziwin* in the research process. In our conversation she expressed the importance of checking with community:

> I decided I just wanted to stand my ground on what I wanted to write on. If I'm going to write on my community, I have to make sure that it's respectful to my community. I have to make sure that people in my community agree to what I'm doing. So which means I have to keep checking back, eh. (Kiskshekabayquek)

Standing one's ground, in Indigenous contexts, means that our re-search methodologies are geared toward operationalizing our worldviews, regaining our humanity and embracing that Anishinaabek/Indigenous way of life.

All the re-searchers unanimously agreed upon respect as a core principle. Respect is a wholistic value and can be enacted at all levels of re-search. Respect is interwoven throughout this entire work. To learn about the history of Aboriginal peoples and develop a critical consciousness is to illustrate respect. To acknowledge and validate Indigenous philosophies and worldviews is to practise respect. Dawn M (2005) promotes this as ethical practice:

> In a nutshell, and in hindsight, this paper promotes another, perhaps Indigenous, methodology for doing coursework and research. Identity is dynamic and situational, knowledge is wholistic and rooted in genealogies connected to the land, and the questioning and sharing of ideas through speaking, writing and publishing can be accomplished more appropriately by greater attention to etiquette, or the ethics of personal relationship. If we can get beyond polarization and competitiveness, acknowledge the dynamic nature of both identity and knowledge, and take to heart the concept of relationship, then we are better empowered to seek knowledge, in relationship, with respect.

Lawrence Gross (2002) agrees that respect is in the Anishinaabe teachings of *minobimaadiziwin*. The life goal of the old Anishinaabe was to follow the Anishinaabe teachings of *minobimaadiziwin*, and respecting the dictates and beliefs enabled this. We need to apply these understandings and teachings today to rebuild and recover from colonial trauma. Respectful research implies a search process with a goal toward creating and living a "good life." In my conversations, respect is enacted when Indigenous worldviews and knowledge are positioned at the forefront. Respect is enacted by following protocols and exercising reciprocity. Michael, in our conversation, talked about the importance of relationship and emphasized how he respects his relationships with Elders:

> One of the most important is relationship. For example, there's one Elder that I met a couple years ago, so I've only known him [for a short while]. And I've known another fellow from there who I met a couple of years ago. They're from different communities, but they're both residing in Saskatoon. And I initially thought, "Well, maybe I could consider talking with them," not interviewing, but talking with them, listening to them mostly. But then I thought I didn't have a strong enough relationship with them. And that's very different than a western point of view, which would say, "Well, you need to break out of that relationship and not let it interfere as much as you can." Whereas whenever I pay attention to Elders and whenever I see learning going on, that's very significant. There's an emphasis on that kind of relationship between people.

The significance of ancestors cannot be ignored. Indigenous people know the ancestors are watching and waiting to share their knowledge. Many Indigenous people pay homage to the ancestors and turn to sacred ceremonies to tap into and seek out ancestral knowledge. Throughout my search, Indigenous re-searchers shared their experiences of accessing portals of knowledge, understanding and direction through dreams, ceremonies, visions, prayer and rituals. The map to get to the ancestors' knowledge is in Aboriginal protocols and ethics and more specifically within Aboriginal epistemology.

Honouring Indigenous knowledge and experience was a central principle guiding my search. I consciously privileged Indigenous sources of information. I talked with Indigenous re-searchers. I read Indigenous re-search projects and I privileged Indigenous authors and scholars. These principles emanate from a need to make Indigenous knowledge and scholarship central to Indigenous re-search. It is Indigenous searchers who enact their worldviews, philosophies and principles in their searches. It is Indigenous searchers who carry memory, history, experiences, knowledge, language and worldviews.

Note

1.   Voices from the conversations are cited with the first name only.

Chapter Six

The Flower Centre: Self as Central

The self is central to Indigenous re-search. The flower centre represents the self and the ways Indigenous searchers include and situate themselves in their methodologies. This includes the re-searcher's location, memory, motive and search for congruency.

What we see revealed through Indigenous re-search is the re-searcher, the self. Within the self exists millennia of Indigenous ancestral knowledge, teachings and Spirit. Willie eloquently reveals the significance of self in the search for knowledge:

> Aboriginal epistemology is grounded in the self, the Spirit, the unknown. Understanding of the universe must be grounded in the Spirit. Knowledge must be sought through the stream of the inner space in unison with all instruments of knowing and conditions that make individuals receptive to knowing. Ultimately it was in the self that Aboriginal people discovered great resources for coming to grips with life's mysteries. It was in the self that the richest source of information could be found by delving into the metaphysical and the nature and origin of knowledge. Aboriginal epistemology speaks of pondering great mysteries that lie not further than the self.

Similarly, Jo-ann (1997) gained an appreciation for "reverence towards Spiritual knowledge and one's spiritual being," illustrating the significance of self as vessel from and to which knowledge flows. Learning about the inner self is the doorway to understanding and gaining knowledge of how to be in mind, body, Spirit and heart in the outer world. When I asked Michael if there was a story behind his research, he replied: "Is there a story behind my search? Somewhat. I'm still trying to unravel it. And the story is 'Who am I?' My identity is always a topic." Dawn M said that, literally, she was all over her dissertation and she linked herself directly to her motives:

> The motivation, "Why am I doing this?" It's about locating myself in my motivations. Like "Why am I doing this? Who am I doing this for?" And of course I'm doing this for myself as well as for these Elders that I've been talking to and for the reasons that many people have for maintaining the teachings and passing them on and ensuring that some of the barriers are challenged. So for me it was about exposing myself so that people can understand me as a human being and about why I'm so passionate about this.

Leanne (1999) and Patricia (2003) both state that we, as learners and search-

The Flower Centre: Self

The arrows depict a strong relationship between the roots and the Self. Self affects the journey (leaves) and varied methodologies in the petals. The strength and supports of Indigenous researchers maintain the pathway between their roots and their centre.

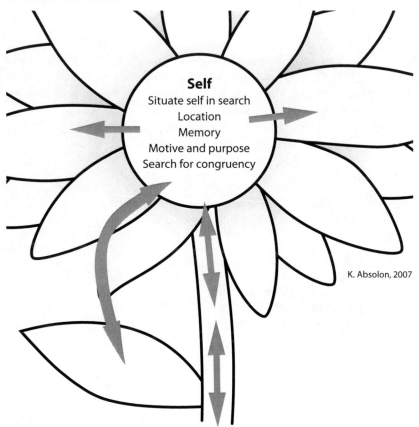

Self
Situate self in search
Location
Memory
Motive and purpose
Search for congruency

K. Absolon, 2007

Indigenous paradigms, worldviews and principles

ers, accept responsibility for our intentions, understandings and knowledge by writing self into our research.

The re-searchers are at the centre of their methodological process. Indigenous worldviews and principles are actualized by Indigenous searchers who are consciously connected to their roots and who have supportive channels to actualize their worldviews. Central tendencies of Indigenous re-search come from the self and from understanding the self in relation to the whole. In many cases, the Indigenous searchers utilized a self-referential and experiential approach to gathering knowledge. Patricia (2003) and Leanne (1999) used culturally based frameworks, where they spoke from their own cultural context and experiences. Our medicine bundle is our own life. Indigenous re-searchers become the vehicle for the expression and application of all that we remember and know. My search is grounded within an Anishinaabe perspective and by an Anishinaabe *kwe* who loves the land and is also bi-cultural. My self is comprised of both Anishinaabe and British ancestry, with a culmination of experiences that resulted from that blend. Our searches become a portal or a doorway to learning about self and self in relation with Creation. The use of self in Indigenous methodologies may open doors that we never thought possible. It connects us to family, community and nation. In that sense, self in the research process cultivates a healing movement of being reconnected and remembered from the dismemberment and disconnections created by colonial policy and actions such as the *Indian Act* and residential schools. Self in Indigenous methodology has no time barriers and will always travel with us as we journey in and out of searches for knowledge.

Other central tendencies in the flower centre further related to self are location, situating self in the search, memory, motive and purpose, and searching for congruency. These methodological tendencies were expressed consistently by the re-searchers. They are not absolute, nor are they separable from one's roots, process, academic goals and/or methods.

Self

Many of the research processes are described as a personal process, and because of our situated-ness, as Indigenous people, our findings come from within. Maggie explains why she situated herself in her methodology:

> This Indigenous methodology that I'm embarking on as an Indigenous woman, it's not just about walking into the university and picking up a methodology that looks good from a book. It's about your own life. It's about who you are. It's about how you have engaged in the world as an Indigenous person, what you know, what's in your story. And if you're going to do this in a way that I think is going to have meaning, and not just meaning to the larger world, but meaning to yourself, you have to go back and you have to go back into story. You have to go back into your own narrative, and you have to find out what pieces are missing for you. And if you're feeling unsettled, why? Why was I feeling unsettled? Why did that book by Silko just throw me for a loop? What was it about that dream that was coming to me that was saying "home is so important"? And so that's part of how my methodology emerged, and that's kind of the funny thing about it. Because I was going down this process where you go. You decide on a topic. You pick a methodology and then you go forward, right? And what happened to me is I was trying to do that. In fact, I had picked phenomenology. But all of a sudden, the more I inquired into Indigenous ways of knowing, the more the knowing showed me the methodology I needed to take. So it emerged.

As Maggie described how her methodology became so interdependent with her life story, I concluded that in Indigenous methodologies, knowledge of oneself is essential to any inquiry. Our knowledge is ultimately what we have when we are on our search. Leanne (1999) identifies Anishinaabe ways of learning and acquiring knowledge and states that we begin with self-knowledge. In her dissertation she integrates personal experiences and perspectives to the body of literature to demonstrate how traditional ecological knowledge is constructed, and she uses her personal voice:

> Indigenous knowledge is personal. It is usually described as "subjective" in the literature, but I think personal is a better description (see Couture 1991). My relationship with each Elder was personal. Knowledge was told to me at a particular time because of who I am and my relationship in the community. When TEK or Indigenous Knowledge resides with the people or its holders, the personal nature of Indigenous Knowledge is left intact.

Like Leanne, many searchers focus on their personal lessons and teachings about the world and their learning experiences. The common use of self illustrates how Indigenous searchers become directly involved in the process. The self is woven throughout the process, linking self to methods. A goal of Indigenous learning and searching is ultimately to learn more about our Indigenous self, history, worldview, culture and so on. Integrating self as methodology, Leanne shares:

> When I initially met the community members that would become my mentors, I asked them to teach me about the land and the environment using their own Anishinaabe ways. They agreed, and then immediately planned to take me out into the bush. We continued spending time on the land throughout my work, because being out on the land, doing ceremonies, dreaming and speaking with Elders were the methods they used to teach me. These methods were *their* methods.

Dawn H (1995) used herself when she worked separately with the Lubicon women in that she provided her own cultural knowledge on the clan mothers and role of women, and this knowledge helped the women get together. She found that working with and writing about the women was easier because they weren't involved in their nation's political negotiations and their like-mindedness made the communication and sharing freer. In Winona's (2000) thesis, the framework and foundation is based on her own *nehiyawiwihtamawakans*, Cree teachings, which come from many sources: family, friends, teachers, recorded oral history collection and a handful of Cree writings. Doing oral history the Cree way is as much about social relations as acquiring information. Oral history, Winona says, is unique from literate traditions because "they are as much about social interaction as they are about knowledge and transmission." She says that oral traditions are living, interactive and participatory by nature:

> A study of kayâs âcimowina, *old stories,* has taken me moose hunting and taught me to clean and prep such fine feast food delicacies as moose-nose and smoked intestine soup. Traditional copyright teachings came in the wee hours of the morning, over cold Tim Horton's coffee in a 4x4 truck heading down the Peace River Highway. One of my teachers has a propensity for second-hand store shopping. Entire days have been spent hopping from one shop to another, mining sale bins for gold... Cree education is based on interactive and reciprocal relations, and all knowledge comes with some personal "sacrifice."

Her expression, "cumulative knowledge-bundle," refers to the valuable knowledge she accumulated over the course of a lifetime. It was transmitted from relatives and was shared with her to use with respect and integrity. The origins of this type of knowledge, Winona further states, do not lend themselves to footnoting according to academic convention.

With confidence, I assert that conscious Indigenous re-searchers are doing re-search *with* other Indigenous peoples, communities, cultures and lands and on issues important to Indigenous people. Raven Sinclair (2003: 119) says "insider research" occurs when the searcher is a member of the researched group and the research meets several criteria such as Native involvement, usefulness to the community and cultural relevance. Conscious searchers are searching topics essential to their own wellness, the goal of living a good life or making the world better for generations yet to come. All the searchers were engaged for a cause greater than the production of a graduate dissertation. We want to make a contribution for the collective good of the community, nation or "Indian situation" in Canada. This is all about saying and being who we are.

Location

All of the re-searchers located themselves, which included things like identifying their nation, name, clan, family, territory and where they receive their teachings. Almost all of the researchers detailed stories about critical life experiences and shared personal aspects of their life. In this sense, searching for knowledge promotes an identification of location, which I think is distinctly Indigenous and goes directly against the positivist eurowestern research presumption that there is only one truth, that neutrality and objectivity are possible and that to safeguard against researcher bias, the researcher's location doesn't (and must not) matter. In Indigenous contexts location does matter. People want to know who you are, what you are doing and why. Peter (2000) identifies his clan and community and talks at length about the landscape, his people and his relatives:

> I am from the grizzly bear clan and the wolf clan my community is n"quat'qua

skatin saktin samahquam xa'stsqa (port douglas) mount currie the old pemberton meadows village and those places up there where people do not live anymore because the animals and fish are gone the forest have been cut down and the water is polluted my community is the towns and reserves along the fraser where my people live.

Dawn M (2005) also locates herself. Such stories are worth telling because our location distinguishes us from everyone else. "You must say who you are when you tell your truth. When discussing whatever phenomenon you are concerned about, you have to speak from your own experience. This is done so that your truth is apparent" (Patricia 2003). Jo-ann says she locates to establish validity for her "self-referential approach." Dawn H (1995), at the onset, located herself in the following way:

> I am a Native woman, Mohawk, Wolf Clan, a member of the Hodenasaunne people of Six Nations of the Grand River. My name is Dega ge ja whistja gay — Flower by the River. I live and walk in my grandmother's footsteps. I walk with my ancestors, listen to them and love them. It is my ancestors whom I obey first — even at the expense of personally loosing a great deal for a greater purpose. I will tell you about this later. Being a Native woman, I also live with all the negative social problems associated with our people: high rates of alcoholism, violence, suicide, ill-health, high mortality, poverty, and despair. They are not statistics to me. They are real — a part of me, my everyday life. Writing this dissertation as a requirement for my Ph.D. in anthropology is also a part of my reality.

I really like this passage because her location is not obscured or hidden in the pages; nor does she try to situate her research independent of herself. We are not left guessing who the author is or where her perspective is coming from. The location is up front, clear and visible. Describing location, in Indigenous contexts, is part of ethical re-search. Because of the biased and obscured history of research on and about Indigenous peoples, visibly locating allows readers to make their own judgements about the research, knowing that there is no such thing as neutrality. Location reveals who we are beyond a family name. It reveals who we are in relation to the world, the earth, our nations, our clans and so much more. Our location reveals a worldview and cultural orientation, which is central to what and how we search.

Locating ourself may occur through a story, a narrative of our name, family and history. Location involves establishing our connection to the land, Spirits and ancestors. Location is central to establishing legitimacy and credibility as a researcher. Laara (2002) shares stories of her name, her Cree identity and her family. She talks about the political, legal and cultural labels of herself and the impact of Bill C-31 on her family, particularly the women. Essentially, Bill C-31 was, among other things, a 1985 *Indian Act* amendment re-instating Indian women and their children to their Treaty Rights. Location exposes us so that our audience can understand the position from which we search. It reveals what we stand for and relates to our motives. Lara explains further:

> In order to situate myself in this dissertation, I invoke an Aboriginal tradition of orality: Atchanookewin (storytelling), albeit in writing. In this section I tell a story about me: where I started my path, where I have been, and where I am going with this research. Like the quotes above, one of the "gifts" of knowledge that I learned from Aboriginal knowings and processes is the importance to acknowledge who we are and tell where we are going.

Location links experiences of the self with experiences of others, facilitates connections and associations and heals relations. Identifying self as an "insider" is important so that the audience can form their own opinions regarding our validity as a researcher in Indigenous territories. They can discern for themselves what they want to harvest from our search and what they want to leave behind. How we locate self can affect the kind of influence we have and who will listen to us. It's a time to share and give back, and we share ourselves and put ourselves forward for these reasons and more (Absolon and Willett 2005; Kovach 2009).

Location varies from person to person, depending on our context. As we grow, change, learn and transform, how we locate changes. This is common because of our colonial history and experiences with residential schools and adoptions. Dawn M (2005) gives an example of how she does this:

> [For years I have] been learning about different ways to think about my own identity. At first, I didn't know I had one; other than mild discomfort and a sense of not belonging in most situations, didn't realize that this concept had real effects in my day to day life… this personal confession is relevant here, to examine the concept of situational identities. What I have described is a brief template upon which issues of identity play out: what my ancestries are, where I'm from, what I speak, the primary conflicts, consequences and conclusions.

Location addresses issues of accountability, validity and reliability, meaning that when we say who we are, the readers can form their own judgements about our credibility and authority to search and write (Absolon and Willett 2005; Monture-Angus 1995; Sinclair 2003). I agree with Margaret Benston (1989), who states that the notion of scientific objectivity, so prominent in western positivist research, is in fact a false notion, arguing that neutrality in terms of gender, race, socialization and humanness does not exist. I believe many researchers falsely present their research as objective simply because they omit locating themselves. Taking ourself out of the picture presents a misrepresentation that the author does not matter and that the researcher's gender, race, class, sex, age or identity has no impact on the research. In reality it is *people* doing the research and *people* interpreting and making meaning; *who they are* does impact the interpretation and meaning and *who they are* does matter. Personally locating ourself, as an Indigenous principle and methodology, counters false notions of neutrality and objectivity (Absolon and Willett 2005; Benston 1989). In our conversation, Dawn M articulated the relationship between location and standing one's ground as an act of assertion and resilience:

> Coming out as Indigenous, you know, coming out as not only Indigenous, but coming out as embracing Indigenous worldviews and ways of being and ways of knowing, and ways of doing things because these things all have operated in my life, all my life. But the old situational identity thing, like I'm a private person and I don't go around telling people what I know and what I don't know and who's taught me what. So in a way this was coming out as putting my private self on display and also putting myself as wholly supportive in identifying with Indigenous worldviews and ways of being. So for anyone who had any doubt about where my allegiances lie, they won't have after reading my dissertation.

Given the reciprocal nature of Indigenous communities, Indigenous re-searchers naturally identify their relations within a community and offer linkages between themselves and the research process (Bishop 1998b; Martin-Hill 2008)). Winona, Dawn M and Dawn H shared their experiences in illustrating the link between location and re-search relationships. Relationality is woven throughout Indigenous scholarship and conveys an understanding that we are beings in relationship with all of Creation (Cole 2006; Wilson 2003). Location is situated in the self and comes from the self, yet it is explicitly related to one's paradigm, or worldview, and is guided by one's principles.

Situate Self in the Search

One day, I realized that Indigenous methodologies are not just about the hows, but also the who! The methodology is just as much about the person doing the searching as it is about the search. Unanimously, all the re-searchers identified the importance of our personal connections to our research. All the re-searchers echoed that when we do re-search we are ultimately doing research about ourselves, families, communities, nations, histories, experiences, stories and cultures. This was a big epiphany for me. Our personal, familial, cultural, traditional and historical connections *are* evident in our searches.

Situating ourselves in our search is distinctive. Our re-search is personal. We are subjective and we want to see benefit to our communities, our families and the generations to come. Kishebabayquek told a rich story relating to her personal responsibility and obligation for situating herself in her research. Her story illustrates how her research journey centres on her and her family and how she came to write about her father's knowledge of the Anishinaabek

Métis. She begins by talking about the survival of knowledge. In the following story, Kishebabayquek speaks with a dialect that is a combination of english and Anishinaabe:

Okay, in my Dad's generation in his family there was two of my aunties on his side of the family still alive, and two of my uncles and three of my aunties were still alive. As far as anybody was making sure those stories survived. 'Cause [my dad] was raised in the Hudson's Bay Post, his father was manager, he was on the trap line, knew life in the bush and he knew medicines. He actually lived out in the bush with people still living in wigwams and actually he knew all that lifestyle. He knew how to survive like that. But out of his whole family he was the only one that was taught that way of life. And then I realized that is why he wrote it down. He might have had 16 children, but as far as making sure those stories continued or the Lake Nipigon land stories, he had to make sure that they continue. And the best way to make sure they continue is to write everything down and because things have changed. People aren't just sitting around listening to old people talk about stories anymore.

Before my dad lost consciousness [in hospital] he told my mother… "Dolly's gotta finish those stories and tell her to get those stories back from this guy. She has to finish them." I neglected that obligation for about 16 years. My dad died in '87 and we started looking at those stories in 2000. So 13 years I neglected my responsibility. I said that I forgot, but I really didn't. It's still hard to talk about sometimes eh! But when I started thinking about it I wondered why did my dad do that (tell my mom I had to finish the stories). He had actually already given the manuscript to this other guy and this guy was trying to figure this out.

I was thinking why me and maybe it had to do with my mom's side. When I was a little kid I'd be hanging out and there are things that I know and the others will ask me, "well who showed you that?" or "how did you know to do that?" For example, I was cutting up moose at my mom's house and my sister comes in and I was looking at her sittin' there and said to her, "what are you doing?" I threw a knife at her [laughs out loud] and said "come here and help me." She says "well I've never done that before!" I say "what do you mean, you've never done that before?" I'm looking at her and so I showed her [how to cut the moose] and she says "you know this is the first time I've done this" and she's one of my older sisters. I said "don't you remember when we were kids, this was always going on?" She said she never had to do it. I said "well this isn't the first moose I cut up" [laughs and laughs]. I learnt this from my dad and my brothers. My mom said that you [Kishebabayquek] were the only one [of 7 sisters] who would do that when you were growing. The others wouldn't skin a rabbit or do anything and she said "you were always there and checking out what people were doing" and so I thought okay my dad choose me to tell stories. I have to make sure that's done properly. So I thought okay… to make my family understand and to make my community understand and this larger academic environment that I was in and the audiences that I have to try and get to. So I put it in a framework… then I starting writing.

Kishebabayquek further talked about accountability, purpose, truth and the relationship between herself in her re-search:

> If I wanted that story that I was part of crafting to be considered true in my family and my community, I had to make sure I was included or else I was just generating knowledge for no reason. And you don't generate knowledge for no reason, 'cause when you start looking at *nandagikenim*, it's an active verb. It's like animate. It's alive and *naandamin*, it just means "know." It's like knowledge, but that you are trying to know something. It is like a verb, *needamin*. It's never static knowledge like in books. It's always something you're trying to get to and you never have people, old men or old women say that they know things. This is going to be based on truth and the way that my family and community determines truth is that people have to be part of the story that you're telling. Also, you have to make sure that you're accepting the responsibility when you do it. You also have to make sure that there's a relationship between what you're trying to know and yourself. So you have to make sure ceremonies are there, even if you are just laying tobacco out, and I think I've done that a few times when I was praying during my masters. I'll probably be doing that during my dissertation too. Making sure that that the Spirits are full. If I'm trying to do this it's gotta reflect, not just well on me, but it has to reflect well on my family and community and that I'm doing the best job possible and in the right way possible. So I did that and I got to the point where I could see that it was gonna be finished and that it was the way it was suppose to be.

Kishebabayquek's story shows that situating self in Indigenous re-search is different from eurowestern research in that we acknowledge and include the relationships between self, Spirit, responsibility, knowledge and truth. Situating self in Indigenous searches positions location, political climate, environment, history and cultural knowledge up front and centre.

Memory

Eber Hampton (1995a) wrote that memory comes before knowledge. In my work, memory comes before motive. In my own search, I have markers in my memory of who I am and where I come from that preceded my motivation. In my memory I return home to that place that is culturally safe to be who I am. As a child growing up in the bush, I was taught to look back so that I would recognize my path in order to return home. Do not get lost was the message! I learnt from an early age to always gaze behind me to etch the landscape and its markings in my memory. I learnt to watch for distinct landmarks along the way and not to wander too far without proper tools and to always be prepared in case I did get lost. But I never got lost; I knew how to walk and navigate my journeys on the land. I feel like this search for Indigenous methodologies is similar. I found that all of the re-searchers journeyed into their memory and began remembering who they are and what they know in their own re-search. In our conversation, Maggie shared:

> I started reading Eber's stuff and that really just threw me for a loop. In particular, his one article, on "Memory Comes Before Knowledge." And to me what that article is about –he talks about his own research, but the main message of that article is you have to go back in — I think he uses the metaphor, "the sacred medicine bundle that is your own life," you have to go and find out what your motive is, what's your story, go back into memory, why are you doing this?

Indigenous scholars, through their search, reconnect to their ancestors, land, culture, traditions, language, history and knowledge. The search, in a sense, becomes a catalyst to remembering who we are and what we know and to bringing those truths forward. In my writing I've thought about how we remember, and when we locate we remember where we come from and who we are. I've used remembering in two senses: one related to memory and one related to reconnecting to our ancestors. By remembering we do two things: we bring our truth forward and tell the stories that we need to tell, and second, we reconnect with our communities because we've been dismembered through residential schools, relocations, *Indian Act* policies and child welfare authorities (Absolon and Willett 2004). We have a history of being brutally dismembered from our families, communities, culture, language, ancestors and so on. So when we remember, we actually become re-membered and reconnected with our history, family members, identities, language, culture and ancestors, and our open wounds can begin to heal. Remembering fosters our recovery of our truth and roots. Remembering our truth is important for Indigenous searchers. Through memory I reconnect with my grandmother and my grandfather. I reconnect with the context I grew up in and claim the knowledge and teachings I received in the bush. I don't forget where I have come from or who brought me here. I include those memories and write about them and talk about them. Dawn M articulated how both her masters and doctoral re-search facilitated a remembering process:

> One of the biggest gifts that I've received is remembering what was taught to me and who taught me — my father and my grandmother in particular. And all those things that they made conscious, in my mind, whereas before they were operating unconsciously, like how to engage with people and what is a respectful way and about that vigilance and awareness and all those little subtleties that are steeped in values; values and ways of seeing the universe and relationships. And so that was a real big gift. By passing on the teachings that I've received, I've become aware of the teachings that I've got and where I got them from. I find how I teach is I'll offer a personal anecdote like, "Oh, that reminds me of this situation" or that, and storytelling, or when so-and-so said this to me and I felt this way. And then people can take whatever they want from it. So the whole process was about remembering what I know. The previous thesis, the MA, was about remembering who I am and this one is

about remembering what I know. Yeah. So it was really empowering in that sense, too, it was a real gift. One of my goals was to start giving back, you know, and start doing things to make changes for the good of all our relations and finding out what I know is a good way to start passing it on.

As Dawn says, remembering occurs within the self and relates to worldview and where we come from. Remembering creates cultural mirrors that validate our life and experiences and those of other Indigenous peoples too. The gift of our searches ends up being in the remembering of ancestral ties, their legacies and knowledge. Our histories on the land go back for generations, and when we remember the territories of our families and communities we become reconnected. Searching becomes a gift that invokes memory, and this both re-members us to our nations, families and communities and brings knowledge forward that was meant for us. If we don't remember who we are, how can we pass that on to our children and families? Remembering means that we stay conscious of our ancestors and grandparents and relations who fought and suffered for our survival. Remembering is giving back and contributing to the continuance of Indigenous peoples' way of life and existence.

Motive and Purpose

Across the discussions, in one way or another, everyone expressed the importance of knowing the motives for their search. For some, the motive came from a family and/or community request and need. For others, the search resulted from a call for more information or knowledge in particular areas to further the "Indian cause." One of our motives as Indigenous researchers must be to show that, despite the ignorance of the western world, our theories and methodologies are concrete and real. They have governed our survival for millennia and will continue to do so for generations into the future. Dawn M talked about the desire of people to share this knowledge to ensure it lives on:

> The most important aspect of the process for me was listening to what everyone had shared with me. Because there was a real urgency in what people wanted to share, wanted to be shared with others. And so like putting that together, putting those stories together in a way that people can hear like the importance of those messages and — so that was a real focal point for me. Because that, to me, was the purpose, was to support the transmission of traditional knowledge.

I agree that the ultimate motive is to make sure our knowledge and methodologies live on. Indigenous academic searches are distinct because our methodologies contain an awareness of and integration of the ancestors and our families. It's about survival. Survival means bringing our history, traditions, experiences, knowledge and methodologies forward. Survival means that our children, grandchildren and great-grandchildren will too know who they are and where they come from. Raven stated:

> Our agenda is premised on survival, it's premised on the mitigation of colonial fallout and harm. And so of course in terms of the principles of OCAP (ownership, control, access and possession), I think there really should be another one there — that's benefit. Maybe it should be BOCAP (benefit, ownership, control, access and possession). (laughs) Because that's the assumption, is that research is done for the benefit of someone, whether it's our communities, the younger generations coming behind us or whatever. That of course fits with our epistemology, our teachings of natural law, that you give consideration to the next seven generations.

We do not want future generations to get lost. My search is about making sure that those methodological pathways survive. The academy is the avenue in which I'm working and making a contribution. But the motive is much bigger than that. It's not for the academy. It's for the people. It's for the other students who are also searching for congruency. And it's for our ancestors. It's for my grandparents because they intended their grandchildren to have this knowledge. People have said that this work is important, and I feel my search needs to be purposeful to my ancestors and the broader goals of survival.

Personal reasons generally underlie motive. Searching, for Indigenous searchers, is more than a project or dissertation. Why do research? Why do we choose the topics we do? Why do we situate ourselves within our searches? Knowing our motives for our searches requires an awareness of our location and consciously situating ourself within our research context. Eber eloquently talked about motive and purpose:

> There's two things that are way more important now that I'm not satisfied yet that I've been able to implement. Those two things are the motive for the research: being very clear in my own mind why I'm interested in that topic. What I found out for myself and for graduate students that I've worked with is that Walter McCollach said "all impersonal questions arise for personal reasons" and that's what I found for myself and a few students I was working with... was that there was some reason that their topics were chosen. And that if I understood what my reason was, that the research would improve. I gave a speech about that once, it got transcribed and published. So the whole area of underlying motivation has become more important to me. Awareness of motivation and a lot of times you know we have this idea of research as a rational process, but I believe it is a more emotionally motivated process and what my academic training did, to a great extent, even my Indigenous training did — was to try and minimize the emotion. It may be just my misunderstanding of some of my training that encouraged me to not even to be aware of what was impelling me or why I was interested enough in something that I would put all that work into it over a long period of time. So that awareness of the motivation and the feelings of the reason why it's important to me is interesting

because the better I understand my motives the more on target the work is.

Where I said there was two things that have changed for me: one is to pay more attention to being aware of my motives of being interested in a topic; the other one is to think more about use. Knowledge for something not necessarily just knowledge about something, and part of that is my fields that I ended up working in, you know education and health are applied fields anyways. So I'm interested in knowledge for something. Being very clear about that within myself when I'm doing that.

Jo-ann (1993) retells a story Eber told her about "re-searching" our motives for doing research and when doing so, asking ourself: are my motives and methodologies grounded in First Nations ways of knowing, being and doing? I think of fasting[1] and recall that before I gave my tobacco to go fasting I was always asked by my traditional teacher to clarify my motives for this search. The reasons, intentions or motives for searching or re-searching inform the process.

The reasons why people are interested in their research topics often lie in a memory — where memory and motive, states Eber (Hampton 1995a), come before knowledge. Our memories give us knowledge and power to undertake what seems impossible. Research objectives influence research methodologies. Indigenous searchers believe in knowledge for something, for a reason, for a purpose, as part of living a purposeful life. We live in a society that has been blind to the fact that Indigenous people have knowledge, memory and motive emanating from philosophical thought, which governs the spiritual, political, social and economical relationships within nations. In this sense, conscious Indigenous searchers have been specific and direct about their motives. The following list illustrates the variety of motives articulated by the Indigenous re-searchers:

• to re-enact respectful research in our searches with our own people;
• to empower and emancipate ourselves in order to regain our humanity, restore balance with Creation and ultimately live a good life;
• to advance, support, strengthen, revitalize and restore Indigenous ways of knowing, being and doing, which create Indigenous methodology choices for Indigenous re-searchers as viable in all re-search contexts; and
• to fulfill family and community obligations when specific requests are presented; the search then becomes a way of giving back and making concrete contributions.

The re-searchers all stated that our motives are connected to our personal stories and experiences. Dawn M (2005) dreamt of an integrated healing centre and so the transmission of traditional Indigenous knowledge became the focus of her search. Kishebabayquek obliged her father's dying request to finish his stories and distribute them to the family. Indigenous searchers write for Indigenous audiences first because our searches are first meant to benefit the Indigenous community.

Motive connects to recovering from colonialism. A search for roots then occurs to recover our people, land, languages, cultures and traditions. The journey back home is often a journey of returning to our roots. Motives are rooted in stories describing a search for identity, group belonging and knowledge for who we are, where we come from and what we know. There are myriad possibilities for Indigenous peoples' searches, but they are most often rooted in our Indigeneity.

Search for Congruency

Searching for theories and methodologies that are congruent with Indigenous worldviews and philosophies preoccupies many Indigenous searchers. Here the relationship between roots, self and methods becomes apparent. Dawn M (2005) sets forth one researcher's experience in this search:

> The best way to do qualitative research with urban people working with traditional-based Indigenous health services was to use theories, methodologies and methods that were congruent with — incorporated the same ways of being (ontologies) ways of knowing (epistemologies) and ways of doing (methodologies) — as those same services. To determine congruency, I called on the knowledge obtained as a person of Ojibway and French ancestry living in Vancouver, the knowledge gleaned from my prior education and literature review, the knowledge gained through prayer and dreaming, and the knowledge acquired by interactions with and feedback by individuals from both the pre-study and research groups of people.

Searching for methodological harmony is a strong consideration for Indigenous searchers. Missisak stated to me that "tensions around finding relevant methodologies are apparent." Laara (2002) writes about the frustrating experience in searching for congruency because of the absence of exposure to Indigenous methodologies:

> My search to look for relevant theories and methods was an experience of frustration, confusion and finally elation upon finding Aboriginal/Indigenous writings as foundational philosophies or "teachings" to support/guide my research process.... I read many books on how to do qualitative research, I digested some and upchucked a lot because I realized that many of these theories just did not "fit" with who I was/am, who my "brothers and sisters" the participants were/are. I struggled to find those methodologies that seemed to at least be "kind," "gentle," "trusting," "inclusive," "connecting," "relational" and "non-intrusive" among other principles.

The search didn't end there because Laara was persistent in looking for methods that honoured and supported an Indigenous paradigm:

> Also, I was mindful that I wanted to find a way to work from paradigms that were grounded in ways that reflected our traditions, perspectives, philosophies, histories, and issues that I could build into this research process. As I struggled through resisting western paradigms and methods of research processes, I realized that there were ways of doing research that honoured the integrity of our Indigenous ways of knowing

Maggie also shared how her search for congruency began:

> There was phenomenology, which I first thought about looking at, which looks at the essence of people's stories, right? But it was coming from a western epistemology [way of knowing]. And even though it was looking at the essence of people's stories, it wasn't giving me good direction as to how, as an Indigenous person, do I use my worldview to go about that journey. So there was no way that I could figure out how to fit in my Indigenous worldview, my Indigenous way of knowing, my Indigenous story, into a methodology that currently existed. So I started working on Indigenous methodologies, "What is it? How does it work?" and that's where my questions grew. So it grew out of a real need to be able to figure out for myself how to do this research in an Indigenous way, how to do it in a good way.

The integral relationship between self and paradigm is also revealed by Laara (2002):

> Hence, my choice to draw from researchers whose methodologies reflected Aboriginal knowings and processes to make sense of the data from this thesis. Furthermore, I honour and appreciate the fact that there are now many more Indigenous and Aboriginal researchers who dare to challenge/problematize western research dominance while asserting our knowledge and ways in research processes.

All re-searchers identified that their search for methods congruent with their Indigeneity was instrumental. Indigenous congruency, I believe, is essential to the research principles, methodology and ultimately the outcome. Because all of the research topics are explicitly focused on Indigenous experiences, realities, needs and histories, the researchers' search for methodological congruency includes a consideration of factors such as cultural traditions, community, people, relationships, Spirit, ownership, oppression, empowerment, protocols and decolonizing. These factors became as much a part of the search as was the gathering of data.

When I was growing up in the bush I learnt to search for berries, leeks, mushrooms and good rabbit runs to snare rabbits. I located the markers on the land and used those to find my way. Similarly, many of us are trying to find the familiar theories and methods so we can bring our knowledge into different contexts to help us navigate our search for knowledge. Kishebabayquek talked about her search for congruent ways to include herself in her re-search:

> I'm dreaming and all these things were happening and I know I'm suppose to do this and I just started writing and I included myself in the picture. So I thought one of the ways I thought that I've been taught to write is from myself. I've been taught I'm responsible for the what I do in the world, my words, the ways that I think, the ways that I speak, and I'm responsible for this! So I started writing and at the same time that I was doing that, I was doing this course on qualitative research and then it just struck me... all these theories don't fit and the reason these theories don't fit is that I'm trying to place myself, my family and my community in this nice little box and we don't fit in that nice little box. So then I thought I have to start looking at how do you develop theory? And soon as I had that in my mind... it became easier and it was almost like a door opened and all of a sudden I had to go to the library and I was on the computer. I found all these articles on developing theory and all the pieces just came together and in Toronto — I kept having these dreams and different things kept happening like I was being guided to that conclusion.

We can become gatherers and hunters for knowledge within the academy or other contexts. We find what we need and bring that knowledge and information forward for others. In her thesis, Joann (1997) explains:

> In my search for a culturally appropriate research methodology (a bone needle) about First Nations storytelling, I started with the principle of respect for cultural knowledge embedded in the stories and respect toward the people who owned or shared stories as an ethical guide.

The search for congruency is about transcending contexts. To me, research in the academy is analogous to berry picking, hunting or gathering. We go out there and scout the land, walk around, search, find and gather a basket full of berries. During our searches we climb over rocks, we jump over creeks, we navigate thick bush, and we weave our way through lands of knowledge. When we bring our baskets of berries home, we sort and clean them, eat them or turn them into jam, pies or preserves, and find ways to share them. I see that our traditional knowledge is transportable from the bush to the city or to the academy. I have been taught the skills to not get lost and have internalized an ability to identify my landmarks along my journey. My landmarks today appear in other Indigenous scholars and their work and in affirmations from those around me. Their nods of approval tell me I'm on the right path. Feeling good about what I am doing is another marker, and my intuition has provided me with the direction I need. Transcendable skills exist for Indigenous re-searchers that enable us read the academic landscape during our search journeys. When I think about this search as a search for berries, I can find my way and feel myself as a researcher, knowing that I continue to do what my ancestors have done. Gather, hunt and search.

Collecting the knowledge and experiences of Indigenous searchers and gatherers illustrates a powerful need to search for congruency. Indigenous methodological mirrors reinforce and validate a way of knowing, being and doing that makes sense when doing Indigenous re-search in an Indigenous way. If Indigenous searchers accepted the status quo, stayed in the mainstream of western methods and ignored ourselves, all these insights and knowings would be lost. A determination to stay congruent with culture, traditions, historicity, worldview, family and community creates methodologies that reflect an expression of self in the research. The beauty and distinction of our work then is a result of all that each of us carries within. The flower centre (the self) is acknowledged as integral to Indigenous methodologies in search for knowledge. Self as a methodological re-search tool inevitably implies a journey articulated in the leaves.

Note

1. Fasting is a time of self-reflection and searching with many variations. It often requires one to spend time alone with Creation without food or water for several days in the bush. In some fasting camps the fasters are given medicine or juice. In this process, one is on a search and is usually seeking guidance, answers or renewal.

Chapter Seven

The Leaves: The Methodological Journey

Photosynthesis, the transformation of carbon dioxide and water into nutrients for the plant, occurs in the leaves. The leaves of our flower represent the transformative and healing process and journey inherent within Indigenous methodologies. Our re-search is a learning journey, not always easy and sometimes scary. In our conversation, Raven said:

> It's a constant process for me, it's a journey. And some of those things I can't really articulate to you. Because even as we talk about it, I would jump into the process and the process kind of resides within my Spirit, in my heart. Even if it's only taking some time in my day to reflect upon my participants and to reflect upon a particular concept that one of the participants brought forth. You might want to call it data analysis, or I could call it honouring the Spirit of that experience.

The other Indigenous re-searchers' work also exemplifies transformative processes. The conversations I had with these searchers and others, such as Maggie, Raven and Eber, show that the stories of the re-search journeys are integral to their methodology; in fact, the essence of their methodology is their process. By process I mean their experiences, journey and transformation. Willie, in our conversation, particularly encouraged me to be aware and attend to my process.

An Organic Process

Process involves a progression, a development, a series of steps toward achieving goals. Process can be either a planned or unplanned series of actions. It can be clearly defined and determined ahead of time or nebulous and emergent. Indigenous re-search methodologies cultivate organic processes, which are unplanned and unpredictable. Organic means to emerge naturally. Although these re-searchers had specific re-search foci and goals, an open-ended process was a large factor in their methodologies. Although indeterminate processes can make researchers anxious, a certain degree of trust and faith enabled Indigenous re-searchers in this book to honour their process. Dawn H (1995) shared that her agenda, or search process, wasn't clear from the beginning. The Lubicon, she said, ensured that the process was first directed by them; any academic goals came second. This could make researchers feel conflicted and nervous. Dawn explains:

The Leaves: The Journey

The arrows depict a strong relationship between the self and the journey. The journey is rooted in worldview. The strength of the stem transports the journey between self and research and methodology. The relationships are interdependent.

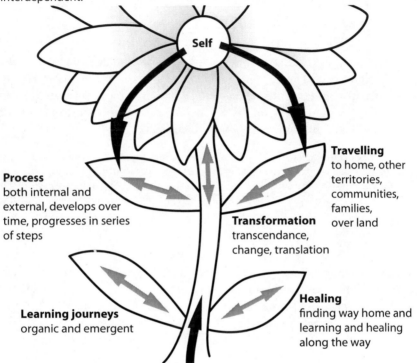

Self

Travelling
to home, other territories, communities, families, over land

Process
both internal and external, develops over time, progresses in series of steps

Transformation
transcendance, change, translation

Learning journeys
organic and emergent

Healing
finding way home and learning and healing along the way

Paradigms, Worldviews, Principles

K. Absolon, 2007

> For over two years, I was unsure of what it was they [the Lubicon] wanted and, academically, I was becoming nervous about the agenda or research focus. It was not until 1991 that I realized they had an agenda all along. They just didn't tell me what it was.

The above quote illustrates that process, when community driven, owned and directed, requires the searcher to relinquish some power and control. I believe it calls for a degree of humility. Our worldview, including belief in Spirit and ancestors, is revealed in our ability to trust process. In Jo-ann's (1997) sharing of how she attuned to her process, the interdependent relationship between process and principles is revealed:

> I have learned from the Elders that beginning with a humble prayer creates a cultural learning process which promotes principles of respect, reverence,

responsibility, and reciprocity. These particular principles are inter-woven into my thesis and their meaning in relation to First Nations stories and storytelling will recur in each chapter, taking on meaning with each use.

Oral traditions are process oriented, and Indigenous searchers manifest orality in several ways. Peter (2000) said he spoke into his computer as he wrote out his words, blending orality with text. As he heard himself say the words, he could feel what he said. He could then see what he heard as he typed. He also spoke into his cassette recorder to have conversations with himself about what he was thinking and writing. I also speak to myself and I talk to the Creator. I am a runner, and I allow the ideas and thoughts to be processed and embodied while I travel over the land. As I run, I churn over my thoughts in my head, heart and Spirit. Learning is a process, and Winona (2000) acknowledges that infinity of developing understanding and knowledge:

> We are a people to whom understanding and knowledge come by way of relationships with the Creator, the past, the present, the future, life around us, each other, and from within. And I am here on this earth to learn... Our searches are neither complete nor wholly representational... they are fragmentary pieces... and most acknowledge they are still learning.

Organic methodology emerges as we attune ourself to our search process. When we listen to our inner knowing, our dreams, the signs around us and our intuition, we become attuned to possibilities that enable an organic process to emerge. For Maggie, this process was a culmination of dreams, journeying home, a pearl necklace, conversations and repeatedly sharing her story. In our conversation, Maggie shared a piece of her story, which provides a poignant example how her journey home became intrinsic to her methodology.

> The methodology came to me in an organic way and not out of a textbook, but out of my own experience and my own feeling of being uncomfortable and reading these different writings by Indigenous people who were saying, "Uh-uh. It's not just here." Like you said, "If you're going to find out about yourself, it's not going to be here in academia. It's going to be out there." And a big thing about the methodology is finding out not just about this objective piece of information that we're going to present to the world that's creating new knowledge, but it's something more connected to who we are as Indigenous people, who we are and what has meaning in our life.
>
> And so what I did was I wanted to talk to people, I wanted to hear other people's stories about research, but I also wanted to capture my own inward knowing and this journey that Indigenous ways of knowing took me on in the past three years. And also what happened as a result of, you know, the dream. It was about a pearl necklace. I was sharing a bit about the pearl necklace and how I was struggling with — I guess for this to make sense I need to go back

and kind of explain my own story of who I am, right? So I'm not too sure how to do this.

Anyway, I was using the metaphor of the white pearl necklace, because when I was a kid I used to wear little pearls for church and — and it was really indicative to me of a very loving, of my White upbringing and the community that I grew up in. I was thinking about a lot of things. I was going back into that medicine bundle, about being adopted. I was thinking about growing up there was a lot of pain around racism. Even though I had wanted to pay honour to the community that I grew up in, at the same time being the only Indian kid in a White school was really hard. And I experienced racism. And so I was thinking about all of this and I was thinking about really painful stuff. And I started to smoke, lost eight pounds in a six week period, which is just not me. I wasn't sleeping. I was reading stuff and I would start crying. I was in a really emotional place. And I was writing, just writing really. Writing from my heart. And so I go up and I just said, "Monty, let's go for a drive. I just need to get out of here." And it was a really beautiful Sunday afternoon. So we went out, we go to the car, and he gets in his side, and I go to my side and there's a pearl necklace. This pearl necklace is hanging from the door handle on my side of the car. And I was just like –we were both stunned, right? I don't want to say it was coincidence because I don't think it necessarily was. I think the universe was giving me a sign.

I knew I had to go home and I knew I had to just be here to write my paper. I knew I had to look into seeing about, learning a little bit about the language. I knew that I needed to be with people, family, both of my families. And I just needed to be home, you know? I wasn't thinking that I needed to come home and necessarily be more than I am in terms of coming home and really trying to engage in ceremony or I just needed to be under the sky. I just needed to see the flatlands. I just needed to see the mothers and siblings, nieces and nephews. I just needed to be here. And I came home.

But that wasn't part of my methodology, that wasn't part of my method. Even when I started thinking about Indigenous methodologies, it wasn't a part of it. It just organically emerged as I was going through this process.

In Maggie's story, the process emerges and facilitates a transformation. Raven said that the process resides in the Spirit and in the heart. I really liked that. In this sense, the process of attuning to protocols, ethics and principles guide the methodology.

Travelling

Process inevitably involves travelling. Who/what is the traveller? Is it you or me? Is it our language, our ways, knowledge, stories or cultural tools? Is it me, you, others? The traveller can be a rock, stone, Spirit, minds, bodies, drums, feathers and, in this case, the words found within the texts and the voices — all these things are travellers. Our voices, words, conversations and thoughts journey from Spirit, heart, mind and body into this work to bring whatever meaning, representation and knowing can be derived from the journey. Indigenous methodologies include stories of who is doing the searching and their journey along the learning path. I really like the way Winona (2000) begins her dissertation with a sense of a new journey:

> She let go of her acreage, sold off the chickens, and gave away the dogs to embark on this PhD program. But she really didn't want to go. Too much work to be done at home — outstanding land claims, watch-dogging federal policy initiatives, the student funding crisis — so many needs and not enough people to do all the work at the best of times. She'd already done two White degrees and really ought to be going back to the bush to pick up her Cree and study more seriously with the Old People. So few of them left. Just couldn't justify the luxury of two years, 2,000 miles south in the land of no winters, for another degree. And for what? Who would really benefit anyway? Done just fine up till now without it. Besides, she was scared.

The journey we embark upon to search for knowledge often begins with inner conflict about leaving community to learn in the big White institution, and this journey may be either criticized or supported by our own people. This journey is full of struggles between the polarities and dualities that we experience from those around us and from within ourselves. It may include physical travel or not.

Dawn H's dissertation involved travelling to South Dakota and Alberta. During those journeys Dawn organized meetings with Elders and Chiefs and held ceremonies. They also deliberated, she said, for many hours over their course of action or directions to pursue. Dawn wrote about seeing eagles and how they were a sign for them, the preparations for sweat lodge and pipe ceremonies and the community of people who all cooperated to do the work they were being directed to do. She talked of the power of the sweat lodge ceremony, the northern lights and sitting with the ancestors after a sweat. Dawn reminds us that being in the community is better because that's where the voices of the people reside. It was important for her to have a community presence. The Chief also told Dawn that being in the community is better. One of her criticisms of writings about the Lubicon is that the voices of the people are generally absent and that the researchers had not visited Little Buffalo or spent any amount of time within the community and with its people.

> I spent as much time with the people as possible. Young and old, everyone had important voices. From the Lubicon and my perspective, this is the contribution of our study. Only the Lubicon could articulate what impact the destruction of the land had and continues to have on them. (Dawn H)

Travelling into peoples' homelands and into their homes to be in their contexts establishes their power base within the research process (Rice 2003). Jo-ann (1997) talks about sharing coffee and stories while meeting a prominent

Elder in her home:

> I met Ellen White in the Spring of 1991, but I knew about her long before
> that… When I arrived, Ellen had made salmon chowder and bannock. As we
> ate, Doug and I teased each other about who drank the strongest coffee — me
> from the Sto:los or him from the Nanaimo Coast Salish. In a way we're related
> by the Lalq'emeylem language, although Ellen's community has dialectical
> differences. They call their language, Hul'qumi'num. We come from the same
> cultural traditions. I felt accepted and at home there; I felt like a member of their
> extended family. Before we began working, I offered Ellen White a Starblanket
> as a gift from the First Nations House of Learning, to thank her for helping us
> with this important work.

Enacting the role and power of oral traditions and the strength of the language is methodology in itself (Colorado 1988; Deloria 1996; Hermes 1998; Young 2003). Indigenous languages are descriptive and action or process oriented (Little Bear 2000). The awareness of Indigenous languages and oral traditions causes a conscious searcher to attend to oral process. Circle processes and circle talk are manifestations of oral tradition and Indigenous ways of coming to know (Graveline 2000; Hart 1996; P. Steinhauser 2001; TeHennepe 1997; Weenie 1998). A circle process can take a person on a transformative journey where engagement, involvement and presence are requisites. Humility in process reflects an inward journey and an attunement to that journey within the collective circle. Consistently, Indigenous re-searchers strive to honour their journey by applying their own cultural protocols, such as offering tobacco, gift giving and, where comfortable, integrating ceremony.

Our journeys are also rich with cultural knowledge, people, sharing, learning and experiencing active processes. Peter (2000) presents a truly inspiring search journey, which he represents through a canoe metaphor. He gets in and out of the canoe as he describes his travels across the lands, waters and oceans and his conversations with people along the way. The journey of our searches is also familiar to me, in terms of travelling here and there with my family. My ancestors travelled by canoe through the rivers and lakes of Northern Ontario. We take many journeys: the journey of the thesis; the personal journey; the writing journey; the making meaning journey; the gathering journey of meeting people and having conversations; and the journey with our families along the way. The swoosh of the canoe resonated with my Spirit, and I remembered that navigating the channels of the academy is akin to navigating challenging river channels. Our ancestors negotiated choppy waters, as will we. The motives, process, learning and meaning in the journey makes it worthwhile.

Transformation

Undoubtedly, Indigenous processes are transformative and transforming. All the re-searchers talked about "process" and the journey. They all inspired me to think about Indigenous ways of knowing and the processes involved. I felt supported to acknowledge my own dream work and ceremonies. I turned inward for guidance when I needed direction. The research journey was described by Indigenous re-searchers as transformative for people, and this transformation began within self. Indigenous-based knowledge quests can be life altering and unforgettable. When the Spirit is invited into the search, the essence of the search moves to another level of faith, trust and process. In Indigenous cultural contexts, we are taught to search for knowledge in the Spirit realm. The process of learning how to do this requires personal commitment, sacrifice and a will to engage beyond the physical. Processes exist that prepare us to be with Spirit, and when we seek knowledge with humility and clear intentions, the Spirit might start to reveal answers through those sacred ways. This deep spiritual involvement and transformation is especially important and contradicts the logic and reason in hegemonic eurocentric academies. We need to resist and transcend this hegemony by becoming aware of it and engaging to actively bring an authentic Indigenous presence and contribution! Taiaiake Alfred describes the "most important role for Indigenous academics: as teachers of an empowering and truthful sense of the past and who we are as peoples, and as visionaries of a dignified alternative to the indignity of cultural assimilation and political surrender" (2007: 23). Resistance is a subtext to the journey: resistance to being silenced and rendered invisible, insignificant, uncivilized, inhuman, non-existent and inconsequential. This resistance means we are "committed to integrating traditional knowledge and bringing an authentic community voice" to our work (Alfred 2007: 23). Transforming the injustices that our ancestors endured motivates Indigenous re-searchers to continue to challenge, confront, preserve, defy, resist, remember, reclaim, rename and work toward the rights and recognition of Indigenous peoples of this land. Not only do we transform ourselves through our research, we participate in transforming the academy.

The journey of gathering Indigenous knowledge requires tools of translation because Indigenous concepts become translated into english written text. Translating Indigenous language and concepts into english requires bi-cultural skills and knowledge. Some researchers state that speaking an Aboriginal language is essential and that only through the language will we acquire a true sense of the meaning of what is being shared (Michell 1999; L.T. Smith 2000; Wa Thiong'o 1986; Young 2003). Fluent speakers say that meaning is lost when translating Anishinaabe concepts to english, which is not surprising because the english language did not grow from an Anishinaabe cultural worldview or epistemology. However, I believe that we must work with what we have and do the best we can without perpetuating guilt or shame for the loss of language among our peoples. All of the searchers in the gathering addressed their perception of language. Whether a person is a fluent speaker or not, language is a significant issue in terms of translation of experiences, terms, concepts and philosophies. This must be a methodological consideration for Indigenous searchers.

New forms of english emerge as Indigenous peoples develop Indigenous concepts using english. Wa Thiong'o (1986) says that to combat the contradiction of speaking the colonizer's language we must commit to learning our own mother tongue and speak it with pride. He says that we must tell our stories in our own language and find ways of recording them in script without compromising their cultural origins. Breaking the rules of language and creating a new language forges another level of resistance to colonialism. "Indigenous english" is a form of english that includes Indigenous phrases and perspectives; it morphs the dominant language into something that the non-Indigenous audience may not recognize or relate to but is understandable to the Indigenous audience. Translating language can be more reflective of a hybrid of english and Anishinaabe worldviews. Peter's (2000) dissertation, which was published in 2006, is a rare delight in the way he morphs Indigenous concepts into english; he makes up words, creates a language and blends words together. To me, his terms make sense in describing ludicrous, insane, ironic, painful, outrageous and chaotic experiences, events and actions. He calls it "Anticolonial isomorphing of stories and epistemologies from Indigenous language into english and back." Peter's dissertation contains many examples of morphing language to critique and ridicule colonialism. On the idea of perpetuating myths he says:

> using the racist term "mythology" "myth" and "mythic"
> well they are mythtaken we have no myths we have only stories

Indigenous methodologies raise Indigenous voices out of suppression. Voices are sounded and the words in the peoples' stories are heard. Conveying Indigenous knowledge, stories and experiences in english means creating a language and a discourse that captures Indigenous perspectives. Indigenous scholars are contextualizing english within Indigenous paradigms and experiences by using english in creative and diverse forms through works of poetry, prose, storytelling and creating "Indigelish." Indigenous re-searchers such as Peter, Winona and myself talk about creating an "Indian english" to aid in the articulation of Indigenous peoples' experiences and worldviews. I often joke about speaking Ojiberish when new words emerge from my mouth.

As we attempt to translate some concepts into english, we tend to use verbs and lengthy descriptions. Because the Anishinaabe language is very descriptive, it takes conscious thought and effort to articulate an Anishinaabe concept in english. For example, the term for a "heat bug" in Anishinaabe translates roughly in english as "singing for the berries to ripen." "Window" in Anishinaabe translates in english as "where the light shines through." Our language in english becomes very descriptive and our thought processes as we write also become descriptive. Winona in our gathering articulated these issues quite well. *Miigwech* translates roughly to express thanks for all that we are given and a hand gesture accompanies that word. The task of translation of language and concepts is challenging, and some concepts and terms cannot be translated because they are contextual and would become decontextualized if translated. I'm told that there are no english words to describe some Anishinaabe concepts and vise versa. For example, there is no word for "goodbye" in Anishinaabe. The concept does not exist because in an Anishinaabe worldview we say "see you later" or "see you around," indicating that we will meet again sometime and reinforcing a cyclical worldview. Worldview is connected to language translation, and context is an essential element to translation. Dawn M highlights that for Indigenous searchers, translation of some concepts and language becomes a strategic decision, in which they weigh issues of meaning, context and ethics.

Healing

Only a few re-searchers, such as Jo-ann, Maggie, Dawn and Michael, explicitly talked about their re-search journey as healing. However, those discussions were strong enough to acknowledge and include. I believe that healing is also implied through methodological concepts of reconnection, remembering, learning, recovering and reclaiming. In a sense, healing is woven throughout the re-search process. Indigenous re-search becomes a healing journey when what we gather helps us to recover and heal a part of our self, life, family, community, knowledge, culture, language and so on. Indigenous searching is healing as it invokes restoration, repatriation, reclaiming, recovering and relearning. It is about healing wounded Spirits, hearts, minds and bodies. Indigenous methodologies facilitate healing individuals, families, communities and nations. Knowledge searches have facilitated a healing from post-colonial trauma and residential school atrocities. Re-search aids in healing from the dispossession of our homeland. Indigenous knowledge is healing through the use of our own culture, traditions, language and knowledge. Methodological congruency with Indigenous history, peoples, culture, worldview and experiences is about healing and making whole what has been fragmented, severed and wounded.

Indigenous knowledges and methodologies hold the key to our healing, particularly in spiritually based methodologies such as ceremony, prayer, healing lodges and sweats. Circle processes can heal and restore relationships. Our journeys are not just about academic knowledge; they are about our journeys home, to our communities, to our ancestors, to our territories, to other territories and to our families. Returning home can be healing as Indigenous searchers' motives are about cultural identity, learning and healing. About her journey home, Maggie shared the following in a reflective soft voice and it was beautiful to hear:

> I remember Monty and I, we were with family and afterward he said to me, "You're different here than in BC." And, you know, we were just laughing and I said, "Well, what do you mean different?" And he goes, "No, you're different here. It really shows." And I said, "Okay, well?" And he goes, "You're kinder here. You're connected to family. You're connected to people, you're kinder, you're not so much a lone wolf," which is very healing for me to hear. To come here has been really healing, to know that I don't have to know everything, I don't have to be fluent in Cree, I don't have to have been raised on the rez and participating in ceremonies from day one. I don't have to do that. What I do need is a commitment to just learn more, just to be present in the culture and that it's okay to be who I am and where I'm at. And, you know, the methodology, for me it's about — it has no time. It will be with me. And that's something that I think — yeah. How do you write that?

The searching journey is just as much about being Indigenous as it is about collecting information and knowledge. Indigenous re-searchers have generously shared aspects of their research journeys with healing undeniably being a part of that process. The Elders and people we meet along our journey can have positive impacts:

> I recalled the good healing kind of emotion I felt after bringing Simon home. He provided me with good things to think about. He had soothed my anxiety. He had also pointed out some markers that I could place on my "journeying" map, to act as "bearings" to help me find my way as I began to explore the territory of First Nations orality. (Jo-ann 1997)

Maggie shared that the journey opened up doorways and portals for her that facilitated her reconnection to her land and family, which were healing for her:

> I started [this process] with thinking I had to know this all or I couldn't do it. That's what my meltdown was about, initially, that I felt I didn't know enough about my culture. I wasn't Indian enough, so I couldn't go on this journey. And what's been really healing about this journey, in talking to people, is that this is just the beginning of my learning. This is like a portal. We talked about portals. This is like a doorway. This PhD has been like a doorway for me to learn more about my Indigenous ancestry, about what it means to be a Cree woman. You know those sorts of things and what it means to be a Saulteaux woman. And so that's the real gift, because it isn't going to stop when I write up the project and hand it in. It's something that I have for the rest of my life. And I mean I think that's the beauty about it as well, that the possibilities of an Indigenous methodology is that it will open doors for you that you never realized could be opened and that it will be with you for long after when the project's over.

Most re-searchers referred to their search as a journey or learning path, but mainly a journey that was challenging at the personal, emotional, spiritual and mental levels of being. These journeys evidence tenacity and backbone within Indigenous searchers.

Chapter Eight

The Stem: Backbone and Supports

Sitting in the forest observing Creation, I realized that the stems of plants are their backbone or spine. Strength resides in the stem, which supports the flower and provides the channel for the flow of nutrients to and from the roots, leaves, and flower centre and petals; it holds everything together. Conscious Indigenous re-searchers enter the academy with a strong backbone, and in this book it characterizes the critical and bi-cultural consciousness necessary to persevere and succeed in using Indigenous methodologies in the academy. The strengths Indigenous searchers draw on to develop this backbone include a critical consciousness, internal resources and community supports. These, I believe, are what enable Indigenous re-searchers to employ Indigenous methodologies in an academic context. The emphasis in this chapter is on acknowledging the stem/backbone and capacities of Indigenous re-searchers themselves.

Critical Consciousness

A critical consciousness was evidenced by all the searchers. In the academy, the research journey is burdened by the dominance of eurowestern ways of knowing. Identifying our supports is essential to remaining grounded to our values and beliefs as we search and gather. The academic and educational context plays a vigilant role in acculturating, assimilating and annihilating Indigenous culture, identity, traditions and wisdoms. Indigenous knowledge sets are perceived and received with antagonism. Michael Marker states: "The efforts to make education serve the status quo have often made the place based knowledge and identity of Indigenous people seem like an antiquated and sometimes contentious perspective" (2004: 102).

Willie (2000) agrees with the need for a critical consciousness:

> The systems of knowledge production and its dissemination in the West has vestiges of influence from a history of colonialism and imperialism. These vestiges of colonialism translate as appropriation and exploitation of Indigenous Peoples' knowledge in the modern context. Current waves of research projects from western institutions, under global economic auspices, threaten to continue the appropriation and exploitation of Indigenous Peoples' intellectual and cultural property. Confronting these neo-colonial practices requires a broad and protracted process of conscientization about research ethics, cultural imperialism, and the protection of Indigenous Peoples' knowledge.

The Stem: The Backbone and Supports

The stem's strength supports the leaves and flower, and the stem is supported by the roots. The arrows depict the interrelationship and interdependence between the stem and the whole.

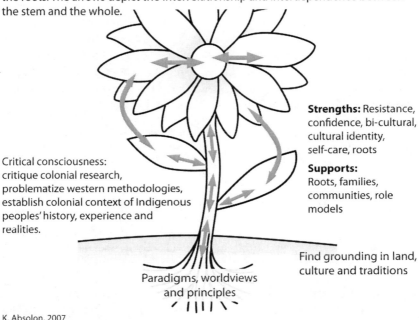

Strengths: Resistance, confidence, bi-cultural, cultural identity, self-care, roots

Supports: Roots, families, communities, role models

Critical consciousness: critique colonial research, problematize western methodologies, establish colonial context of Indigenous peoples' history, experience and realities.

Find grounding in land, culture and traditions

Paradigms, worldviews and principles

K. Absolon, 2007

All of the research projects critique the failure of western methodologies to reflect the strengths of the community, culture and traditions of Indigenous peoples. They all insisted on the need to critically address eurowestern re-search theory, methodology and ethics. We need to ensure that our re-search methodologies include critical analysis of the histories of Indigenous-White relations, the construction of knowledge and power, and socio-historic truth (Duran and Duran 2000). A critical understanding unveils the oppressive nature and intent of research on Aboriginal peoples and critiques the old order of scientific empiricism, which squashed methodologies of acquiring knowledge through the senses, by experience and observation. Critically conscious Indigenous searchers see Indigenous peoples' searches in the spiritual, cultural, historical and current colonial context. Eber, in our conversation stated:

> We have to start with the colonialism, with the attack on our identity — everything. That's the first step to creating that ground that you were talking about. Oh geeze how come every time I sit down to write something I gotta moan and groan about the atrocities that have been done to us, you know... pisses me off... I know it's like I end up doing that and in a way it's like clearing the air — establishing my perspective, my take on the world. A lot of it has to do

97

with that colonial experience and for me to acknowledge that up front seems necessary.

This means that we critique and problematize eurowestern research theories and question their reliability in Indigenous contexts. Willie's thesis establishes a strong critique of eurowestern research. In our conversation, Willie talked about community contexts of knowledge production and eloquently questioned bringing Indigenous knowledge into academic settings that refuse to recognize and respect that knowledge. He sees the western system as underdeveloped in comparison to Cree knowledge systems:

> In my master's education I've gone to look at western culture and what it's all about and how come it doesn't recognize or accept Cree being. What makes it so narcissistic? So I came full circle back to the community. I see western people as little children. They're still growing. The wisdom and agedness coming from the Cree world are not respected by the little children. They don't know enough. How can we interact with children or more underdeveloped children? I see university institutions and western systems are just children developing these processes and so I have a fundamental problem with approaching Cree thought in a way that is trying to subsume that thought in a western paradigm.

When Indigenous searchers enter the academy to do their research, Willie says, communities miss out on the development of our own forms of knowledge production. And when Indigenous peoples attempt to develop Indigenous forms of knowledge within the academy, they are marginalized by the theories and methods of western science. Similarly, Leanne (1999) says:

> Indigenous Knowledge is constantly being measured by the western yard-stick.... If you want your knowledge to be legitimate in this society, you have to prove it is legitimate on western terms, using the western knowledge system. This is not only epistemololgically unsound, it is also racist.

We can't dismantle colonized forms of knowledge production using colonial methodologies; we need to both develop a critique and then turn our gaze toward Indigenous tools and knowledge. Critiques of colonialism in research, historically and currently, are paramount in contextualizing Indigenous re-search today. We must make our oppressions visible and tell the stories of how the intellectual authority powerhouses try to shapeshift us into eurowestern thinkers and reproducers of their worldviews and paradigms. We must unveil those experiences and stories of the academy's attempts to silence us, to reshape our unique creative works of intelligence and art into "something understandable" and something colonized. We are observed, recorded, analyzed, synthesized, managed, organized, categorized and then problematized and pathologized. How dare the academy force colonial methods into our searches.

Dawn H (1995), like others, critically acknowledges that western science has been used to assert, justify and perpetuate colonial oppression, and she talks about necessary first steps toward uncovering Indigenous wisdoms:

> Post-colonial intellectuals are beginning to rethink, reconstruct, and revise ethnocentric social scientific paradigms. The ontological has given way to the epistemological. Monopolies of truth are crumbling as more and more Natives, Africans, Asians, and women begin to enter the western intelligentsia. The post-colonial era of social science is a reflection of the current political and social reality. Social agents of the "other" kind are inquiring into the subjective, biases, and ethnocentric assumptions made about "them"....
>
> The western yardstick used to measure all "others" is beginning to reveal its ethnocentricity. Development, industrialization, and technology—all formerly considered signs of advancement of a civilized society—are beginning to be revealed as destructive forces which endanger all life forms, not just Natives. Some scientists are turning to Indigenous wisdom to raise the consciousness of western people and their institutions....
>
> The theoretical crisis in anthropology, or in the social sciences in general, is developing around the issues of resistance, representation, authority, textuality, analysis, and post-colonialism.

Dawn's critical review of the historical representation of the Lubicon reveals misrepresentations and a blatant absence of the voices of the people. Colonizing anthropological research, she points out, omits the real stories. To counter the omissions, she focuses on Indigenous sciences, asserting that they are an initial tenet to Indigenous methodologies. In essence, Dawn, like other critical Indigenous re-searchers, includes the cultural and colonial analysis of resistance to colonialism within the search.

Indigenous scholars' ongoing critiques dismantle colonial research motives, theories and methods (Duran and Duran 2000; Ross 2005; L.T. Smith 2000; Talbot 2002). Luana Ross (2005: 60) asserts: "We need to deconstruct old, tired methodologies. As researchers we have an obligation to rework methodologies with various worldviews and unequal power structures in mind." Critical reflections and discourse set a pathway for freedom to be attained without replicating or empowering colonialism and eurocentric hegemony (Alfred 2005). Maori scholars Linda Tuhiwai Smith (1999) and Russell Bishop (1998b) have made invaluable contributions to the Indigenous critique of colonial research. Bishop (1998b: 201) identifies a Kaupapa Maori approach as "the philosophy and practice of being and acting Maori." Kaupapa Maori is self-determination, collectivist (not individualistic) and assumes the social, political, historical, intellectual and cultural safety and legitimacy of Maori people (Bishop 1998b; Smith 2000). This involves , a rejection of hegemonic belittling and a commitment to a critical analysis of the existing unequal power structures and to consciousness raising and politicization. Kaupapa Maori also means accessing, defining, validating and protecting the knowledge that existed before european arrival. Maori research is epistemologically based within Maori culture (Smith 2000). Russell Bishop illustrates these two necessary elements of Maori Indigenous knowledge creation. First, he speaks to the presence and commitment of maintaining congruency with cultural knowledge:

> One fundamental understanding to a *Kaupapa Maori* approach to research is that it is the discursive practice that is *Kaupapa Maori* that positions researchers in such a way to operationalize self-determination... for research participants. This is because the cultural aspirations, understandings, and practices of *Maori* people implement and organize the research process. (1998b: 202)

And he also speaks to the necessity of developing a critical analysis:

> Such understandings challenge traditional ways of defining, accessing, and constructing knowledge about Indigenous peoples and the process of self-critique, sometimes termed paradigm shifting, that is used by western scholars as a means of "cleansing" thought and attaining what becomes their version of the "truth." Indigenous peoples are challenging this process because it maintains control over the research agenda within the cultural domain of the researchers or their institutions. (202)

By virtue of researching in academic corridors, we explicitly navigate two knowledge sets. Willie, in our conversation, elaborated on the tensions Indigenous people experience when they are critically conscious and choose to enter academic contexts to re-search Indigenous knowledge and communities:

> Now what do you think? You come from a community and developing that community knowledge in different contexts. Think of that community as a living organism of its own. It needs certain things for it to function. The collective/community is one context. Language is another context. You're doing this in a universal language and it's not a universal language. The context of that organism is that there's a certain language that belongs there. Using someone else's language to describe that organism is a language out of context. The oral tradition is very process oriented. People have to be active for the oral tradition to survive. In the western context everything is written. In the Cree context, the oral tradition and where I see community — it has to be a process. It's like the heartbeat. The oral tradition is a process and it needs active participants to keep moving. It needs a community. That process of that energy and anything that makes that community function as a community — as a Cree group — is dependent on people contributing to that and within that context. That has to be there to understand the functioning of everything, the interconnection and interdependence. That's context!

And while the re-searchers and critical authors echo that re-search for and by Indigenous people is needed (McPherson and Rabb 2001), just clearing the mind of colonial constructs is not enough. Decolonization is the common descriptor for unlearning racism and colonization and relearning and recovering Indigeneity (Calliou 2001; Fitznor 2002; Graveline 2004; Simpson 2001). Indigenizing your search is to move beyond the critiques and centre your search from who you are as an Indigenous person. *Context* is understanding the intertwining of being both cultural and colonial. Contextualization requires an integration of the critique of colonialism and the domination of traditional research in the process of conceptualizing and mapping out our own research methodologies (Bishop 1998b; Fitznor 2002). Cora Weber-Pillwax (2001) says that you must contextualize yourself and own the location from which you research. Consequently, Indigenous re-searchers must know their history (cultural and colonial) and the role that history has played (Kenny 2000).

Winona (2000) presents a critical encounter with eurowestern hegemony and illustrates a strong case for oral history research from Indigenous ways of being and Indigenous worldviews:

> Charging that mainstream historical literature "imprisons Indian history" through the silencing of Indigenous perspectives and voices, and "by the rhetoric and scholarly inventions of empire" Native American scholars argue for a new articulation of Indigenous scholarship grounded in tribal intellectual traditions.

The stories are limited in their presentation because so much time has to be spent countering eurowestern hegemony. Winona presents a critique of post-colonialism and post-modernism and states that Indigenous scholars are expected to meet two standards: that of the university and that of their communities, and inevitably, at times they conflict. Patricia (2003) talks about narrative life history and her father's manuscript on the life of the Anishinaabek Métis. Dawn H (1995) felt conflicted between the academic need for a research design prior to her project and the Lubicon people's way of doing. Her process became the "Lubicon way" because the Lubicon people resisted verbalizing what "collaborative" research would look like and insisted on showing rather than telling. These scholars echo other Indigenous scholars on the challenges of navigating both academic and Indigenous community demands.

As Indigenous searchers navigate dual agendas, the channels become narrower and more difficult to steer through. We not only have the responsibility to present our findings and knowledge in the most respectful and authentic manner possible, but we also have to establish our context, argue for our methodology, expect cynicism on its validity and then present it to both the academic and Indigenous audiences.

The Indigenous scholar's position at the confluence of worldviews is crucial in the work required to assert and realign perspectives about Indigenous Peoples and their knowledge. Developing and disseminating Indigenous Peoples' perspectives about society and knowledge is crucial in advancing not only critique, but also in developing new forms of knowledge. (Willie 2000)

Indigenous and academic perspectives differ on both methodology and research agenda. The efforts to create a discourse on the articulation of Indigenous methodologies challenge myths that Indigenous methods are unsystematic and not concrete. Raven was passionate about being an active "myth buster" when she expressed the following:

> Indigenous re-search methodology isn't just kind of "willy-nilly" eclectic approach, because there's that foundation or the philosophy that it draws upon and that's — depending on what nation you're from, those are very, very clear. There's no ifs, ands or buts about that, like in terms of what's protocol. This is very clear. And it's quite universal. At least ethical reciprocity is universal in Indigenous cultures, we know that. So it's dispensing away with that myth. And that it actually makes it harder, because it can't be approached, this research endeavour, from just a cognitive academic frame, intellectual frame of mind. I have to be wholistic, so I have to consider things like Spirit and emotion.

Patricia (2003) makes the important point that ethnography has typically been to guide outsider researchers when studying another culture. However, when we are searching within our own cultural paradigms, we need to follow our own cultural guidelines and experiences in our own social world. Indigenous re-searchers in this book represent the duality and challenge of searching from an Indigenous worldview within a colonial eurowestern context. Needing to present our critiques and justifications for doing Indigenist re-search compromises space to present what we actually want to say.

Hopefully, one day we will be able to move directly into our knowledge searches using whatever Indigenous methodologies fit the context. Currently though, critiques are still a necessary part of the process. Dawn H (1995) states this when she says:

> Before I can make room for "our" voices to tell this story I must engage in a non-Native academic dialogue to simply get to "our point." I will do this for the sake of the dominant institutions for whom I write, so you understand why this is not relevant to "our" discourse.

Being critical of the master in the master's house is risky business. Critically conscious Indigenous scholars are critiquing colonial academic structures and forms of knowledge production in the very setting where we are conducting our searches. Inevitably we will be perceived as antagonistic and threatening to the academic status quo. We knowingly bring a critically conscious mind and presence into the academy; we enter with a consciousness of our roles and responsibilities.

The Role of Critically Conscious Indigenous Scholars

Dawn Marsden describes Indigenous re-searchers in the academy as "shape-shifters," both within our research methodology and within the academy. All the re-searchers identified that their research and methodology was an important part of their presence in the academy. Conscious Indigenous re-searchers and re-search have a profound impact on the academy and are contributing to changes in curriculum, research methodology, programming, scholarship and faculty.

> Critically conscious Indigenous scholars have a role to play in developing the conditions required for appropriate research discourses and transformational programming in educational institutions. Indigenous scholars are perhaps in the best position to chart the appropriate pathways to emancipating and transforming knowledge. The critical Indigenous scholar can readily occupy the ethical space that is characterized as the confluence of two worldviews. (Willie 2000)

We are both Indigenous and scholarly. Our re-search, within the academy, coins us as scholars. Without question, the academic environment holds burdens and responsibilities for critically conscious Indigenous scholars. Peter (2000) states that, as First Nations, our responsibilities are to factor in accountability, not just measurability, of our relations with all of Creation and to follow our original instructions as they were orally passed on. Today we are challenged to continually relearn ceremonies and languages and to regenerate mutual relationships by Indigenizing methodologies. Our awareness of our place in Creation is our responsibility. Indigenous frameworks are ethical and spiritual considerations, and the codes of conduct are those guidelines provided to us by the Creator. Peter also reminds us of our responsibility to own the history and knowledge that is ours and use our methods to retrieve and communicate them:

> I am talking about first people writing our own contact stories (if we choose to) rather than sharing ours with people who want to make a name for them/selves who want to become "experts" on this or that "tribe."

In owning our knowledge, we must acknowledge the history and roots of our teachings, or the origins of our accumulated knowledge. Many of the researchers acknowledged those leaders and mentors who have tenaciously asserted Indigenous knowledge and/or methodologies in their re-searches. This acknowledging is an important practice. Dawn M refers to this as the genealogy of our knowing. Laara (2002) acknowledges leaders such as Pam Colorado, Russell Bishop, Fyre Jean Graveline and Verna Kirkness for the paths they have forged that enabled her to continue to integrate Indigenous knowledge and process in her search:

These leaders demonstrated leadership about how research is thought about and conducted for, and by, Aboriginal/Indigenous peoples. This was a relief for me as an Aboriginal scholar... because I struggled with mismatched western ways of taking up research on Aboriginal peoples. I did not want to repeat processes that might dishonour our relations.

The Indigenous re-searchers are my mentors and have provided me with the leadership, strength and vision to continue to champion Indigenous ways of searching as legitimate means. Willie (2000) talks about our responsibility to invest some of our energies into rebuilding Indigenous resources and knowledge:

> This may mean enacting the responsibility of researchers to research their own communities to find their resources for healing and transformation. It may also mean making researchers available for the benefit of Indigenous communities and other marginalized peoples that have experienced the full violence of colonialism and nevertheless have maintained the vision of the possible.

Through my conversation with Willie, I was reminded that if we are too involved in our academic research our communities may lose out on what we have to offer. When working with our communities, there is no doubt that we serve. Dawn H (1995) shares: "After five years with the Lubicon, I realized they have maximized my presence in all areas: as a woman, a Mohawk, and a professional. I no longer ask them what they want from my collaborative research project." I also believe that other Indigenous peoples and communities will benefit from the individual and collective efforts of Indigenous scholars tenaciously working to indigenize and rehumanize academic methods of knowledge production. Willie (2000) elaborates:

> The heavy academic involvement of Indigenous scholars with university interests and priorities denies and unfairly limits Indigenous communities' access to their own resources for research programming and development... The broad task for Indigenous scholars is to transform research scholarship beyond the colonial and neocolonial standards that are now the established order and to work at the cutting edge of knowledge production through empowering discourses and paradigms that model and enshrine the human potential of all peoples.

Although research hasn't always benefited us, we now have a responsibility to ensure that our re-search agendas and goals do. Michael (1997) stated that we have a role as learners and advocates simultaneously:

> As Aboriginal people I believe we need to respect and stand up for our own practices, our own approaches that guide these practices, and our own views that determine our approaches. In order to do this, we need to continue learning about our history from our perspectives. We need to continue to overcome the belief that has been instilled in many Aboriginal people that these practices

are irrelevant, or worse, to be feared. We need to continue turning to our own Elders and healers as legitimate providers of information and resources. We need to continue learning who we are as Aboriginal people.

Indigenous scholars are not in the academy to simply espouse rhetorical word games but to ensure that research methods create change which benefits communities.

> The role of these Indigenous professionals is similar to the role played by the first generation of Indigenous teachers and nurses and by the first generation of medical doctors and social workers in Native communities, a difficult role of translating, mediating, and negotiating values, beliefs, and practices from different worldviews in different political contexts. (Smith 2005: 96)

Indigenous re-searchers are assuming control over our future, and in doing so are transforming the way knowledge is produced. Missisak, whose name in Cree means horsefly, talked at length about her role in transforming Indigenous forms of knowledge production:

> I like to bug the system and I like to bug people at the committees, you know, reminding that we're here and you need to acknowledge us, you need to even have the word Aboriginal on your agenda or in your admissions or something, to encourage Aboriginal people to come, respect its histories and so on and so forth.… I think that name was meant to give to me to help me in the work that I'm doing, because I am a bug on the system. I like to challenge the system. Well, I don't like to, but I do it. I counter, I correct, I do those things.… We're here to stay. They're here to stay and they're a reminder that we're here to stay.… We're part of Creation, in other words. So stop getting rid of us. Stop trying to get rid of our language, our knowledge, you know, stop trying to assimilate us — so it's that kind of story. So it's been kind of an interesting story how it unfolds. I really use that a lot and try and develop methodologies or using methods that are, again, Aboriginal friendly or relevant.

Our perception of ourselves as re-searchers or searchers or gatherers comes from and is rooted in our traditions. Long before we were in the academy, our ancestors were conducting research and relied on Indigenous methodologies as they sought out knowledge. Today, reclaiming Indigenous methods of searching for knowledge embodies our own learning and healing, and this knowledge is transferable.

> I think somebody can do a paper where they're strictly citing Aboriginal scholars, but they couldn't do that before, you know, without doing this kind of comparison, "This is why I'm doing this, because this is what I found I have to do" and explaining certain parts of my methodology and saying that, '"Well, this is like a focus group," so people understand what a sharing circle is, for example, you know, and so that they would have that — well, it's kind of

saying you're still getting data, you're still getting information, but the method that you're using, the process, and the guiding principles are slightly different.

We challenge myths, as Raven says:

> We engage in Indigenous re-search or the soft qualitative type research, we're not being objective enough. I think that's a myth. And I say that because, when I follow my traditional ways of being, my traditional teachings, I'm required to be objective, and not only about life around me, but about myself. I'm required to reflect upon my location in terms of my environment and don't make assumptions and treat other people the way you want to be treated and — and those things, you've got to be damn objective. You've got to be damn objective to sit there and listen to an Elder tell you, "Well, you're just being bossy right now" or, you know, for them to mirror something to you that you need to learn in order to grow and mature. You've got to be objective or you're going to spend a lot of time, you know, in a little ball, curled up crying and whining by yourself. Those teachings are not easy and they demand objectivity. They're experiential, but they require reflection and weighing all of those perspectives. Yeah — we're all about myth busting!

Within the academy, the role of Indigenous re-searchers is to transform systems of knowledge production, to be congruent with Indigenous worldviews and to play a role in producing knowledge and information that is useful, beneficial and purposeful toward Indigenous emancipatory goals. Winona (2000) talks about the challenges of actualizing these goals:

> The challenge for Native American scholars in the social sciences then, is to transcend the influences of "structuralism, modernism, and the dualism of subject, object or otherness" and to deny "paracolonial discoveries and representations of tribal literatures." The challenge for Native American historians is to create space for innovative articulations of the Indigenous past that bridge the old and the new.

Resisting academic acculturation is an inherent role in a conscious scholar's mind. From her searches Raven learned that resistance to western research domination has been occurring as Aboriginal re-searchers' secretly apply their own worldviews, protocols and practices:

> I guess the main finding was that they had all incorporated their cultural practices and protocols into their research, but they just hadn't shared it with anybody, because they didn't perceive that there was any, there were any forums in their methodologies or in their research processes within those institutions to share that information. So, for example, one of my participants said, "you know, I couldn't share that I had gotten my dissertation topic from my kokum in a dream, because she is deceased, eh? How would my committee take that?"

Some searchers do not tell their supervisors or write about their methods in their thesis. Yet they still honour their own protocols and practices because they must. Indigenous methodologies have often been forced underground, and this oppression evokes frustration and anger. At the same time, there is no doubt that change is here and Aboriginal methodologies are quickly gaining momentum and respect. Resistance, in these examples, is not so much about making concessions as it is about avoiding academic bureaucratic potholes. They are strategic decisions, and Indigenous scholars must make them, to honour their responsibilities.

Strategic thinking is embedded in our languages. The Cree concept of *keemooch* is an expression used by Missisak to characterize the undercurrents of resistance in our work and the subversive or sneaky way we navigate the academy to operationalize our agendas:

> I would *keemoochly* bring something in or I would raise it or would write it up anyway so that it's embedded in my writing. And I think in terms of teaching, I'm more assertive about using the concept of *keemooch* and saying what that is. The undercurrents, the conventional structures [in academia], they're very western. That's the framework and there's flushing content. To me we can bring the *keemooch* stuff and the flushing and the content. This is Aboriginal content. Sometimes we bring it into the very western framework. But once we bring the Aboriginal content into this western framework, we then push the margins of transforming that western framework into more Aboriginal and Indigenous ways of research and teaching and doing. And that's what I do. It's constantly speaking on it, addressing it, talking about it wherever I am. Even if I'm not on the agenda, I find a way to piggyback on someone or say, "Well, how does this affect Aboriginal peoples?" To me it's going against the grain. Raising critical issues. I think in many ways it kind of follows those concepts, except that when I say, *keemooch*, I'll do it in a way and sneak it in. We'll make sure that the Aboriginal position is there, even though it wasn't initially thought about. That's why it's *keemooch*, because it wasn't planned. "We're just going to do it *keemoochly*." So I think in that sense a lot my work still really ends up being that, and that is a *keemooch* way of working. And then also we're bringing in people I know that will support that too. I think part of it is what permission we give ourselves, allow ourselves to do at what times too, and what will fly. Like you see the fly is there again. So the fly is constantly in my life.

As we occupy academic spaces and develop our research goals, questions and proposals, we are assuming our roles as activists and advocates. We are here collectively crossing borders, disciplines and faculties.

> Indigenous re-searchers are "becoming" a research community. They have connected with each other across borders and have sought dialogue and conversations with each other. They write in ways that deeply resonate shared histories and struggles. They also write about what Indigenous re-search ought to be. (Smith 2005: 89)

I consciously selected critically conscious Indigenous scholars because of their roles as advocates, facilitators, coordinators, helpers, healers, educators and much more. Clearly, Indigenous re-search involves an anticolonial, liberatory and emancipatory declaration of being. "Implicit in such a definition is that Indigenous re-searchers are committed to a platform for changing the status quo and see the engagement by Indigenous re-searchers as an important level for transforming institutions, communities, and society" (Smith 2005: 89). Maggie told me about the journey through which her methodology emerged, and her story will impact how methodology emerges in the academy. Missisak's role as an advocate for advancing Indigenous perspectives is clear. Jo-ann communicates a Sto:lo and Coast Salish approach of storywork. Peter advances Indigenizing methodologies through a canoe journey as a warrior through his anticolonial discourse. Michael's commitment to his family, community, Elders and culture is also clear. Raven is a myth buster. Dawn M conveys her role as a catalyst to retrieve, collect and retain community traditional knowledge in healing. They all contributed a critique of colonial research methods and strengthened the presence of Indigenous knowledge in the academy. Activating our roles and maintaining a strong backbone involves strengths and supports that accompany Indigenous re-searchers who enter the academy. We are not alone as we carry our supports with us.

Indigenous Searchers' Strengths and Supports

Conscious Indigenous re-searchers' methodological gumption includes personal strengths, cultural strengths and community supports. These strengths and supports already exist for the re-searchers and they simply carry them within. I'd say they all have a strong backbone to just do it, but they also have powerful support systems.

Surviving the academy requires a vision beyond the academy, a sense of purpose, a grounding in identity, external supports and internal allies. Indigenous scholars resist forced fragmentation and do not want to check identities and worldviews at the door of the academy, nor should we have to. Suggesting Indigenous scholars leave integral pieces of themselves out of their research is unethical and oppressive. Within the academy we are, at times, navigating chilly, intolerant, hostile and assimilating channels. The re-searchers spoke of the obstacles and challenges they faced as they actualized Indigenous methodologies. We survive and get through because of a strength in knowing who we are and where our supports come from.

In thinking of our strengths I returned to the bush and remembered that dealing with obstacles was normal. It is rarely easy to walk in the woods. These memories helped me feel less agitated about obstacles because they reminded me that the earth has taught me to be a persistent problem solver because, if you are alone, no one will help you in the bush. You have to figure things out and utilize your own resourcefulness. I offer one of my own stories:

I remember as a child, my brother and I being out in the bush a lot. Like many other days, we were exploring the land and imagining the life of our ancestors. The trails we walked were lined with birch, poplar, pine and maple trees. It was spring and the sun shone through the trees. The leaves weren't quite budding yet and the earth hadn't started birthing. The woods were full of song birds, squirrels scurrying here and there, insects and other small creatures. I truly loved being in the woods. The bush was easy to walk through and we could see over the terrain. We were heading for a favourite spot: a rock cliff next to a nearby lake. There we would sit and gaze over the sparkling water. There we'd have our snack and goof around. Along the way though, we came across a wide creek with fast flowing water. It was spring and the water was high. We gazed up and down the creek to see if we could just jump across, but we didn't see a narrow enough spot. We looked at each other and then turned to search the ground to see what else we could do to get across that creek. Trouble shooting made the journey more interesting and fun. We wandered around searching for a log or something to make a bridge. Finally we found an old log and dragged it over to the creek. Despite its weight and size we managed to toss it in the water. We did it! Our bridge was made and we carefully crossed the creek balancing ourselves on that log. Having made it to the other side we triumphantly and happily continued on our way. Fortunately, there were no fences there to stop us, nor were there gatekeepers there to keep us on one side of the creek.

We become stronger in confronting, coping and problem solving obstacles we face, and those strengths can define us as warriors. Today, Indigenous re-searchers re-write our stories and histories from resistance and strengths perspectives.

Internal fences keep us boxed into particular ways of thinking, being and doing. Even if there were an opening, our internal fence would prevent us from seeing that opening. Internal fences can confine and limit our perceptions, behaviours and actions. Internalized racism and colonialism are fences that have resulted from government policies and structures meant to oppress and eradicate Indigenous peoples. Systems such as residential schools, churches, reserves and Indian legislation perpetuated internalized racism. When oppressive messages are forced and repeatedly imposed, people internalize them and comes to believe that they are inferior and the White people superior. Conscious Indigenous searchers have worked to develop and heal their minds from internalized oppression and racism. Our searches are about Indigenous peoples' survival, and in order to survive we remember who we are and what we know. Our search for knowledge is ultimately connected to an emotional and personal search related to: Who am I? And Where do I come from? Many of these researchers faced internal fences. Their consciousness of these fences is a powerful tool in their searches. Decolonizing our minds and thus our re-search is a journey and a process of learning, healing and critical reflection.

During the time in which I took up this work, I started to think about my life in the bush and began going back into my memory. I started to think about what I learnt from my mother. I was reminded of her teaching: "don't get lost." My clan brother also encouraged me to not get lost by advising me to take my whole self with me and remain congruent. So I started thinking about how my mother taught me to not get lost:

> Every time we'd go in the bush, my mother would always make markers along the way. The markers took the form of broken branches, placing rocks strategically or she would teach us to turn around and look at where we came from so that we would recognize the landscape coming back — whether it was a tree or a creek or rock. She was even nicknamed "princess broken branch" because of her practice of creating markers to not get lost. Every time we walked further into the woods she would tell us to turn around and memorize what the land looks like because when we returned to come back home we would need to recognize it. "Turn around and look at where you've come from," she'd say. We would walk in the bush and then we would have to turn around, pause and memorize that pine tree, that rock, that creek — walk further along, turn around, and memorize, so that when it was time to come back, we would recognize the landmarks from where we've been. She taught me to always turn around and to look at where I'd come from so I'd know how to get home and not get lost.

Teachings I received growing up in the bush give me strength today, and I know that I have the ability to identify my markers along the way. In the academy, I think our research is about finding our way home. There is urgency and a very strong pull to reclaim our birthrights as Indigenous peoples before they are lost. A majority of the participants indicate that their searches fulfill a strong desire to find their way back home again. For some, the academy is the means in which we are finding our way home. Through the academy, we are searching for our knowledge, histories, cultures, traditions, stories, names, identity, community and family. We require congruent methodologies so we don't get lost. Indigenous knowledge and methodologies enable us to conduct our searches so that we find ourselves.

Academic channels can become murky and muddy and can bog us down and distract us from actualizing Indigenous worldviews and methodologies. The following is another teaching that I carry because I know that gathering requires strength, knowledge and skill to get through obstacles and thick terrain. One time I almost got lost because of the barriers:

> The bush is full of barriers and obstacles and we learnt to get around them somehow. Obstacles do exist, but when we stop and open our minds up to the possibilities, we usually find another way of continuing on our journey. It is no fun walking through pickies or thorny bushes. No one wants to cross the river at the widest or roughest part; we search for smoother places to cross waterways, or we journey on land that is more compatible to walking. Necessity instigates journeys into thick bush or through rough waters. Only

in pursuit of those low bush cranberries or that bush of lush blueberries will I cut through a thick piece of bush. I see what I want and I bushwhack it to reach my goal. I keep my eye on those lush blueberries because that's what I'm after and they won't be around indefinitely. One day I journeyed deep into the bush in search for blueberries. I was gone all day. On my way back home I didn't recognize the landmarks. I turned in different directions and it all looked the same. Sometimes in the bush the landmarks begin to look the same after a while. I got a bit confused and didn't see the landmarks that I tried to memorize. I wondered if I was lost. I stopped and listened and heard sounds and I saw that the sun was in the far west and I knew that I had to walk in a southeasterly direction to get to the road and then go home. So in a pinch, I cut straight through thick bush and struggled to walk as I pushed branches aside one after the other to avoid scrapping my eyes and face. The thought of being lost necessitated "bush-whacking." My reasoning was correct. I eventually came to a road and recognized where I was and knew then how to get home.

Choosing our path means we have to "bush-whack" it from time to time to reach our destination. I believe Indigenous scholars are, at times, bush whacking it in the academy. We are cutting trails and leaving clearer paths for others.

Sometimes resistance and persistence draws our strengths out. There is strength in resistance. Our languages and cultures affirm our ability to search strategically. This is in Missisak's term *keemooch*, a concept I love. Also, I belong to the Marten Clan, and one of our clan teachings tells us that we are strategists. Thinking strategically is similar to *keemooch*. Persistence and defiance as forms of resistance enable Indigenous re-searcher to proactively search in culturally relevant and meaningful ways. Coping within the academy calls for strength and resistance to being colonized. It is clear from the searchers that resistance takes many forms.

All Indigenous re-searchers who maintain their identity within the academy are bi-cultural, having what Leroy Little Bear (2000) calls an "ambidextrous consciousness." This ambidextrous consciousness allows us to negotiate the dualities of being Indigenous in a euro-colonial society. We occupy multiple spaces and are consciously bi-cultural. There is diversity within. We are skilled at carrying dual knowledge sets. This is an advantage. It enables us to move in and out of and between our worlds with relative ease. Winona (2000) writes:

> The irony of my "education" is that I spent 19 years studying my own peoples' past in universities, from outside perspectives, using eurocentric sources, according to foreign conventions, when my own people have intellectual traditions of our own.

We occupy complex spaces where contemporary, cultural and traditional realities intersect. Linda Tuhiwai Smith identified this space nicely:

The issue of diversity is not just about people who eat differently and speak another language; it is about people who think differently and who know differently. Furthermore, it is also about people who, because of their education, can think like a student from a metropolitan university and think like a student from a tribal college and environment. (Smith 2006: 551)

Our resource lies in our ability to draw on these dualities and ironies when we engage in research as Indigenous peoples first and then as scholars. Our cultural identity precedes our academic identity. We are both Anishinaabek and scholars. One does not exclude the other. Our challenge is to achieve a balance within this blend. Dawn H (1995) talks about this:

In this context there is a contradiction in being Native and an anthropologist; being the subject/object and an "authority" is, of course, impossible. As a Native woman I have been socialized to defer to Elders as the "authorities." I have been raised to be humble and respectful. Academia urges me to be "critical" and, therefore, disrespectful. Going for the jugular is rewarded. Anthropologists pressure me to define a Native perspective or build a grand Native paradigm. My conscience tells me only the Creator has that ability…. The key is not to be consumed by the hegemonic or to alienate myself in either world, and, more importantly, to redefine my role as an anthropologist.

At a personal level, what supports Indigenous re-searchers is their worldview, clarity and inherent belief in what they are doing. All the Indigenous searchers are highly motivated and in touch with their intentions. They are aware, purposeful and clear about their search motives. Their search agendas are not nebulous or ambiguous. Missisak says her strength is her confidence in what she is doing. She states that we have a way of perseverance, resistance and defiance, which, I agree, has helped us to survive the atrocities and resist being assimilated. We know what we know.

I think its confidence that this needs to be there and a little bit of defiance. Because I just think, you know, like as Aboriginal people in a decolonizing framework, is that if you really, truly believe that, we constantly have to push the limits and raise what we see as valid knowledge, to keep reminding people, keep putting it on the table. And sometimes I do that just to see how people will react. Being a little devil. (laughing) My name is Missisak. Well, I do talk about that in my story, in my thesis. When you look at that, you will see that. But what I've said is that with that name — my grandfather gave me that name as a child.

Some re-searchers talked about an internal drive and passion to participate in creating change toward the validation and recognition of Indigenous knowledge and methodologies. Some want their work to be practical, useful and beneficial to the communities. Others use Indigenous knowledge and methodologies with a clear intention of creating pathways for other Indigenous scholars so that the cumulative effect of our collective efforts will be a clearer and less arduous path for Indigenous searchers in the academy. Indigenous methodologies intersect with our life. Researching in the academy calls for a personal sense of diligence, discipline and wellness. Undoubtedly, living a healthy and balanced life and taking care of ourselves is essential because the search demands our whole self.

When dealing with the anxiety and stress of doing Indigenous re-search in the academy, most of the searchers found grounding in their spiritual practices. Winona (2000) identifies prayer as a source of strength:

> One of the primary differences between writing and speaking is that speaking takes place in a social, interactive environment while writing is a lonely, detached activity... For many Indigenous peoples, social science training and the solitude of writing, can be alienating... Writing about voices speaking is a lonely venture but only at times when there is no one around to talk it through with. And when I found myself alone, meditation and prayer filled the void.

As I wrote I too felt isolated. I, like most of the participants, found support from Spirit through prayer, ceremony and other sacred rituals. Sometimes smudging with sage provided stress relief. Talking to Spirit through tobacco or singing a song moved my energy to calmer states.

It was not unusual for these researchers to experience anxiety and panic during phases of the research journey — especially when uncertainty and confusion entered. Being connected to the land kept some Indigenous researchers from getting lost in the academy. Taking time to return to the land and feel the essence of the earth grounded their mind, body, heart and Spirit during uncertain and stressful moments. Some people returned to their home territory and felt their ancestors' presence to remember and reconnect with them and who they are. Some talked about fasting as a means of reconnecting with their vision and purpose. When panic entered researchers often turned to the elements of Creation such as wind, water, earth and fire as grounding forces.

I wrote earlier of the significance of Cocomish and Shaumish in my life and in the creation of this book. Many of the re-searchers found similar supports. They often spoke about the ancestors as a source of strength and guidance and felt their presence in dreams and visions. We are close to those ancestors and continue to feel their Spirits calling us to honour our traditions and heal from the colonial attacks. Our history is held within our bodies, our families, our ancestors, and these histories and ties are deeply felt.

Our ancestors' legacy is in the lands, languages, traditions and cultures that they safeguarded. These enabled our ancestors and us today to survive genocide, assimilation and attempted annihilation.

> I believe that sources of fundamental and important First Nations knowledge are the land, our spiritual beliefs, and the traditional teachings of the Elders. To understand Elders' teachings, the values and actions of patience, responsibility, respect, and reciprocity are essential. (Jo-ann 1997)

Jo-ann points out that our Spirits are strong and the strength of the Spirit and culture we rely on is insurmountable. I simply do not have the words to describe the strength of Spirit of these researchers. Their words speak for themselves. We talk about who we are. We are Spirit beings. We search for who we are. We identify and locate and connect ourselves to our nations, our Spirit names, our clans and our land bases, and we have many expressions of gratitude for such gifts.

All the re-searchers practised reciprocity by making offerings in gratitude for knowledge acquired and gifts received. Sacred acknowledgements are expressions of gratitude and appreciation for our culture, our life, our ancestors and many other things. So we acknowledge those forces that support and help us, and we acknowledge our allies too. This "attitude of gratitude" reflects the value of reciprocity, where we give thanks for all that we receive. In these teachings and practices, balance and harmony are achieved, which enables us to continue with our searches and our work. Those are personal internal tools and resources.

Some Indigenous searchers just knew that honouring their Indigeneity as a methodological guide would lead them in the right research direction. Maggie talked about searching from her worldview:

> And then it shifted to looking more at the cultural practices and knowledges that as Indigenous people, gave us information and guided us, but weren't necessarily part of the kind of knowledge that you would use in the academy in a basic methodological approach. So things like dreams, intuitions, these sorts of things, and how you bring that all into the academy. So that's how I started doing this research, just initially.

Undoubtedly, Indigenous re-search methodologies are empowering to Indigenous peoples. When western culture is so pervasive in life, the ability to employ Indigenous search methodologies in our searches is in itself a supportive, affirming and rewarding process. Dawn Marsden said that creating the Wampum Research Model was "one of the most affirming parts of the research project and the research process. And there was a lot of prayer involved in the research process." All of the re-searchers who participated in this project genuinely enjoyed doing their research despite the many challenges they faced. Maggie talked with enthusiasm about her search:

> I like to take the Cree course and to go check into different sacred sites, medicine wheels, or just visit with people. Going up at FNUC is really cool, personally for me, because, there are a lot of Crees and Saulteauxs there. And

it's just being around my own, like going out to Okanese and Pasquas and being able to be a part of some of the ceremonies. Being able to participate in some of the community meetings. Being able to go out to Cupar, which was where I was raised, and spending time with my mom and my niece and nephew has been just really, wonderful. And those things I think are part of Indigenous methodology, because they're about family, about relationships.

Our re-search is about us and it's situated in our real experiences, it's about empowering real people, and it's about finding our way home. The re-emergence and articulation of Indigenous knowledge and searching for knowledge in an Indigenous way, to me, is about turning around and finding the familiar landmarks through our dreams, through our stories, through our experiences, and we're finding our way back home. We are trying to get un-lost. We know when we're home because we can feel it; we feel that familiarity when our process fits who we are. There are supportive signals and landmarks around us. As Maggie shared, there isn't so much dissonance about our process when the methodologies honour who we are as Indigenous peoples. A major insight was that Indigenous searchers, like myself, are enjoying their search for knowledge when we employ Indigenous methodologies because our learning, recovering, reclaiming and re-asserting is relevant to our Indigeneity. It's all very purposeful and connected to a greater intention. We insist on using our own processes for the survival of our knowledge and ways. Raven's passion is clear:

> What drives my passion now is that I want to contribute my voice to that increasing and that growing discourse that is ours, that articulates to the world, that we have always had a way of being in the world that was extremely intelligent, because we operated on certain principles where the end result was balance and harmony. My passion then is to contribute to that reassertion and that remembering and that recreation of our discourse that is going to inform other people in the area of research. That knowledge is as ancient as the stars. We just happen to be the people that get to say it and to be the reminder for the topic. And so that discourse is happening not just in research, but in other areas. I mean in education too. There's lots and lots of dedicated scholars who are doing the same thing. They're trying to operationalize Indigenous knowledge and Indigenous pedagogical forms into the western education systems and curriculum. And that's pretty powerful.

Many re-searchers felt supported by their community. They knew they were not alone, and this is a significant support when researching in isolation within the academy. Community may be the Indigenous academic community, the family community, a community with similar interests and goals, a reserve community, an urban community and/or a community of Elders. Michael shared:

> For me community is pretty broad. I have a commitment to my community.

My understanding of part of our traditions is that you be the best person you can to benefit your community. So what keeps me moving forward is I've got to do the best I can to support those in my community, so that we can all move forward together. So that's another really big motivator to keep me — I would hate to think, for example, if I dropped out right now and just had nothing more to do with any of it, because of the sheer amount of energy and life that's been invested in me by my community to keep going forward. And so that's a loss to the community. Also, things like — like even today, in the sweat this morning, those remind me that I'm on track and help me move forward in the way I want to move forward. So those, things such as sweats, driving around with Elders and just having those conversations, those things help me move forward. And a lot of times conversations are about — okay, we're not talking about moving back into tepees, we're talking about how do we live today in this reality, but in a way that we still know who we are as Indigenous peoples. So those kinds of conversations, ones like just sitting here with you help me move forward. So when you asked me to do this, well, of course I'm going to do it. It supports me. (laughs) So those are supports. When I think about it, it all relates, it goes back to our people.

Many of the re-searchers talked about wanting to do the best they could for their community and that they persevered because of their community. Community relationships and loving supportive relationships are often the glue that helps Indigenous re-searchers negotiate the obstacles and "bush-whacking" that the academy demands. Michael, like many others, talked about being supported by his First Nation to be able to complete his work. I too have been thoroughly supported by my family, community and Flying Post First Nation throughout my doctoral journey, and I feel immense gratitude to my community and my ancestors. The support I have felt from my relations instills me with determination to do the best I can do for those around me. Indigenous re-searchers' communities are diverse, but all of the re-sarchers spoke or wrote of community support in their re-search. Rarely do Indigenous searchers search alone: "The faith, support, and expectations of family and teachers sent her on this learning journey" (Winona 2000). At a personal level, the community includes children, partners, families and friends. When I asked Michael about his supports as an Indigenous scholar, he said, "It's my boys, my family, and the people around me and in my life that helps me to keep moving forward." Maggie sums up her supports nicely:

Well, I think what's really important to me, that keeps me going, and that keeps me inspired — I'm surrounded by really loving people. Like I really feel fortunate in my life that I've got a partner, I've got families, I've got friends, I've got people at the university, a committee that genuinely care about seeing me do okay through this process.

Hearing life stories from our relations has helped some of us understand our experiences within the academy and provided anecdotes to use in our survival. Today, we have the privilege of witnessing other Indigenous scholars finish doctoral programs and successfully defend their searches. Role models are important supports. When we read our colleagues' theses and observe their dissertation defences, a cultural mirror is created, myths are busted open, and we can perceive ourselves in such places. The impact is empowering. It debunks the idea that Indigenous people don't get PhDs. We do and we have the role models to prove it.

The stem as a methodological backbone emanates from the researchers' sense of self and identity. The backbone or force of Indigenous re-searchers and research is explicitly grounded in worldview, cultural and tradition. Conscious Indigenous re-searchers are aware that our presence carries a role to resist the pressures to conform and this requires a strong backbone. We know the burden and responsibility of standing up for who we are. Wounds of colonial trauma and a survival drive to heal those wounds propel Indigenous scholars to adamantly assume their roles and responsibilities. Our vitality invokes a resistance to colonialism. Our power comes from the supports and strengths of family, community and nation. Undoubtedly, the stem links the roots to the whole while lifting up the leaves, flower centre and petals. It is the backbone that supports Indigenous re-searchers to actualize their worldviews, histories, knowledge and experiences in their research methodologies within the academy.

Chapter Nine

The Petals: Diverse Methodologies

The petals represent the diversity and complexity of Indigenous methodologies. They include the Spirit, heart, mind and body because Indigenous methodologies are wholistic in nature and encompass the whole being. Each petal represents tendencies of Indigenous re-searchers on their searches. Petals that are hidden represent Indigenous methodologies yet to be articulated because there are many more potential methodologies. There are also petals that overlap because Indigenous methodologies are interdependent, relational and reciprocating. The petals also change from season to season. They are not stagnant or formulaic.

My search immediately revealed that Indigenous methodologies are alive; they aren't set forth in a research textbook. Indigenous methodologies are much more wholistic and all encompassing than I originally thought. Methodology is within every process of our search. Just by being Cree, Anishinaabe, Mohawk, Sto:lo or whatever nation — to some degree we are Indigenizing our methodologies. Our very presence in our journey enacts an Indigenous methodology. Our gestures, ways of thinking, being and doing enact an Indigenous methodology. And we are all employing Indigenous methodologies to varying degrees in our searches. The Indigeneity of our re-search is held within our own Spirit as our search for knowledge is regarded as a sacred process. It's not just a matter of offering *semaa* — Indigenous methodologies are far more expansive. We need many, many petals to demonstrate all the aspects of Indigenous methodologies. One thing for sure, Indigenous methodologies are concrete, complex and complete. Peter (2000) represents his methodology as a journey woven throughout:

> the traditional academic practice of methodology being in a particular chapter
> would certainly not be in keeping with anything my culture could work with
> for us thought and ethics and action were not add-ons not post-ordained bridges
> for methodology had to be part of the weft and weave and darn and logjam
> it would not be just an informing of practice the backstop of method
> methodology had to be more that a wake or Chinook arch
> a whethering a forecasting of how research would take place
> methodology is throughout   what is absent too   is important

When doing Indigenous re-search within the academy, as Willie, Peter, Winona and Michael warn, there is a danger that Indigenous methodolo-

The Petals

The arrows depict methodological grounding in the roots, via stem, self and leaves.

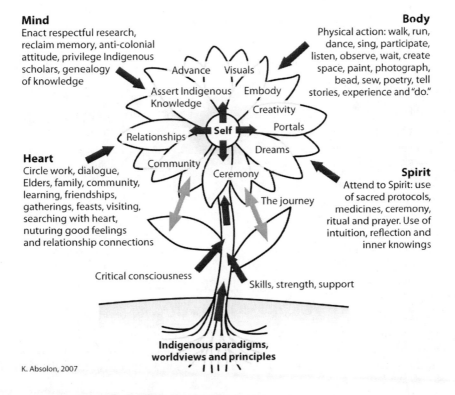

Mind
Enact respectful research, reclaim memory, anti-colonial attitude, privilege Indigenous scholars, genealogy of knowledge

Body
Physical action: walk, run, dance, sing, participate, listen, observe, wait, create space, paint, photograph, bead, sew, poetry, tell stories, experience and "do."

Advance   Visuals

Assert Indigenous Knowledge   Embody

Creativity

Relationships   Self   Portals

Dreams

Heart
Circle work, dialogue, Elders, family, community, learning, friendships, gatherings, feasts, visiting, searching with heart, nuturing good feelings and relationship connections

Community

Ceremony

The journey

Spirit
Attend to Spirit: use of sacred protocols, medicines, ceremony, ritual and prayer. Use of intuition, reflection and inner knowings

Critical consciousness

Skills, strength, support

Indigenous paradigms, worldviews and principles

K. Absolon, 2007

gies will be seen as addendums to western methodologies, marginalized as alternative or othered. Within the cultural and colonial academic contexts, Indigenous methodologies and their emancipatory goals are products of Indigenous worldviews, principles, values, beliefs and experiences. Maggie and I enthusiastically talked about Indigenous methodologies as distinct viable options for students, organizations and communities. Maggie was jazzed when she said:

> If people want to use an Indigenous methodology, they can, and just as if they wanted to use a feminist methodology. Do Indigenous methodology, yeah. And that gives me shivers, in terms of just being really excited about that because I think it's so important and I think it is really breaking trail. There's been a lot of really good work done before. But to actually put it out there as Indigenous methodology, as an entity on its own, I think it's really important and that's why the research I'm doing, the research we're doing, that's really going to be a part of that movement. That's a way of really, directly giving back and it will have practical application for other people.

I can see it even beyond academia and graduate students. When people are wanting to do an ecological study with one of the communities here, then the idea is, "Okay, well, what's your methodological choice?" The community can say, "We want to use an Indigenous methodology" that follows a Cree worldview and use Indigenous methods like a sharing circle, like sharing stories or whatever methods they want to use. But communities can say to government, "Well, if you want to do research with us, we really need you to use an Indigenous methodology." And so in that sense we're the worldview, that's the power of the methodology.

Dawn M shares her Wampum Research Model, and like the petal flower, it is wholistic. Peter uses prose and a canoe journey. Laara uses narrative and circles. Jo-ann uses storytelling, as Patricia uses her voice and personal story. Raven attends to Spirit, and Maggie journeys home. Dawn H uses her dreams and visual artwork.

Because Indigenous knowledge is wholistic and cyclical (Cajete 1994; Little Bear 2000; Nabigon 2006), Indigenous re-searchers describe their methodologies as multi-perspectives or having polycentric perspectives (McPherson and Rabb 2001). Indigenous re-search methodologies must therefore be pluralistic, eclectic and flexible (Sinclair 2003). They need to reflect the many facets of our existence today, while reflecting the cultural integrity of our ancestors.

Petal flowers have many diverse and beautiful petals, and there are many varieties of petal flowers. I came across an abundance of ways of coming to know and needed to sort them out. The methodologies are further organized using the elements of the four directions — Spirit, heart, mind and body — to assist in creating some clarity in articulating the methodologies. I have organized the methodologies according to my teachings of each element. They are not mutually exclusive of one another, and overlapping concepts occur. The overlaps simply reflect the wholistic, inclusive, relational and interdependent nature of methodologies. Indigenous methodologies, like the whole being, require all elements of Spirit, heart, mind and body to be strong and well. I begin with petals that are in the direction of Spirit and work my way around the petals in a way that is akin with the four directions of our being.

Spirit: Protocols, Ceremony and Honour

Pam Colorado (1988) derives four dynamics that she says we ought to attend to in our methodologies: feelings, history, prayer and relations. If we are to conduct research that is ethical, humane, relevant and valid, our methodologies must be culturally congruent. Spirituality is central within Indigenous culture, and its expression is relative to each searcher's nation or combination of nations and oral traditions. Undoubtedly, Spirit is a source of strength and directs re-searchers to conduct their searches in specific ways. All of the Indigenous searchers talked about incorporating Spirit, prayer, ceremony, dreams and cultural protocols, and this essentially means to care about how we conduct ourselves. Raven reflected back to me the attention I paid to Spirit:

> Like for example, you have this project to do. But the first thing that you did was you set up, you made a comfortable environment and then you attended to the Spirit — through the act of giving the tobacco. And that tells me that everything that this is all about is a — this is a spiritual act, this act of research that you are engaging in — this gathering of knowledge. Your intentions are here in this (tobacco). And the way that you created this was about your intention, but it's also about all of those things for you that have come from your spiritual paradigm, sacred epistemology. And this is the physical manifestation of that. It frames this whole and has created this research activity. So that's the foundation. And then the rest is about being creative.

Establishing respectful relationships with Spirit forms a basic methodological principle. Carolyn Kenny (2000) recognizes the need to be creative and to create safe spaces to conduct re-search in accordance with our own worldviews. She highlights the four stages of preparation, enactment, validation and transformation in integrating the concept of ritual practice into research. Specific methodological tendencies in all of the search processes, to varying degrees, included the use of sacred medicines such as sage, cedar, tobacco and sweet grass. The principle of reciprocity is actualized with offerings such as tobacco and gifts, depending on the cultural context and the searcher's preference. Offering *semaa* evokes spiritual intentions, and the protocols of enacting such intentions are taught through ceremony. At least twelve of the searchers gathered people together and offered berries or other foods as a gesture of reciprocity and gratitude. Indigenous methodologies exemplify concrete ethical standards and practices, and Spirit is treated with the utmost respect and reverence. Leanne (1999) offered tobacco and gifts during initial visits with Elders and left the "academic skills" at the door. Her interactions with the Elders were guided by cultural protocols, and she states she listened and observed, did not interrupt to ask questions and tried to be patient and wait for answers.

The journey of our search is a spiritual process, a major methodological concept for Indigenous searchers. It's not something that comes from the mind. This spiritual depth is nurtured and encouraged within Indigenous culture. We are taught to honour our Spirit. It's not something we say we've learnt outside of ourselves. It's a process that flows from within us, and that pathway is often identified as a sacred pathway, a pathway of the Spirit. This understanding relates to our Creation stories and our view of where we originate. I've heard my Elders say that we are spiritual beings, and in our Creation stories we are descendents of Spirit. Every living thing has a

Spirit and a purpose, and we have a contribution to make. Raven talked about how her Spirit guides her methods:

> The sacred epistemology — my spiritual frame of mind is my left brain. That takes precedence over anything else. So, for example, I thought I was done my data gathering, and I did a ceremony and put out tobacco, and I was like, "Okay, now I'm done." (claps hands and laughs) I got two phone calls the next day from participants who wanted to share their stories with me. And I wrestled with that very, very briefly and then I remembered. Nothing happens by accident. If those voices are meant to be in this research, then it's my responsibility to interview them. And it took, you know, just a brief, split second for me to say, "Okay."

We recognize an intuitive knowledge base that's connected to our ancestors, which is connected to the Spirit world and other realms. There are certain things that we understand and know because we're Aboriginal, or Anishinaabek. Anishinaabek Elders say the gift that the Anishinaabek carry, I mean all Indigenous people, is a wholistic understanding and knowledge, that gift of vision — we can see all of life. We have the medicine wheel, we have the circle and we have wholistic paradigms. Indigenous re-searchers talked intuitively about the wholistic perceptions, connections and relationships that we bring to our search.

The search for knowledge is also a spiritual relationship with learning and knowledge production. When we are searching for ancestral wisdoms or traditional knowledge, the search process must acknowledge Spirit. The searches were learning journeys, and of the fifteen sources, thirteen wrote or spoke about being guided by dreams, visions, ceremonies and prayer. Raven is adamant about these being concrete methodological searching tools:

> Spirit, intuition, reflections, dreams are very concrete and tangible. Dreams may not be tangible until we break them down and then it becomes, you know, in the written form. But whether it's concrete or not depends upon how you have been raised and your worldview and just your understanding of dreams and the role they play in your life. But that's very concrete.... I think, really, what we mean to say or perhaps what we ought to be saying rather than not concrete is it's not yet fully articulated. Because we're working with two very different entities, as Willie would explain it, and in some ways they operated in dialectical opposition — and Willie's article [Aboriginal epistemology] is really helpful because he talks about the two worldviews or ways of being. Find another way to articulate whatever it is that's happening around that lack of clarity or that confusion or that inability to express and articulate what it is. Because it's very clear. I'm doing my dissertation and the framework is Indigenous methodology and case study. Lots of other people have done Indigenous methodology. So I mean logically it doesn't make sense to say it's not concrete, because we're doing it. Yeah, so I just got lots of energy there around that.

Prayers, ceremony and dreams are concrete manifestations of how Spirit has a presence in Indigenous searches. Jo-ann (1997) employed Spirit in her methodology by "tracing respect from cultural protocol, appreciating the significance and reverence for Spirituality, honouring teacher and learner responsibilities, and practicing a cyclical type of reciprocity." In stressful times during thesis work, prayer provided comfort and support and was a source of strength. Ceremony is an expression of one's spirituality, and according to Leanne, ceremonies are a source of knowledge — knowledge that comes directly from the spiritual realm — and are sacred, so Indigenous searchers limit what they detail. Ceremonies provide a channel to heal, cleanse, seek knowledge and gain insight to help make decisions throughout the search process. Ceremonies and dreams assist in the synthesis and processing of our searches.

Guidance by the dream world and Spirit beings moves Indigenous methodologies beyond the mind to include the Spirit, heart and body. Dawn M (2005) eloquently shares how dreaming is a research tool.

> To validate dreaming as a research tool, we must remember that dreaming is where we symbolically process, synthesize and resolve the information, questions and experiences that we have had each day, with the knowledge we have accrued so far, to produce knowledge "new-to-us." Some dreams, which many call visions or gifts, are especially helpful in answering our questions, guiding our actions, or making sense of the world.

Jo-ann (1997) also stated, "When I was beginning to formulate my thesis topic, I experienced a dream. Traditionally, Sto:lo people had dreams/visions while on an important 'quest.' I told a good friend about this dream which gave me courage and direction for my research." Maggie shared that her dream about home being important fuelled her journey to come home and that became part of her methodology. Also, Dawn M (2005) dreamt the Wampum Research Model after praying for direction because she felt overwhelmed with all the knowledge and information that had been shared with her. Leanne (1999) said that she repeatedly shared, interpreted and used her dreams to make decisions about her work. It's common in Indigenous cultures to acknowledge and integrate the insights, messages, teachings and events from the dream work into the waking world. Dawn M (2005) agrees:

> The shift required to make dreaming a useful tool for research, is to accept your dreams as a valid way of obtaining knowledge. Because you may not understand how dreaming works, doesn't negate the information they are conveying. Just call them gifts. Dreams are valid according to the sense they make to you, in the symbols that are important to you.

Heart: Relationships, Reciprocity and Community

Research with a consciousness of Spirit also implies an awareness and understanding of enacting research with heart. Several concepts such as relationship, circle process, community, Elders and working from the heart are methodological tendencies of Indigenous searchers. All of the search-ers attended to relationships in their search, calling for the enactment of Indigenous protocols to identify themselves and their purpose, create good settings and reciprocate the sharing and witnessing of their search processes.

Laara (2002) highlights the "various Aboriginal knowings and processes I utilized in my research journey." She identifies teachings she gained from family, culture and traditional teachers about working at the grassroots with people, with goals of self-determination and control. Research relationships were regarded as friendships, with sharing encouraging words and reciprocal ways of relating. Creating positive research settings involves gatherings and meetings that reflect friendships, food, cultural/spiritual ceremonies and conversations about the future, families, communities and children. Within this process, people share stories, laugh and sometimes cry. Specifically, these methods require adaptability, flexibility and fluidity with the relationships they were engaged with.

At least eleven of the Indigenous searchers had existing relationships or mutual connections with the people they spoke with and learned from. In other cases, new relationships were formed through their research. The research relationships are continuing and influence the gathering process. Michael (1997) states that, because he is a Cree man and on the "inside" and participates in traditional activities, his location influenced the amount of knowledge available to him prior to actually gathering information:

> By not recording during the events, I was able to become totally involved in the environment. My focus was on my experiences, physically, emotionally, spiritually, and mentally. Not recording the events as they happened also respected the view of many Aboriginal peoples who participate in traditional ceremonies that recording should not take place. However, the sharing circles that I participated in occurred through a significant span of time. In order to maintain my memory of the circles, I did make some reflective notes after the circles occurred.

In my case, I already knew most of the re-searchers to varying degrees. This is partly because the circle of Indigenous scholars is still relatively small. It is also because relationships are recognized as an important strength and resource for Indigenous re-search, and we make new relationships through our re-search. We use our relationships to move forward. We create space to spend time and do thing together, and our relationships cross over different paths. Our relationships extend the boundaries of family, friendship, colleague, helper, teacher, advisor and so on. Our relationships are formed out of diverse community contexts. Jo-ann (1997) recalls the learning friendships she developed throughout her research:

> I have known Vincent for seven years, but have watched him work at numerous gatherings over many years.... Establishing relationships within this research context has become a way of establishing and sustaining lasting friendships with deep caring and endless stories and talk. Learning to listen with patience, learning about cultural responsibility toward the oral tradition, learning to make self-understandings, continuing the cycle of reciprocity about cultural knowledge, and practicing reverence are some of the lessons I experienced with Chief Simon Baker and Elder Vincent Stogan.

Searching for knowledge and the consequent transmission of Indigenous knowledge happens through relationship connections (Battiste and Henderson 2000b). Teaching is done and knowledge is transmitted by relatives through storytelling of real life experiences (Little Bear 2000). Relationship connections exist between the spiritual, physical and human realms. Russell Bishop (1998) encourages Indigenous re-searchers wanting to develop good relations to seek the help of Elders for guidance and to learn correct spiritual frameworks or protocols. Pam Colorado (1988a) says that learning the protocols is essential and asking for direction from the Elders is integral to Indigenous re-search. Further, she summarizes guidelines for preparing to enter into an interview relationship with people. Some of the key elements include the following: prepare well, care about the people, visit and take time, choose a good location, nurture good feelings, relax and build trust, listen and watch, and bring your knowledge and mind with you. "Personalizing methodology" calls for compassion, sensitivity and subjectivity (Ross 2005). Personalizing and reciprocating relationships in Indigenous re-search create a process that is mutually beneficial. It is our responsibility as searchers to be prepared by developing understandings about oppression, power, race, class, ethnicity and gender and to use our knowledge and experiences in a respectful and humane way. Ross (2005: 61) states: "When I interview people, I communicate in a meaningful, sincere manner. I share myself and my life — I am not simply 'gathering data.' Moreover, the people I interview are not objects — I see them as real people." Laara (2002) talks about her ethics and protocols in honouring her relationships with people through the use of tobacco as a sign of gratitude to the Aboriginal people who helped along her re-search journey:

> Because I was relying on Aboriginal people to "help" me with this research journey, I decided to use tobacco to demonstrate my gratitude to them. For example,... I asked the participants to give of their experiences, their knowledge, their thoughts, and their commitment to make this thesis a reality. I also informed them that I would provide a copy of my thesis to each person that

was involved: a gift to acknowledge their contributions. By understanding the research outcomes, they knew that in giving their time and energy to this project that they are contributing to a body of knowledge that is needed to contribute to the improvement of Aboriginal Peoples. Also, in preparation for the sharing circle I offered tobacco to the Elder as a way of asking him to carry out a certain responsibility.

Relationship-based processes are becoming common methodological choices for Indigenous searchers (Bishop 1998a; Weber-Pillwax 2001). Sharing circles, also known as talking circles, have provided culturally congruent channels for sharing stories, cultures, experiences, histories, perspectives, lessons, mistakes, knowledge and wisdoms (Archibald 1997; Fitznor 2002; Hart 1997; Marsden 2005). The medicine wheel has been used and applied to social work and educational contexts by Indigenous educators and social workers such as Fyre Jean Graveline (2000), Herb Nabigon (2006) and Michael Hart (1996). Sharing circles have always been a mechanism from which to heal and search for knowledge. Laara (2002) utilized sharing circles to gather stories and took her turn last in the circle so that she did not influence the tone or direction of the sharing. Interrupting, monopolizing and dominating are not issues within sharing circles because of the process of each person speaking in turn while everyone else is expected to listen. This results in everyone experiencing the sound of their voice and listening to others. Michael (1997) explains that the circles he participated in did not have time restrictions and varied from twenty minutes to two days. He was flexible with the circle location, which was determined by the community involved. His format was an informal relaxed gathering with open-ended questions proceeding in a conversational manner, versus structured questioning, which Peter (2000) calls "interrogative." Dawn M (2005) articulates specifically her use of talking circles because they provide a process to facilitate storywork and because this methodology is founded on the concept that we are all related and interconnected:

> One of the most interesting things about doing storywork in talking circles is that the researcher has no control, beyond introducing the research focus and questions, over the contributions that participants will make. The direction of stories shared can be written or deviate widely from researcher expectations.

Another methodological tool that Dawn M used was called "witnessing protocol," in which four people simply witnessed and observed the talking circle. This process follows a Coast Salish tradition described by Dawn:

> At the beginning of the talking circle, after prayers and songs and instructions, four participants were invited to stand as witnesses to the day's events. At the end of the day, they were invited to share their observations.

Working with talking and sharing circles can include the preparation and serving of food, offerings of tobacco bundles to express gratitude and good medicine shared, person-centred voice, storytelling and humour, while generating mutual sharing, understanding and learning, and non-interference of dialogue, all and within an Indigenizing framework (Fitznor 2002). Dialogue is a core feature of relationship-based processes and involves more of an active engagement between people than a question-and-answer format. Dawn M (2005) identifies having dialogues with individuals to add strength to the storywork process, and she invited participants to meet her individually after the group gatherings.

> Each dialogue was initiated using a shorter version of the unfinished story, first used at the first gathering. The unfinished story served as a good reminder about the goals of the research project, how the main research question came to be, and led naturally into the asking more specific questions.

The individual dialogue reproduced a form of the talking circle. Indigenous people who are familiar with circle work are more comfortable and at ease with circle as a methodology for gathering knowledge. In my search process, I had conversations with people, and in the learning circle a space was created for dialogue, sharing and connections to occur.

Our families and communities become involved in our re-search. Dawn H talked about her family developing connections with the Lubicon Chief. In my search, other family members were present at various times during my conversations. In addition to gathering participants, Indigenous scholars acknowledge family kinships as Indigenous methodology. Situating herself in the community is also important for Mary Hermes (1998: 165), who states that "the relationships, of reciprocity and respect, ordered the methods." Linda Tuhiwai Smith (2000) articulates working principles for research from a Kaupapa Maori research perspective. Genealogy of families and historical relationships with family, land and the universe are central to a Maori worldview. So the issues for Maori research begin with how researchers think about Maori people generally in terms of the kinships, interrelationships and genealogies. Smith further describes principles related to language, customs, control and ownership of knowledge and the extended family. The work of Maori scholars in articulating Kaupapa Maori research and family models of research has been critically refreshing and liberating, and this research is drawn on to support the Indigenous re-search agenda in Canada (Bishop 1998a, 1998b; G.H. Smith 2000; Smith 1999; L.T. Smith 2000).

Community relationships are another common strength of Indigenous methodologies. Consistently, conscious Indigenous re-searchers agree that our searches be purposeful and beneficial to community (whatever that community is and represents). My re-search community is comprised of a diverse representation and includes Indigenous educators, scholars and searchers. I also have my traditional community, geographic community and nation community. I have a clan family and a circle of people who I choose to be in relationship with and who lovingly support me. Some searchers may interpret community to be their reserve, their First Nation, Indigenous peoples generally, their land base, their cultural orientation or their lifestyle. Community is determined and defined with respect to the searcher. Our searches generally occur in collective contexts and not in isolation. We need to be in the community context to continue developing Indigenous methodologies.

Leanne (1999) articulates the community-based protocols that she followed. She relied on community experts and went to the fishers, hunters, medicine people, trappers, youth and children who were considered experts in specific areas. The Elders of the community asked Leanne if she would go to talk with other community members who have knowledge. In giving her direction, the Elders acknowledged that other sources and resources for knowledge exist. A diversity of understanding was gathered by spending time with these other community resources. In other words, the scope of her findings broadened and opened up doorways to knowledge. Dawn H's (1995) methodology was influenced by her cultural background. Talking with Elders was steeped in Indigenous traditions of reciprocity and community connections, and this influenced the type of interaction she had with the Lubicon peoples. Working within a community requires a specific knowledge set on how to work with Elders, and for this knowledge, we must be involved in our own traditions and communities, because we share commonalities between nations on establishing connections. Dawn recognized and respected that the search would occur the Lubicon way, with the Lubicon people positioned in authority over the process. She visited the community and stayed there for months. Even though she was searching in a different community context, she was assisted by an Elder from her own community who accompanied her to Little Buffalo, the land of the Lubicon nation.

Elders are the ones in the community who are recognized to have acquired knowledge and hold wisdom in areas of Indigenous ways, philosophies, theories and methodologies. They are the historians and record Keepers. They not only have life experience but also an understanding of life. Elders are the ones who know the land and the "old ways," they have lived and survived. They have stories to share, and these stories contain knowledge and wisdom. Leanne (1999) worked closely with Elders, was directed to Elders by the Chief and council of the community and visited the Elders over an eight-month period. Her relationship with the Elders existed on two levels: one was as a searcher for the community; and the other was as a learner about Anishinaabe ways and Anishinaabe identity. As a result, she says, she developed more of a personal relationship with the Elders. In her search, she worked with a core group and had monthly meetings. The group directed her search, introduced her to Elders and other community experts and organized trips onto the land and ceremonies. The community group became her teachers:

> I held them in a position of power, and our relationship was characterized by respect, friendship and open-ness. All the members of this group were involved in various activities surrounding traditional ways of community healing. We all shared a traditional belief system and were at various stages in the process of reclaiming our cultural traditions. It was these individuals who I spent the most time with, in sharing circles, speaking about dreams, camping, hunting, fishing, participating in ceremonies, storytelling, learning by doing and working on various community projects.

Most of the searchers have a heart connection to their searches and passionate feelings about them. They enjoyed their searches and found them to be meaningful, purposeful and relevant. We deal with real issues, important concepts and ideas, and the learning is both healing and stimulating. They all found that their searches affirmed their identity and helped to fill knowledge gaps that were targets of cultural annihilation. Indigenous re-searchers feel strongly about gathering historical narratives, traditional knowledge and language skills. Collecting information, knowledge and understanding from individual and group experiences are invaluable searches for the ongoing survival of our cultures. Often the researchers themselves are inspired by the people with whom they are searching and from whom they are learning. Enacting re-search with a good heart is one pathway to *minobimaadiziwin*, the good life. Doing research in "relationship" reconnects us and remembers us to ourselves and one another. Perhaps "reclaiming" and "reconnection" as methodological search processes begin as early as searchers' connecting with one another and initiating a joint graduate thesis. Collaborative dissertations are not common, yet from an Indigenous perspective ought to be considered in enacting relationship-based searches.

Mind: Respecting Indigenous Knowledge

Respect for Indigenous knowledge is the main tenet of this group of petals. Enacting re-search that is respectful of Indigenous ways means that Indigenous re-searchers work to advance Indigenous perspectives, worldviews and methods in all areas of education, searching and scholarship. We articulate Indigenous methodologies *keemoochly* with confidence, persistence and defiance. We bring these methods into how we research within the confines of the academy, where we develop a critical consciousness, find our role, recruit allies, recognize our skills and supports, and negotiate barriers.

Indigenous scholars reference and privilege other Indigenous scholarship, knowledge and literature. The reason is simple: we need to grow and develop and articulate Indigenous theories and methodologies. Within the academy, we have been forced to privilege non-Indigenous theories and methodologies for too long. To continue to force such assimilative standards into Indigenous knowledge quests is unethical, racist and colonizing. We need to refuse assimilative standards and to make strategic decisions to not only include and assert Indigenous knowledge but to be aware of what, how and why we include certain knowledge. Thinking strategically is a state of mind. We carry an attitude to work against colonialism. The defiance of colonialism and attempted annihilation of our lives, families, culture and land permeates Indigenous re-search agendas. Colonialism has contaminated our minds, and this abuse must stop. This attitude comes from a place within that screams for our way of life to be actualized. Is that my grandparents calling out? Is that my Spirit calling out? Is that our ancestors calling out? Certainly, we are not disappearing and will continue to assert and carry a warrior's attitude into our work. By enacting our Indigeneity we make a contribution toward realizing our knowledge and methods. Respectful searchers propagate and protect who we are, our identities and the way of life our ancestors gave us.

Respect of Indigenous knowledge is manifested by Indigenous searchers through asserting Indigenous knowledge and methods, acknowledging their genealogy of knowledge, advancing Indigenous perspectives, privileging Indigenous scholars in their searches, making strategic decisions and negotiating academic gatekeepers. Indigenous searchers make conscious and strategic decisions about their searches because the academics who guard the elitism, power and privilege of the academy do so to maintain their control over knowledge production. They regard their gatekeeping role seriously. For the searchers, a respectful search process is contemplative, reflective and thoughtful. Conscious Indigenous searchers engage in their academic searches deliberately incorporating their knowledge and making conscious decisions about what knowledge they share. Dawn M describes the impact of asserting Indigenous knowledge and methods:

> There are different Indigenous theories and there are different Indigenous methodologies and there are different Indigenous methods. I wanted to be clear. I wasn't lumping everything all together, but saying, "Here are some commonalities amongst traditional based Indigenous wholistic theories and traditional based methodologies," and "These are just some." I hope people are left thinking, "Well, what other Indigenous theories are there and what other Indigenous methods are there and what other Indigenous methodologies are there?" Suddenly, all this knowledge and information that's already been shared in research and in literature everywhere, you know, people can take another look at it and say, "Oh, okay. Here's a theory for that" and "There's a theory for that," and suddenly Indigenous knowledge, Indigenous people

are no longer the savage, ignorant, blah, blah, blah, stereotyped people with nothing to offer, but here we are on a level playing field. I mean how many non-Indigenous scholars would appreciate suddenly being thrown into an environment where everything they had to share was quaint?

Enacting respectful re-search is imperative to the searchers, who have said that Indigenous knowledge inquiry is rigorous. It simply takes more time, energy and effort to search the "Indigenous way." For instance, one spring I felt compelled to take my children, Aki and Cody, on a fast. I had to follow Anishinaabe protocols in conducting this fast with my children. There were specific processes I engaged in because we were now working with Spirit, and in order to facilitate our fast in a "good way," I was responsible to ensure that the ones fasting were taken care of. Our environment had to be tended to and the time of year was another factor. I had to prepare and teach my children. The grounds had to be made ready and our fasting camp set up. This example shows that the knowledge and processes in which we engage to search are rigorous, ethical and dictated by tens of thousands of years of tradition and survival. The process of going on a fast prepared us to receive knowledge. Willie said "knowledge" is our friend, and we need to prepare ourselves to receive this friend and not be afraid of learning. Indigenous methods of knowledge production are based on culturally appropriate protocols initiated with conscious preparation.

Acknowledging our teachers and where our knowledge comes from is another common tendency of Indigenous searchers. From my search I learnt the importance of respecting the genealogy of knowledge. Dawn M wrote and spoke about the genealogy of the Wampum Research Model. Maggie spoke about the genealogy of the organic emergence of her methodology. I shared the genealogy of the petal flower as a wholistic representation of Indigenous methodologies.

Another aspect of recognizing how and where we learn is in creating space and visibility in our documents for the people who shared their wisdom and knowledge with us. Indigenous searchers discuss the desire to openly acknowledge who they spoke with and who was involved in their search process as an ethic of acknowledging the genealogy of our knowledge.

I agree that I have a responsibility to speak about what I have learned and that much of that learning comes from experiences; however, much of what I have learned also comes from others. Even though I speak from "me," the circles of influence from my family, community, and nation also shape "me." (Jo-ann 1997)

In oral traditions, when we stand up and speak, we acknowledge where our knowledge comes from and acknowledge our teachers, helpers, mentors and guides. This affirms our relationships and interdependence with others in our life. We live in relationship and learn from our relationships; this is the genealogy of how we learn and acquire knowledge. Confidentiality, as an ethic, then becomes relative. I wanted the genealogy of knowledge within this book to be acknowledged, and all the people I spoke with affirmed this notion and agreed to be named. Indigenous searchers recognize the need to honour as well as protect those we have learned from. So confidentiality may at times not be appropriate and at other times be necessary.

The searchers spoke with me about wanting to integrate past stories, knowledge, experiences and conversations they've had with Elders or family members. Michael talked about integrating previous knowledge, talks and experiences into his current search. He called it a "back door methodological approach." Other searchers identified that our knowledge also comes from our past and has traditionally been orally passed from one generation to the next. This knowledge passes through us and is carried on because we remember what we were taught and then we pass it on. It's important for us to reclaim our own knowledge traditions because "they took our memories from us, now you just go on and take those memories back, and make them ours again" (Winona 2000). Indigenous searchers do this by pushing the back doors open and challenging the academy to accept those channels of historical knowledge. Some researchers are going back into their memory and retelling stories they've heard or traditions they've witnessed. Again, the relationships are revealed in that methods of going into our memory are directly related to use of self as a methodology. Some of our original teachers have made their journey to the Spirit world, and that knowledge is retained in our memory banks. The only way to tap into that knowledge, for its survival, is to tap into our own memory and then begin a process of verification with other community members or Elders.

Body: Doing, Working and Creating

Enacting Spirit, heart and respect for Indigenous knowledge ultimately leads us to "doing," becoming involved and active. Physical and body work as methodology actualizes the Spirit, heart and mind of the search. Indigenous methodologies incorporate all aspects of our being and all connect to each other.

Doing and being creative are operative here. There comes a point in our process when we need to go beyond the writing and move from the cerebral, heart and Spirit into the doing and being (Rice 2003). Words alone are not enough in a culture that is experiential, wholistic, land based and connected to all of Creation. Indigenous searchers have enacted a physical element in their searches.

You know, there was no interest in my research until I started using, incorporating visuals in my research. The Wampum Research Model was the first one that I brought out. I use all these processes, but I wasn't writing about them, initially, until the Wampum Research Model. And then I brought it out and then suddenly, like everyone can identify. Of course it was predominantly Indigenous audiences. But, words are boring a lot of times and they're not very good at getting across meaning like visuals can. (Dawn M 2005)

The body elements of Indigenous methodological tendencies include physical actions and creating movements. Indigenous methods of searching and gathering generally involve "doing." As I stated earlier, in June 2006, I attended and presented at a conference called Shawane Dagosiwin (being respectful, caring and passionate about Aboriginal research) in Winnipeg, Manitoba. The third phase of my search occurred at that conference, where I facilitated a learning circle on Indigenous methodologies in search for knowledge. The learning circle was significant in my search as a means of sharing what I had gathered and learned. I prepared a giveaway with my search and did something physical while I was trying to make meaning of all that I had gathered. The act of making meaning became an act of embodying what I was learning and led to physically creating a tapestry of the petal flowers represented here. I needed a concrete representation and something visually stimulating.

Also at that conference, I listened to Brian Rice present his doctoral-search, in which he retraced the journey of the Peacemaker in the oral traditions of the Rotinonshonni. His presentation was about walking the Path of the Peacemaker as a methodology for writing his dissertation in traditional knowledge. His dissertation was on the oral stories of the Peacemaker and before he could start writing he needed to embody these stories; he felt compelled to retrace the Peacemaker's journey to do so. He walked an impressive thirty miles a day for a month. Ceremony, prayer and visits to Elders in their lands prepared him for his walk. In his presentation, he showed slides of his journey and told stories of the landmarks, the people he met and his own journey. Brian writes about his Rotinonshonni methodology and stated his rationale for doing the walk:

> The writing that I did during the colloquiums was still without any spiritual essence. This aspect would have to consist of some form of work that went deeper than the writing and learning process. For this reason, I chose to do the walk in the territory of the Rotinonshonni following the story of the Great Law as best I could. (Rice 2003: 177)

Embodying our search is a concept I heard echoed in my conversations. We embody our searches in different ways. Some people do so in ceremony, and others take journeys such as Brian Rice's walk or Peter's canoe journey.

Dawn H's (1995) re-search with the Lubicon is another good example of an active methodology. Dawn participated in sweat lodge ceremonies, seasonal tea dances, round dances and other meetings with the Elders, who took time to explain things through one-on-one discussions or formal interviews. Dawn elaborates:

> I continually hounded Chief Ominayak and the council to assist me in articulating our "research project," the design goals, time frame etc. I was never given an answer, just silence and grins. In time I came to realize that the Lubicon chose to "show" me what they thought important rather than "tell" me.

Either we find ways or those we work with find ways to embody our search, to internalize our process and tend to the physical aspects. I travel, have conversations, do ceremony, sew and bead. I also run to feel the earth beneath my feet, breath the air and take space to process my search. In our conversations, Dawn M shared painting as part of creating her re-search model:

> The Wampum Research Model is one of the most affirming parts of the research project and the research process. And there was a lot of prayer involved in the research process. And I was at a point of being overwhelmed by all the information that had been shared with me and thinking about how to write about the research process, because it was — it's very complex and there's not a lot of models out there, as you know. And so I put some *semaa* down and prayed, and that night I woke up at about 3:15 in the morning and — it was one of those things where it was tossing and tossing and tossing in my dreams, like all the details were there. And so it was like I had to — and it was prompting me to wake up. So I woke up. And the skills most available to me are painting and I'm very visual. Because it was all visual in my dream. And so I just got out this big thing of, that paper that you cover tables with, and just started drawing. You know, I just got the lid of the margarine bottle and — it was all in my head and all the information was there. So I actually wrote about it later in a paper, about all the details. So I painted it all out.

Learning by doing is Anishinaabe pedagogy. Leanne (1999) used several forms of "doing" in her research:

> Learning by doing was a central method chosen by the Elders and community experts to teach me. For me, it meant participating, experiencing and reflecting in a number of activities in spiritual, emotional, physical and mental dimensions. I went on hunting trips, out to fishnets and to check traps. I travelled old canoe routes. I visited sacred sites and participated in sweat lodges and shaking tent ceremonies. I camped on the land a number of times with community members, and observed healing and sentencing circles. I participated in a number of smudging ceremonies and sharing circles. I was also asked to share my dreams and visions.

Working together is what Leanne identifies as an Anishinaabe methodology. Specifically, an Anishinaabe method follows the seasons and works within its cycles, follows the decision-making methods of leaders, and honours the clan system.

> The Anishinaabe methods of inquiry I have used as research methods in this dissertation include; Anishinaabe collaboration, apprenticeship with Elders and community experts, learning-by-doing, ceremony, dreaming, storytelling and self-reflection. (Leanne 1999)

Leanne worked with a core group, meeting on a monthly basis. The group directed her research, introduced her to Elders and other community experts, and organized ceremonies and trips onto the land.

> During the initial stages of the community research project, a band councilor in the community in which I was working, who is also an Elder asked me, "Will you go to the fishermen, the hunters, the medicine people? Will you go to the ones who know? Will you ask the women? suggesting that I needed to consult a variety of people to generate a clear picture... I was directed to a number of community experts by the Elders and the members of the environmental group. Community experts that emerged during this research included hunters, trappers, fishers, youth and children who were the experts in a specific areas of knowledge. I usually visited with these people. (Leanne 1999)

Working with Elders is critical to understanding and knowledge transmission in Indigenous ways. The Elders, after all, are the historians and record Keepers. Leanne was directed to the Elders and visited them often during her research. During her initial visit, she offered tobacco and gifts, identified who she was and what she was doing or what she wanted to know (although she didn't state she told them for what purpose). Her relationship with the Elders evolved on two levels: one was as a searcher documenting for the community; the other was as a young person learning about Anishinaabe ways and Anishinaabe identity. As a result of this way of working, she developed more of a personal relationship with the Elders.

The physical element is also about creating space, change and a supportive committee, being creative and undergoing methodological shapeshifting. Indigenous scholars, without question, are pushing for methodological shifts and astutely assert a need for space. Laara, Dawn M and Winona all spoke explicitly of the need to find a supportive space in the academy. A critical resource for any searcher is a committee of allies because a committee will help create space, as expressed by Missisak:

> That's what I've done, is to keep bringing it back and bringing it back, "Well, what about this?" "I would like to do this," "I would like to do this" and then just being fortunate to have somebody like P. who would never resist it, but would say what the institution might support or not support. So in the end I got supportive people on my committee.

Creating space opens up possibilities. Maggie's going home created space for her to just be herself, grow, heal, think, search and write. Her space allowed her to study the language, be in relation with family and friends and feel more at peace with herself. This space nurtured congruency, which I believe is pivotal to being able to produce authentic knowledge. We have to be careful to not be too rigid or dogmatic because we can't write a prescription for what home means or what groundedness means or what being centred means. Indigenous re-searchers work from their own sacred place. For Indigenous methodologies to manifest, they must have space for that to occur. Creating space allows shifts to occur so that Indigenous searchers can forge pathways for Indigenous methodologies in Indigenous searches.

I feel like a methodological shapeshifter as I vision and dream about how to represent my search in a congruent manner. The petal flower has helped me to shapeshift from considering linear boxes and text to a representation that I can understand and relate to because I understand that our original teachers are of the earth. In a sense, Indigenous searchers are shapeshifting the way Indigenous knowledge is conceived, perceived and received. The act of making meaning of our searches lies in the question of how we represent all that we have gathered. Dawn M (2005) contributes to the methodological snift by detailing a "beaded representation of the research process… this came after praying for assistance to comprehend all of the complex influences and considerations." Her model was generated during the making-meaning stage of the research, which for me occurred after all the berries were in the basket and the sorting of the search began. Analysis is a strictly academic term. Making meaning can be a physical process. The beads woven together represent the influences and relationships of more than three relevant groups: the Indigenous re-searcher, Indigenous community and the institution. Dawn's beads and weaving together represent knowledge that is as old as our ancestors:

> This Wampum Research Model is a research tool that can be used and modified to represent, design, analyze or present complex influences and relationships in qualitative research and is a rich example of the potential or revived traditions and visual arts for expanding and extending perspectives into other domains of being and knowing.

Recent Indigenous searchers have presented some very inspiring representations of their searches. Peter (2000) radically shapeshifts out of grammatically correct english to prose, poetry, dramatizations, canoe journeys and conversations. Sharilyn Calliou (2001) identifies four methodological frameworks by five Indigenous scholars (David Kwagley, Eber Hampton, Marie Battiste, Roland Chrisjohn and Sherri Young), which briefly are: acknowledging work with Elders, honouring our memory, use of medicine wheel teachings and critical discourses on dominance in research. She calls them "give aways," and she also names ten methodological principles "graffiti slogans" because her research focused on landscapes, creativity and graffiti artists and draws analogies to researchers creating "thoughtscapes." Some of these principles are to know our landscape before proceeding, research from the heart, know our motives, and data are not objects. Dawn M's most recent work incorporated visual arts and painting. "Painting is just one of the ways that dreams can be expressed, but as a visual, is especially effective as a communication tool, or starting point for designing, analyses or discussions" (2005: 53). Visual manifestations reflect an embodiment of methodologies. Avenues for giving voice are created through painting, beadwork, tapestries, sculpting, poetry, prose, stories and photography. Visuals help lift the words off the page because our searches are multidimensional and wholistic. Dawn M (2005) stated that words can be boring and we need to keep conversations and words in their context and provide a context to the words:

> The theories, methodologies and methods used in this research project were: Indigenous wholism, storywork, talking circles, Indigenous protocol, prayer and dreaming, unfinished story method, dialogue, audiotaping, Ojibway and Coast Salish practices, and visual arts.

Stories are oral landmarks that are passed from one generation to the next. They contain knowledge of histories, traditions, events and life experiences. Winona (2000) expresses that collecting stories can be physically demanding:

> The study of kayâs âcimowina, old stories, has taken me moose hunting and taught me to clean and prep such fine feast food delicacies as moose-nose and smoked intestine soup…Cree education is based on interactive and reciprocal relations, and all knowledge comes with some personal "sacrifice."

Indigenous searchers talk about storytelling as a methodology to help our people tell their stories so they can leave their mark. These stories help us to not get lost. We build on our stories and each other's stories, and eventually our stories weave together as we share them.

> Collective storywork, as a research methodology is the active process of sharing, telling or engaging with multiple stories, for the purpose of documenting consistent and important themes. Collective stories are the final products or versions of what has just been processed, through reflection, analysis and conclusion. (Dawn M 2005)

Creating a collective story involves beginning with our own story and then inviting participants to add to the "searchers story." Weaving our stories together brings us out of isolation, and when we share our stories we realize we have common stories. Michael says that when we meet, talk and share our stories, they "would be weaved together. And that's something that becomes really important as well, is weaving our lives together and making something strong out of it. The similarities become those patterns in whatever we weave together." Today, our stories have changed to acknowledge what beautiful mothers, fathers and grandparents we have and what strength they have given us because they fought the fight. In our stories they came out, not in negative images, but shining, and we can see their beauty and strength. As we share our stories they transform from stories of defeat to stories of survival and resistance. In that sense, we're shapeshifting our stories. Working ourselves into our narratives and collective memories is an Indigenous search methodology (McLeod 2005). Jo-anne and Peter extensively employ stories as methodology. A restoring and re-storying methodology facilitates healing and reconnections. Weaving our stories together leads to a weaving of work and a building on each other's knowledge. These are examples of Indigenous modes of knowledge production.

Indigenous methodologies create doorways to self-discovery and other unanticipated journeys. Indigenous searchers found doorways that revealed possibilities of healing, knowledge, history, truth, identity, culture and much more. Like gathering berries or food, those who read this book will take what they need and leave the rest. The searchers throughout this book describe many portals which are related to their context and search, and themselves. We need to continue to acknowledge one another and not compete for knowledge ownership because "researchers are not developing new paradigms and methodologies; they are simply acknowledging the existence and validity of knowledge creation and transmission in Indigenous Knowledge systems" (Winona 1999). We are all working toward a collective goal of acknowledging and validating Indigenous knowledge and methodologies such as prayers, dreams, fasting and ceremonies.

The diverse methodological tendencies represented by Indigenous searchers doing graduate research in the academy are a sum of a Spirit, heart, mind and body enactment of wholistic Indigenous methodologies. Brian Rice states: "Traditional Knowledge provided the framework, the vision, and the process for the work. Traditional Knowledge methodologies are valid in their own right, and can be used to create a dissertation that combines western and Indigenous epistemologies" (2003: 182). They are interrelated, dynamic and fluid and dependent on the context of the searcher and their search. The roots of these methodological tendencies for conscious Indigenous searchers are in their worldviews, ancestral histories and languages.

Chapters Three through Nine detail a wholistic view of Indigenous re-search methodologies and tendencies. They are diverse and varied, interrelated and interdependent. Not all are present at once but are actualized to varying degrees and in diverse forms. Any petal flower could represent

Indigenous re-search methodologies, and its collective elements would represent their wholistic and relational nature. Their distinction lies in their intimate connection to the worldviews, histories, cultures, languages, experiences and contexts of Indigenous re-searchers. Space is abundant, and there is unlimited room for their ongoing articulation and developing discourse. My intent is to contribute to and participate in developing Indigenous discourse hoping that others will do the same.

The environment of a petal flower affects its life. The environment also impacts how searchers and gatherers work. I don't go searching for berries on Clarks Island in Georgian Bay because there are rattlesnakes there. I won't go berry picking in a storm, nor can I pick in cold climates. I love searching for berries along the rivers where I can take a break and go for a swim. Petal flowers bloom with the right amount of rain, air and sunshine. The environmental context is not separate because it affects Indigenous re-search methodologies in the academy. I talk about this environment as a separate chapter because we enter into the academic context, and this context does affect Indigenous re-searchers and their re-search methodology. It presents issues and challenges.

Chapter Ten

The Enviro-Academic Context

The petal flower is affected by its environment, and similarly, Indigenous re-searchers are affected by our environment in the academy. For our graduate studies, we enter the academic context, interact with it and then leave it. During the time we are there, we both affect and are affected by the academic context. The Indigenous searchers in this book faced controversy and challenges as they entered the environment of the academy and began asserting their methodologies. Anticipating challenges, some took precautions beforehand. Winona (2000) writes: "Before she packed up her pick-up truck for Berkeley, he [Harold, an Old Man] took her to the mountains for ceremony to protect her Spirit from the harsh environment she'd be living and learning in." Within the academic environment there are a number of important dynamics, including academic gatekeepers, allies and the research committee, textual writing of oral traditions and developmental issues that are challenging and unique to Indigenous re-search.

Fences and Gatekeepers

As Indigenous re-searchers nudge their way toward empowering Indigenous theories and methodologies, "old order" power holders of western forms of knowledge production may become aggravated, irritated and annoyed. Fences are erected, and gatekeepers vigilantly stand guard to maintain the power and privilege of who can know and how this knowledge comes to be. Power is rarely relinquished freely (Pinderhughes 1989). Controversy and conflict are sure to arise, and Indigenous searchers have demonstrated ingenuity and determination in confronting barriers.

Indigenous scholars who are primarily schooled within western positivist frameworks are taught to divide, categorize, standardize, reduce and remove human nature from the process. We are warned against having a personal involvement/stake in our re-search. When courses on Indigenous re-search methodologies are not available, the starting point for many Indigenous re-searchers is to recognize the limitations of western research frameworks, critiquing them and then choosing to make adaptations or to let them go. Raven talked about this:

> I've always been in the western education system at the same time as going to ceremonies and meeting teachers and learning different teachings and having

lots and lots of experiences, cultural experiences as an urbanized Cree woman. And so some of the teachings and things I got out of context. And I had some bad experiences where there was abuse of power. I guess just a flagrant abuse of power. I grappled with all of those sort of experiences. In my master's we did what was called the designer thesis. I did a thesis on a research methodology. So I didn't actually go out and do any qualitative or quantitative data gathering; it was text research. And so when I got into my doctoral work, of course, you have to take research classes and what was missing for me was again the cultural mirrors. I mean I had gone through my undergraduate at the First Nations university so I was out to experience a little bit of what it's like to try to infuse a western curriculum with Indigenous thought and knowledge. And at the PhD level that was really missing. Everything was purely western.

The big question is then what do we replace it with and how do we do Indigenous re-search? Letting go of western methodologies opens doors to recognize that other real choices exist. Maggie too recognized the limitations and searched for an Indigenous methodology. From her search process, a Cree/Saulteaux way of coming to know emerged. In the buffet of methodological options, Maggie says that one of her goals was to ensure that Indigenous methodologies are present and visible. Location, situatedness, relationships and motives are central to wholistic Indigenous re-search agendas. That does not mean that we are not objective or rigorous about what we are doing. On the contrary, as Raven asserted, our protocols and methodologies are ethical, objective and respectful. It's difficult to be critical of western methodologies when we have internalized western definitions of knowledge and science. So to become progressive Indigenous re-searchers we have to become conscious of the history and impact of colonizing methodologies and oppressive theories. We have to learn our cultural history and knowledge. We have to undertake a journey of learning, unlearning and relearning, and this journey is difficult because we are inundated with the continuing effects of colonialism every moment of every day. Some of the re-searchers acknowledge that it would have been simpler to just do western research, stay detached and get it done. Raven explained:

> I mean if I could, I probably wouldn't choose it. But, if I had druthers, it would be kind of nice to just be that, a distant, removed researcher doing a case study, where I just had to interview my participants or something. No, no. I'm in this journey and it's very, all encompassing, because it's a personal one, it's an academic one, and it's a spiritual and stuff like that.

Doing Indigenous methodologies in the academy sometimes means taking the road less travelled and bush whacking it from time to time.

External fences are structurally, institutionally imposed and enforced and create obstacles and challenges. Indigenous re-searchers become hoop dancers as we jump through bureaucratic hoops that defend colonial education structures, programs, content and procedures. As Dawn H (1995) notes:

> Post-modern theories have acknowledged their own power positions, subjectivity, and historic moment in the process of social analysis…. Thick descriptions of post-modernism and anti-imperialist literature continue to drown out the "others" voice. The notion of grasping the Native point of view is obscured by self-justifying, self-reflection, and global interpretation of the self rather than the other. There is little room for the other to make a true presence within the theoretical debates over analysis currently underway…. The problem with the Native voice entering into the debates constructed by the "dominant" discourse is in danger of intellectual assimilation… [and in this manner] the Native point of view will always be a construct of and by the ethnographer.

Many of the Indigenous re-searchers expressed frustration and anguish over their search. Even though they found useful elements within feminism, phenomenology, critical theory, narrative and participatory action — they couldn't find a full fit for their work within western research frameworks. Missisak shares her tensions and frustrations:

> Our struggles with the institutions, our struggles with our respective workplaces, with colleagues, the resistance to having even Aboriginal people, you know, coming in to take up a position and with bringing anything with Aboriginal perspectives. Like there's a difference today than there was back then. And that's not to say that it's still not happening. So it's the whole idea of the acceptance by Canadians in general to welcome, you know, Aboriginal perspectives and processing it into their work lives and into their institutions, the parameters and that. So that's where I shifted from thinking about doing that research with teachers and with a multicultural focus, shifting to work strictly with the Aboriginal educators. And that's where I became stuck, because I was not comfortable using or relying on the different methodologies I had been reading about. There are some, of course, that are friendly, like what do you call, the narrative inquiry. There are methodologies that are attentive to what I would call friendly that we can use and adapt. So, you know, and to say something is totally an Aboriginal methodology I don't think is there. Because we're caught up in having to write in english, so in that sense it won't be there. We're caught up in having to look at what's been done before, and what's been before have been both Aboriginal and non-Aboriginal.

Within the western academy, conscious Indigenous re-searchers require two knowledge sets. One knowledge set is grounded in western knowledge paradigms, and the other is grounded in Indigenous cultures and systems of learning. Indigenous searchers constantly have to deal with criticisms about the rigour of Indigenous methodologies. Dawn M shares her frustrations:

> What fires me up are the western accusations. Like for me the whole dissertation, the whole process, it's about our ways of seeing reality and it's like, "Damn the torpedoes, damn the rigour torpedoes." You know, just because, you guys have no concept of these other ways of knowing or being, you know, about the

universe — it doesn't mean that they're not valid. And so the whole way that I wrote was that these are valid ways. Then I remembered the multiple purpose of it. So I'm not apologetic. At the same time, I'm very aware of the accusation of lack of rigour, because there's no recognition of spiritual ways of knowing, you know, in western academia. And yet it's so, so real. These are whole ways of human being. And you know what? You talk to any non-Indigenous people, you know, on a deep level and they're talking about the same things, but their whole western framework of who we are as human beings is dehumanizing to us. So it's about regaining humanity, you know, regaining who we are and all our attributes and all our abilities as human beings. There are way more abilities than are categorized in academia, you know, way more knowledge than is categorized in academia. And prayer and dreaming and our visual expression, through whatever people chose, those are so important. They're the missing pieces in *who* we are. How can we say we're developing knowledge if we cut out everything but what's physically observable?

Like Raven stated, Indigenous methodologies and knowledge are concrete and strong enough to be challenged because they are rigorous and methodical. Because of institutional racism, there are still few Indigenous scholars in the academy. We are struggling and persevering to do re-search projects in the absence of cultural mirrors, Indigenous content, Indigenous curriculum and Indigenous mentors. Many Indigenous graduate students are designing their own courses and research programs and doing so with minimal support. It raises the question of why we pay for this!

Working with Indigenous knowledge and methodologies involves complex tasks and processes. Re-search relationships are long-term commitments, and working with Elders requires a knowledge set particular to the Elders' nation and cultural context. Non-Indigenous academics may not understand this. Although Elders are regarded within Indigenous communities with respect, academic structures create barriers and limitations to having Elders participate in a genuine manner on thesis committees. For Elders, the academic schedule can be problematic; therefore research must be flexible to ensure involvement by Indigenous communities, Elders and people. Dawn M (2005) intended to include Elders on her committee but time pressures prevented that. And when I was doing a graduate research course, one of our instructors told the Indigenous students that the only Elders to be on PhD committees would be those of the academy.

Knowledgeable and skilled Elders should be given a similar status to university faculty, to ensure that research by and for Indigenous peoples is undertaken, guided, and approved in ways appropriate to Indigenous worldviews and methodologies. In addition, while Elders have often guided students in their research and been credited through acknowledgements, there has been little acknowledgement of this guidance in formalized ways, in ways that would raise the intellectual capital of Indigenous peoples. The requirement to make a persuasive case for the inclusion of non-academic people on committees, prevented me from involving Elders, because of the length of time already used during completion of courses, exams and research proposal; I didn't think building a case would have been successful, quickly enough, to include Elders on my committee, in a full and respectful way, given the short time remaining for the completion of the research.

Considerable knowledge is required of Indigenous re-searchers. Working with Indigenous methodologies carries substantial responsibility and obligation. Indigenous epistemologies, which are derived from natural and spiritual laws, instigate strong ethical practices in Indigenous knowledge production. The knowledge acquired in any search can be overwhelming and daunting, and Indigenous re-searchers shared their feelings about doing their best to be conscious of their own process, ethics and protocols.

The most notorious character at the fence is the non-Indigenous gatekeeper. Indigenous re-searchers repeatedly voiced their frustrations with the academy's gatekeepers. Institutional racism creates and perpetuates glass ceilings, and those limitations are reinforced by non-Indigenous gatekeepers, who watch over the academy to ensure that you play by their rules — all the while reminding you what a privilege it is to be in their academy attaining their degrees. These gatekeepers strive to keep us preoccupied and distracted with defending, justifying, arguing and anything else to block our gaining a place of legitimacy, recognition and power within the academy. The only way to not become caught is to recognize gatekeeper tactics as neo-colonialism and keep asserting, integrating and standing up for Indigenous knowledges and methodologies. Like the petal flower with its stem, we need our backbone to deal with gatekeepers, who can be draining, demoralizing, offensive and disrespectful. Strategic searchers move past them, around them, over them and through them and are cautious of the trap they present. Problem-solving skills, ingenuity, *keemooch*, resistance and persistence all are strategies evidenced by the Indigenous searchers in this book. They had all met academic gatekeepers who they identified as impediments to actualizing Indigenous theories and Indigenous methodologies. Kishebabayquek tells a story of the tensions she's experienced in the academy while struggling to do a thesis on her father's knowledge:

> I looked at post-modern theories, post-colonial, I looked at feminist, standard sociology theory, and some of the phenomenology stuff, some of the narrative stuff, but they were still treating people as if you going into a situation and you're studying something. I was studying something, I was writing about my family and I couldn't do that. At the same time that was happening, I was looking around for this theory and method that was going to fit what I wanted it… and a general idea of what I wanted… and one of my professors when I told him what I wanted to do… he just sat back and basically looked at me… and said "basically what you want to do is to write about your father." I said "ya… is there something wrong with that?" He said "oh come on Patricia"

and then I realized this wasn't a favourable thing. This was a problem for him and I asked "so what problem do you have with that?" And he said "come on Patricia this is your family. You're going to write a thesis on your family?" I looked at him and I said "I want you to just close your eyes for a minute and think of me as a Canadian student walking in here with an unpublished manuscript by a traditional Ojibway, Métis man from one of the communities in this area. What response would you have?" And he just looked at me like I slapped him. I said "now I want you to think about what you just said to me and I want you to think about what I just said to you." I said "there's something wrong. If I have to be divorced from the research setting... if I have to... if any other grad student were writing about this, this wouldn't be a problem, because they're coming in from an outside perspective." I really felt so insulted. So he says something to the effect, "well there is a branch of studies where they talk about the subaltern" [her voice is questioning this word] and the subaltern speaks for something. I say "when did I ever give up the responsibility that I have to speak for myself, because I didn't do that." So I thought to myself... well okay... he doesn't get it!

Kishebabayquek's professor thought she was too close to her research because she was Indigenous but would have accepted a non-Indigenous person to write about her father. So then why is it too subjective or biased when Indigenous people write about Indigenous people: our families, communities, teachings, histories and experiences? We must confront academic double standards because they exist to maintain the power and privilege of those who have benefitted from being coined (dubbing themselves?) "Indian experts." The dominance and authority wielded by non-Indigenous gatekeepers is problematic, and some Indigenous re-searchers have been forced to abandon their searches because of this abuse of power in the academy. Oppressive actions occur when Indigenous scholars are denied their right to cultural congruency and when Indigenous scholars have to battle every inch of the way through their search.

The university contradicts itself when it claims to be here to foster new learning and create new knowledge, and yet enforces conformity of approach. Raven shared that Indigenous re-searchers *do operationalize* Indigenous methodologies, they just don't articulate what they do in a way that western methodologies recognize. In Indigenous contexts, it is not optional to ignore spiritual or natural laws. Despite pressures to conform, Indigenous re-searchers who want to integrate Indigenous methodologies into their search will do so, but they may not identify that in their text. Once again, we are forced into strategies of resistance for the ongoing survival of our ways.

Indigenous re-searchers, I found, like me, were frustrated when pushed by western academics to make their research comparative. Non-Indigenous gatekeepers often push Indigenous scholars to utilize western theories and then draw comparisons to Indigenous epistemologies, paradigms and methodologies. I see this as meeting more the interests of western academics.

To push Indigenous scholars to make comparisons is problematic on two fronts:

1. the non-Indigenous gatekeepers don't have the cultural competency of Indigenous worldviews and knowledge to understand what Indigenous scholars are articulating; and
2. comparative analysis becomes a major distraction from the Indigenous intellectual and methodological advancements that are motivating Indigenous re-searchers.

Most conscious Indigenous re-searchers want to focus on the development of Indigenous knowledge and methodologies and to contribute to their on-going articulation. My interest is in asserting the application and validity of Indigenous methodologies. When Indigenous re-searchers are working from an Indigenous theoretical and methodological standpoint, comparisons are unnecessary. Comparing Indigenous approaches with dominant research approaches is not helpful in this project and can in fact undermine it.

Earlier, I cited Dawn H's (1995) caution against what she calls "intellectual assimilation." Indigenous voices across the land are echoing that we must continue to assert our knowledge and power as Indigenous peoples by speaking in our own voices and providing a space for the voices of our people to come forward. We ought not to be silenced or to be afraid to speak in our own voice for fear of reprisal or criticism. Non-Indigenous gatekeepers try to steer us in research directions we don't want to go because they don't understand or see the significance of what we want to research. The gatekeepers may see our focus as "too personal," "too emotional" or "too subjective" — so they discourage research that appears, in their context, as non-objective. Five of the re-searchers had professors who didn't understand the nature of their search and who said that their re-search was too close and personal and they were too involved in their work. The following was shared in one of the conversations and reveals the discomfort and oppression experienced by Indigenous re-searchers:

> When I think about Indigenous methodologies, I feel like my master's program is removed from that to some degree, probably to a fair degree and mainly because I was forced, both internally thinking I was forced, and just by watching what was around me, forced into a methodology that wasn't our own, but at least wasn't overly oppressive, for lack of better words. So when I think about my masters, I think about ethnography and that history in terms of anthropology and ethnography is pretty — it isn't too nice. You'll get snippets in there about what in my sense was real for me. And what I mean by snippets is I had to write out who I was, but it still came in, in parts. When I reflected back in other sharing circles, I participated on facilitating. That's in there, but not overtly. So that part about who I am, the participation, the ceremonies,

the ceremony part to get ready to do it, the turning to ceremonies to help me keep moving, if I got stuck, for example, and all of that was present. But in terms of how to write it so that I could pass, I probably edited out — just by watching the dynamics around me [at the university]. I'm always hesitant, because — well, I'm still in the process. I did my master's and I'm doing my PhD at the same place, so I'm hesitant — and I'm working at the same place. I'm hesitant, because if I become offensive, then I'm burning bridges. So I have to watch in that way. In terms of the PhD, I still have that internal part about being really cautious. It's a little different on two ways, cautious about going too far about revealing our own thoughts and our own ways and still trying to figure out that line and what does that mean. But also cautious that if I push the envelope too far, then am I gonna be shut down.

Indigenous scholars in the academy talk about fear and hesitancy to do their searches in their own way or in ways that feel more congruent to their life and worldview. Many walk cautiously around the academic mine fields.

Non-Indigenous academics' ignorance about Indigenous peoples' histories, experiences, worldviews, theories and methods is quite restrictive. If you don't know what you don't know, it's difficult to recognize your own level of ignorance. Indigenous searchers are subjected to academics who are not competent on Indigenous matters, yet judge and measure us using western standards. We need the space to develop, create, search and theorize about Indigenous ways of knowing, being and doing. The limitations of the academy in these matters means that Indigenous scholars often are pressured to be both a learner and an educator of their supervisors. Four of the re-searchers talked about the need to educate their supervisor about Indigenous perspectives, and while some supervisors are open to such opportunities, it is time consuming and draining to do this during an already demanding doctoral process.

We also have personal fences that exist because our lives are busy and full. Many Indigenous re-searchers are academic leaders, community leaders, educators, family members, spouses and parents and experience pressure in all these roles. With employment, community, cultural protocol and family pressures, the research itself gets pushed aside because there is no space or time to attend to the required processes — so the research process can take a long time. Doing Indigenous re-search requires more time with process, relationships, community, reflection, Spirit and protocols. The academy has time limits, the community has time limits, natural and spiritual laws are time specific. Being Indigenous in this society also infers that our lives are complicated. The stressors of life as Indigenous people can complicate the search process as we may also be coping with extended family issues, life and death situations and health issues. It is no secret that being Aboriginal in Canada is complicated with stressful experiences because of racism, colonialism, politics, poverty, discrimination, stereotyping and basically living in climates of intolerance and injustice. Do we occupy a blockade or work on the dissertation? Do we attend ceremonies or work on the dissertation? They are all part of the whole, and so we make choices on a daily basis of where we engage and place our energy. I agree with Raven, who shared that at times it would be quicker to do re-search that was non-involved and detached. That really isn't an option though, because once knowledge is achieved we can't go back to ignorance. And we often can't walk away from a project because of the involvement of Spirit, community, Elders and the importance of the work.

The journey from the head to the heart is said to be the longest journey a person might take. Searches for knowledge using Indigenous methodologies are often Spirit and heart driven. They are not easy journeys. Often the methodologies emerge organically as the search process unfolds. The process can be fluid and difficult to articulate. This is not to say that our methodologies cannot be articulated, just that it is challenging. Text is often not enough, and many Indigenous re-searchers are challenged with issues of knowledge translation related to Indigenous concepts, experiences, languages and processes. Diverse mediums, which include the arts, visuals, video, graphics, songs, poetry, prose or storytelling, are often required for creative representations.

Allied Theories

All of the re-searchers struggled with the dominant nature of western methodologies. Most Indigenous searchers seem to begin with western methodologies and then integrate Indigenous processes, not because of issues of value but because "you don't know what you don't know." When they began their work, a search for congruency of methods emerged, coupled with their own ways of knowing, inevitably leading to shifts. Allies are essential, but understandably, we walk with caution. The danger seems to be in accepting theories and methodologies that are after all still cloaked in colonialism — albeit softer forms of colonialism.

> The danger of routing Indigenous discourses exclusively into western social science doctrines is that the more inclusive context of the Indigenous Peoples' experience and the right of Indigenous People to name their own experience according to their worldview will once again be marginalized. (Willie 2000)

Allies can and have supported conscious Indigenous graduate searchers. The Indigenous re-searchers I spoke to and read for this work acknowledged the allies who too resist the oppressive nature of dominant research methodologies. Allied methodologies supported the searchers until a leap could be made toward asserting the rightful place of Indigenous methodologies in Indigenous knowledge production. Few Indigenous re-searchers began by asserting Indigenous methodology. Michael (1997) gives an example:

In light of the participatory nature of ethnography, utilizing this approach also supported me in meeting the previously highlighted points. First, I was able to include my own, as well as the participants', subjective views. Second, I was able to fully involve myself as a participant. Third, I was able to incorporate reflection, insight and personal experiences.

Dawn H (1995) also wrote about her deliberations:

Is there any room in social analysis for the Native method or should I twist reality to fit the language and consciousness of the oppressor as Lorde states? In terms of exactly which method, I used both. Operating in the material world, I used video and tape recorders to conduct one-to-one interviews even though who I interviewed and when may have been spiritually and culturally guided.... The interviews in the Lubicon section [are] directly transcribed from the audio tapes. The collection of interviews is structured according to families and kinships systems.

Laara (2002) sought out allied theories and ended up modifying qualitative methods to fit more within Indigenous contexts, using sharing circles instead of focus groups. She states: "I adapted qualitative methodologies (pilot study — own observations; questionnaire that was grounded in Aboriginal context; group interview — sharing circles; interviews — conversations) that were relevant to this group."

Our methodologies are concrete and strong enough to guide our knowledge production today, as they did with our grandparents and great-grandparents. Eber stated: "One of the ways that I think of Indigenous people around the world and myself as an Indigenous person — is that we're relatively close to our old cultures — we're relatively close in time and in generations to our traditions of being human." We are not so far removed from this knowledge, yet today our context is different and we are not alone in our struggles. I believe we need to strive to make Indigenous methodologies central, with allied theories and methods as secondary.

To what degree is the inclusion of euro-theorists and allies considered? Peter (2000) states that he included the voices of euro-theorists to have a balance in his dissertation. I disagree with his decision because the reverse is not true: euro-theorists have not recorded the need for balance by including the scholarship of Indigenous peoples. Such reasoning also insinuates that our scholarship is imbalanced if we choose not to include the work of euro-theorists. Peter also states that he chose to include euro-theorists whose work was in alliance/allegiance/support of Indigenous peoples or who wrote in a respectful way. I find this a more valid reason for including eurowestern references which support our work. Peter chose

certain ones who had edited collections of our words in respectful ways
others who had left our words unmanaged within their own work our research

and those adopted into indigenous communities lives geographies
and those who "try to move outside normal 'regimes'
of academic / professional academic discourses,
in search of less-well-colonized spaces, where Other things can be said
...where other things can be said Differently"
eurotheorists are included in my comprehensive examination in outrigger positions
and in this journey as ballast   jetsam   for a balance/imbalance dynamic

Today I consciously privilege Indigenous authors as a political and academic act of validation and goal to "lift up" Indigenous knowledge. My aim is to position Indigenous scholars as voices of authority regarding Indigenous issues. Laara (2002) agrees, explaining: "I found that Aboriginal scholars were problematizing western mainstream ways of doing research while rekindling *and* asserting Aboriginal/Indigenous paradigms."

The Committee

Academic support is essential for Indigenous searchers who assert their location and personal involvement in their research projects and employ Indigenous methodologies within the academy. Indigenous searchers stated how much they appreciated and valued support received from Indigenous faculty, even in other institutions. Indigenous faculty offer culturally relevant support and their presence on committees provides role models and cultural mirrors that are too often absent. Few Indigenous re-searchers have yet had the benefit of an all-Indigenous committee, and so non-Indigenous allies within the academy play a paramount role. All the Indigenous re-searchers had a committee comprised of both Indigenous and non-Indigenous faculty, every re-searcher talked about supportive non-Indigenous allies within the academy. Such support received not be underestimated. Michael talked about this:

> At the same time, there's a small group of people that are supportive. And the way they're trying to be supportive is by making room, so that they're trying not to impose things. I believe people who are on my committee are trying to do that.

Ultimately within the academy we must work with allied academics who understand colonialism and who can "act as gatekeepers of knowledge in order to ensure that western european thought be kept in its appropriate place" (Duran and Duran 2000: 88). They can help keep colonizing methods out of our search. Some of these scholars' research helps us to understand the institutions we must navigate. Their presence on our committees or in the academy assists with opening doorways and windows to create "methodological space" so Indigenous re-searchers can do their work. They respectfully do not impose contradictory requirements of western theories or methodologies.

Maggie talked about how important her committee was in helping to create space:

> Why I feel really grateful about my process is that I was fortunate to have people on my committee who said to me, "Do what you need to do, Maggie. We've got your back." And structurally, from a university perspective, one of the things that I believe that was helpful to me is that on my committee I had the Dean of Education, I had the Director of Social Work, and I had Leroy Little Bear. And so I had senior people, who have been around and who could give me that space.

Committee members may have the authority to create "academic space" for Indigenous processes and methodologies to emerge. Maggie's committee supported her to go home to do her research. The possibility this creates for Indigenous re-searchers to work in a congruent manner is crucial. Space allows us to breathe, to be in our process, where our Spirit and heart can have life. That space means we don't have to leave our identity, culture and worldview at the door. It means we can remain congruent and thrive as an Indigenous scholar. In that space, we don't have to waste our time or energy arguing, explaining, justifying or defending our worldview or why we're doing what we're doing. This frees up spiritual, psychological, emotional and mental energy to grow and develop. If we are consumed with defending and arguing, then we are in basic survival mode and not able to grow.

The make-up of a re-searcher's doctoral committee is of crucial importance, and some participants made strategic decisions[1] about their committee because the thesis takes years of work and committee support can diminish or enhance our progress. Several of the re-searchers talked about the number of committee members they went through to find a committee that would support and work with them. Some re-searchers replaced an antagonistic committee member or even changed academic programs when faced with wasting valuable time dealing with unsupportive and even antagonistic committee members. Dawn M shared her experience with valuable time wasted.

> So one of my advisors after six months admitted to me that he couldn't support this kind of research because of the political situation, that it was under threat, even though he was currently supporting a couple other dissertations. His main focus was to — I think it was to turn mine into an anthropological, another anthropological work, where he wanted me to look at the content of traditional ceremonies. And, you know, that's not my place. And, you know, like for me it was about looking at the framework, like "What supports are there? What are the structures and the barriers in the political realm?" Yeah. So that was difficult, because it wasted, you know, half a year for me.

Alternatively, respectful and supportive committee members in positions of power are helpful in navigating the academy's bureaucratic roadblocks. I have been fortunate to have non-Indigenous allies as committee members who, rather than insisting on irrelevant western criteria, use their position of authority to expand the parameters, definitions and interpretations of academic research and policy. Indigenous re-searchers need to constructively talk about their thesis work, receive appropriate feedback, have appropriate challenges and receive support.

Writing Oral Traditions and Other Ironies

Academic writing presents challenges for Indigenous re-search contexts for reasons related to language and oral traditions. Four of the larger issues that were identified were related to:

1. academic writing and creating hybrid languages;
2. what to include from oral traditions in written text;
3. translation of knowledge, concepts and language; and
4. representation of knowledge.

Gatekeepers uphold western forms of academic writing and often force Indigenous scholars to write in a particular manner for the academy, which is often a non-Indigenous audience. Michael Marker states:

> One of the central problems for Indigenous intellectuals is that words — in english — are presently owned by an academic culture that has some consensus on the legitimate definition of these terms and activities. Indigenous scholars must either invent new words and then struggle upstream against the prevailing current to wedge them into the academic lexicon, or expand the meaning of conventional terms to include Indigenous perspective. This means seizing a word and saying, "this is what we meant when we say science, or epistemology, or respectful methodology." (Marker 2004: 103)

We need to create words and language that accurately reflect our intentions and are meaningful to the Indigenous audiences we write for. Writing for a non-Indigenous audience can take the form of changing our language to english, changing the tone, "white-washing" our findings or changing our terminology. It creates pressure to fragment information by creating themes and categories, thus forming a reduced and de-contextualized analysis, whereas Indigenous approaches would keep stories and voices within a wholistic context and let the readers make their own conclusions and interpretations. When writing for non-Indigenous audiences, the gatekeepers may require descriptive writing justifying and explaining Indigenous methodologies or long explanations of the basics, which limits Indigenous scholarship to introductory concepts.

Eber talked about keeping in mind that sense of audience; who we write for as we communicate our research:

> A real important part to research is the communication — is the conversation — is the publishing — is the communicating sharing knowledge. And so I guess the one way I think we are, as Indigenous re-searchers who are in the process of inventing or reinventing Indigenous re-search or claiming it — even claiming that tool — is by treating each other as our audience. So if we're actually writing to Indigenous people — the extent to which I'm actually writing to Indigenous people — I think that's one way that automatically changes the research. That sense of audience.

Our educational and research goals are self-directed and aimed at gaining a deeper understanding of our experiences from our locations. If our goals are to emancipate ourselves and contribute to Indigenous knowledge production that benefits us, naturally our commitment is to write for an Indigenous audience. What to write and how to write it leads to other considerations and challenges.

Discerning what is okay to write about and what is not okay to write about, in the academy, are ethical and strategic decisions made throughout the search process. Dawn M says:

> We're trying so hard to break new ground in the academy, but we have to do it carefully. And there were other strategic decisions that were made about this dissertation in that same vein, because there is this whole about — one of the biggest attacks against Indigenous re-search is rigorousness and validity. So that was a consideration. It wasn't in an oppressive censoring kind of way, it was definitely in kind of a strategic defensive kind of way....
>
> Some of them had to do with spirituality as the basis of Indigenous, traditional based knowledge and stories that supported that. Like there's a whole realm of conversations and I would say all of the decisions — were influenced by the group that I was working with, research group, individually and in multiplicity. One of the decisions was to take out references to some of the beings that we know about, that wouldn't be strategic to put into the dissertation, because that's another conversation that will have to take place later. And not only do we have this fundamental spiritually based view of reality, where everything is connected through Spirits, but that means that through Spirit there are these other beings, both Spirit and manifest, that are walking around. So all those discussions about... and all the terms and terminologies for people who walk between the worlds, that, for people who aren't human and aren't the beings that most western Canadians are familiar with, yet they influenced the process and influenced what was said, yet we left them out.

We are careful to not remove certain knowledge and teachings from their context. There are two reasons: One is that non-Indigenous academics, as Dawn points out, are not familiar with certain phenomena. Second, non-

Indigenous gatekeepers tend to take our critiques of colonialism personally and defensively and urge a rewording to soften the stance.

Writing within the academy is difficult as I search for words, phrases, analogies, metaphors and language to describe my worldview and the meaning I ascribe to it. Although I know I am capable, it's the making meaning of my thoughts in english grammar that gives me trouble. Even though my first language is not Anishinaabe, it was my mother's language and she transmitted her worldview through her communication to my siblings and me. Consequently, my worldview is Anishinaabe, yet my language is english. Many of the researchers, too, felt the limitations of the academy to receive our way of coming into knowledge. Winona says just do it and write from where you are. Dawn H (1995) articulates what, I believe, many Indigenous searchers anguish over while writing:

> Trying to remember all that I had seen and heard, I wondered how I was going to write about my involvement in these ceremonies and closed political meetings. My role as researcher had been redefined by the Lubicon. They had shared so much with me; they had included me in their lives. How was I to remove myself from these events in order to construct a presentation that revealed intimate thoughts of the spiritual beliefs of these people? They had revealed so much to me that was sacred and profound. How could this relationship be translated into the White man's world? As I listened to the drums I pondered these questions, feeling so very lost between many worlds.... Chief Hubert Buck sat with me for awhile. I told him of my dilemma and he responded, "Write the truth, that's all." So simple was his answer I had to laugh at myself.

Peter (2000) talks about why he transported his dissertation in a canoe and describes his language usage as an "anticolonial isomorphing of stories and epistemologies from Indigenous language into english and back." Leanne (1999) discusses in-depth the issues of textualizing Indigenous knowledge and transforming oral into written:

> Once Indigenous Knowledge has been filtered through western conceptual models and definitions and constructed into TEK, it is textualized. The textualization process has the effect of mis-translating knowledge across perceived conceptual universals, transforming the knowledge from process to product, de-contextualizing the knowledge, de-personalizing knowledge by separating it from the people, and transferring authority from the people to the content of the text. Textualization ultimately produces Indigenous Knowledge in a form that is completely accessible to the mainstream society.... Indigenous knowledge cannot be separated from the people. The people cannot be separated from the land.

Eurocentric thinking perpetuates the belief that something is not valid unless it's written down. Yet, Indigenous values are reflected in Indigenous languages in oral contexts. The translation of language, content and concepts sometimes requires more explanation and description. Indigenous languages are largely descriptive and verb based and reflect a particular worldview. English reflects a european worldview and, at times, is inadequate to articulate Indigenous methodologies, philosophies and concepts.

Issues of authority and translation plague Indigenous scholars who are faced with transcribing oral traditions into written text, where living stories that were once heard take on the stillness of the written word. Winona (2000) states that our challenge is to transcend the influences of dominant paradigms, objectiveness or otherness and to deny colonial representations of Indigenous peoples and cultures. She writes that we need to have opportunities to "re-imagine and re-express" the oral into the written and to find ways to "vivify the text." I really like that Winona calls words that are full of meaning and connotation "bundle words"; these are words that have a philosophy behind them. We use and create bundle words in english in an attempt to translate knowledge, concepts and contexts. We must resist falling into internalized colonialism and we must re-emerge in our stories. Winona gives an example: "A literal translation of 'truth' from english to Cree is tâpwêwin. But like most attempts at translation tâpwêwin means far more in Cree. It is one of those 'bundle' words that comes attached with deep open-ended philosophical understandings."

Translating the oral into the written is paradoxical too. Jo-ann (1997) shares her dilemma:

> I felt at a disadvantage because I do not know the Hul'qumi'num language enough to appreciate the connotated meanings. I noted that I should examine further the problems related to language differences, especially with translation and changes of word/concepts meaning with Ellen and other storytellers who are fluent in an Aboriginal language.

Many of the searchers discussed the contradictions of telling or describing oral histories in written english and how inappropriate it was to have to use english to describe Indigenous worldviews and contexts. Patricia (2003) describes her struggle to tell her father's stories and argues that telling his story was as legitimate a research process as is western science. She describes her thesis as a hybrid of how she was taught to speak culturally with how she is expected to write academically:

> Some academics may refer to this dissertation as the subaltern speaks, as this supposedly specifies that the people who are usually studied, the other, has developed the capacity to speak for one's community. I differ. In this dissertation, there is a recognition that this story and other similar Indigenous based stories must be told. If we are to meet our responsibilities to future generations, we have to use available contemporary tools to ensure that these stories, told from our perspectives, live on. They can offer a counterbalance to the historical records and add to the development of Indigenous-based written theories and

methods. Given the oral tradition of Indigenous storytelling, this may seem a contradiction, as is my writing in english.

We tend to create hybrids and characterize them as Indian english. The challenge of translating from visual and oral into written english is an interesting one we grapple with, and I have seen in the theses how creatively that challenge was met. The researchers wrote in prose, told stories, used poetry and integrated voice and personal narratives. I enjoyed reading the dissertations as most of them included personal voice and narrative. It was like reading languages that blend english with Indigenous worldviews. Indigenous people who use only english "do so in a distinctly Indian way, so that some knowledge of cultural communication patterns is requisite to an understanding of conversations" (Winona 2000). I have often referred to myself as orally dyslexic, and Winona talks about non-fluent speakers who are also insiders who "have the kinship links necessary to reintegrate and learn, and to varying degrees have internalized cultural communication patterns."

Clearly, as we translate between languages and contexts, we are conscious not to compromise, sacrifice or lose significant knowledge, understandings and teachings. Patricia (2005) writes that within her literature search there was no historical verification of Anishinaabek identity and that most studies deal primarily with negative social indicators of Indigenous peoples. The lack of accurate Indigenous representation is an issue when, as Patricia states, "nothing reflected either my reality in the world or how I negotiated my path." None of the researchers wrote as dispassionate objective observers, as all their searches were rooted in the personal and subjective. In fact, all of the Indigenous re-searchers were acutely conscious of how they represented their search, despite the issues that academia and writing present.

Representation, for Indigenous scholars, is not just a question of academic validity; it is also a question of family, community and nation integrity. Our audience becomes inherently involved when we begin to consider communicating our findings, and all of the researchers considered representation integral to how they presented their search. We want our work to speak to Indigenous people, not just academics. These are not light issues. We often write one way but are pressured to write another, and yet, as Patricia notes, "we are aware of the criteria for being accepted and offered full membership into the exclusive club of western academia. The concern I have is what we must sacrifice to join this club."

Leanne (1999) grapples with the irony of representing live and dynamic features of traditional knowledge that she received from the Elders. Documenting a knowledge that is active, personal and creative becomes difficult when written text appropriates that voice and freezes that knowledge in a particular time and context. We must be very careful with documenting traditional knowledge because it makes it more accessible to non-Aboriginal peoples for mis-use and mis-representation, which can be damaging to Indigenous peoples in Canada. So Leanne made conscious decisions about not documenting certain things, such as Anishinaabe environmental knowledge, descriptive accounts of her community experiences and reports done with the community, because all that knowledge needed to remain in the community. Leanne's dilemma makes clear that writing oral traditions becomes an issue of not only what we choose to include but also what we exclude.

> Initially, transcribed interviews were to appear in this dissertation. It was a constant worry to me. Above all else, I didn't want to hurt the people who had shared so much with me. By taking their words, and publishing them in my dissertation, I was also assuming responsibility for the knowledge. I was making it accessible to the dominant society, and there were no guarantees that this knowledge would not be used at a latter [later] date against the community. I came to the realization that I could not ethically publish those transcripts.

The conflicts, as Leanne says, arise around what we feel is ethical to publish or not. Intolerance and antagonism are reported by Indigenous researchers trying to write in our own way. Other academic pressures include guilt, different approaches to learning, reducing knowledge and time constraints. Jo-ann (1997) states:

> Some of my uneasiness of guilt feelings are also based on the possibility of financial gain. I benefit from this research work by completing a thesis, thereby obtaining a university degree which could influence my career and possibly my financial earnings. The guilt arises because I see how many of our Elders and cultural people live — near poverty — yet they are the ones with the high degree of cultural knowledge.

Regarding academic pressures, Peter (2000) had to change his abstract in order for his dissertation to be accepted because of the prose it was written in, which was an interesting contradiction given that his defence was successful. Peter writes:

> it seems the forces of colonization are ever at work
> even in terms of format now the very shape of my knowings must be transformed
> must adhere to what is acceptable to dissertation abstracts international
> a clearing house a data base cognitive head quarters international for *res academica*
> I append below my original abstract together with an email
> from the graduate chair of education at simon fraser university
> who let me know why it was not acceptable as *was/is*
> I choose to not filet analyze or interpret the letter he sent together with
> a supporting one from mr enrique cruz but I am curious at the choice of mr cruz
> providing me with as acceptable exemplars one being the ed d abstract
> of a document written by wendy ellen burton...

...I certainly hope that that example is of an aboriginal woman writing a thesis...
...I think it is time that what is constructed as being "acceptable"
move from western epistemological deemedness in terms of "correct"
to a place in which other cultures besides western academic ones
are welcomed into the conversation

colonialism imperialism consumerism these have been given much space
and time
many millions of books have been created in these camps of western intel-
lectualism
it is time that universities and governments and business moved from places
of racism
to places of shared partnership.

Like Peter, Indigenous re-searchers who attempt to counter western methods often experience backlash and intolerance within the academy. Michael
(1997) writes about the possibility of his research being criticized because he
may not have appeared objective or distant enough. He talks of Aboriginal
science and the notion of epistemological humility:

> Wholistic learning is a requirement of Aboriginal science. If I maintained dis-
> tance from the participants, informants, and events on the ground that I was
> avoiding "going Native," I would not be exercising epistemological humility. I
> may even be falling into Gilchrist's (1994) concern of internalized colonialism.

Some of the re-searchers expressed frustration with the "expert" syndrome in
academia. Dawn M (2005) identifies some difficulty writing about traditional
knowledge in an academic context and feeling pressure to write for publication and to become the "expert." I think it significant that she discusses her
resistance to the importance imparted to individual authors when she wrote
about the genealogy of concepts in her thesis. Her resistance acknowledges
that over time concepts and knowledge are collectively developed by many
people. People discuss and make interpretations and meanings of the knowledge they acquire. In other words, knowledge has a genealogy of its own.
Many, many people contribute to someone's knowledge and to cite only the
person who wrote about it negates those Elders and teachers who contributed
to the knowledge.

> I am also insulted by the implied assumptions that I cannot arrive at ideas or
> conclusions without reference to a published author.... The attempt in this
> thesis was to use my own ethical responses to academic pressures to ascertain
> difference, conflict and relationship between the desires of the academy and
> my integrity as an Indigenous graduate student. (Dawn M 2005)

A final irony is that we write in isolation about building community, reconnecting and collectivity. Writing a dissertation is a lonely exercise, and bringing

other voices in helps to break our isolation and build collective consciousness. Integrating Indigenous peoples' voices into my work was a commitment to acknowledging Indigenous traditions of orality, but in written text. Despite the alienating conditions of writing a dissertation, Indigenous searchers find comfort that a broader sharing of the harvest or dissemination of information will bring balance. Michael and I, in our conversation, speculated on Indigenous scholars engaging with each other to do joint dissertations, allowing us to engage in searches with others and create joint projects.

Writing about oral traditions and other ironies involves making judgements and strategic decisions as we negotiate the complexities of the issues. Frustrations, antagonisms and conflicts are a part of the search experience in the academy. I hope that articulating these experiences and perspectives will create awareness and change so that Indigenous re-searchers will be able to take their rightful place in the academy.

Thorny Prickly Challenges

Thorny prickly challenges are those bits and pieces that are difficult to grasp, need be left alone, too tricky to touch and leave us feeling uncertain. All the re-searchers identified thorny prickly challenges. I believe the difficult issues we shared are also developmental. As Indigenous methodologies are articulated and worked out, clarity emerges and so does wisdom. My goal here is to identify and create awareness of some of the challenges that arise. Answers and clarity will emerge for each person as their work progresses. Some of the challenges explored are negotiating our dualities, dealing with spirituality and sacred knowledge, knowledge extraction and appropriation, methodological traps and quantitative methodologies.

Employing Indigenous methodologies within a constrictive academic environment leaves us, at times, in agony and conflict. The experience of being torn between two worlds or pulled into two different directions is, I think, a form of what Ngũgĩ Wa Thiong'o identifies as "an existential human anguished condition" (1986: 22). Leroy Little Bear writes eloquently of jagged worlds colliding and that no one is either 100 percent Indigenous or eurocentric but that we have been forced to develop "an integrated mine, a fluxing and ambidextrous consciousness" (2000: 85). When we live in a world that rejects our humanity and identity, we end up doing odd forms of emotional and mental gymnastics to compensate and cope. It creates a split in our minds between who we feel and think we are and how society perceives and treats us, resulting in states of distress and dis-ease. Gregory Cajete (2000) claims that in order to honour our humanity and heal this split in our minds, we must acknowledge the human being in ourselves toward a reconciliation of self. Reconciling the dualities of our realities cultivates an ambidextrous consciousness (Little Bear 2000), which means being able

Thorny Prickly Ones
What do you do if the flowers have thorny prickles, aren't as nice or are too beautiful to pick?

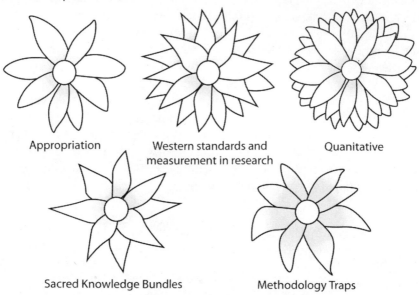

Appropriation   Western standards and   Quanitative
measurement in research

Sacred Knowledge Bundles   Methodology Traps

K. Absolon, 2007

to productively negotiate two realities/abilities at once. Knowing both an Aboriginal worldview and a eurowestern worldview and mentally moving between the two worlds on a daily basis requires such a consciousness. An appropriate metaphor for this is having your feet in two canoes and somehow maintaining a balance. Indigenous re-searchers talk with pride about our ability to maintain this balance and our bi-cultural understandings of two knowledge sets in two worldviews. These dual knowledge sets create within us a unique hybrid knowledge. Doing any Indigenous work within a western european context entails naming and dealing with our dualities while affirming our bi-cultural orientations.

Spirituality in the search process is a considerable challenge as is the question of what to write about when it comes to sacred knowledge. The cultural context for sacred knowledge production is worth noting. Our teaching lodges and sacred medicine lodges belong in the community for our people and children and they are protected from the academy. We must be careful what sacred knowledge methods we bring into the academy. We have to be very careful about what we say or write about. There are sacred pathways that can't be scrutinized by the academy. Indigenous re-searchers query whether or not to include certain Spirits and sacred knowledge because writing about such things can be controversial. Indigenous searchers respond to these issues by making strategic decisions with regard to what to omit and what to include in their descriptions of their research process, and they often exclude references to sacred beings and sacred knowledge of the spiritual realm. Indigenous re-searchers continue to search for an ethical and strategic balance to acknowledge the Spirit of/in their work. Some check in with their Elders and traditional teachers to achieve this ethical balance.

Indigenous re-searchers likely have different perspectives regarding what sacred knowledge to share. Not all Indigenous knowledge and methodologies are meant to be articulated within academic text. Some flowers are rare and precariously beautiful, and the urge to pick them is there — but should we? Some need to remain in their context because that's where their beauty and power comes from. Willie reiterated that point clearly. To extract them would be to disempower and dismember them. We have some powerful knowledge keepers and medicine people who hold sacred bundles and the means to sacred knowledge. Eber stated that there are more ways of knowing than can be categorized within the academy. What we articulate within the academy is only a fraction of the knowledge that exists within Indigenous peoples' cultures and traditions. Some things can lose their essence when they are documented and decontextualized. What is defined as a sacred knowledge bundle may be unclear and requires guidance from sacred knowledge holders. There are many methods to access this knowledge, and not all are appropriate for academic research contexts. I believe we need to receive guidance from Elders and sacred knowledge keepers regarding the inclusion of such knowledge in academic text.

Knowledge extraction and appropriation are also prickly issues. For decades non-Indigenous people have done research on and about Indigenous peoples. Today, we encourage collaboration, partnerships and protocol agreements between Indigenous and non-Indigenous re-searchers. Indigenous people do Indigenous re-search, but, can only Indigenous people employ Indigenous methodologies? Are methodological groundings of Indigenous worldviews, paradigms, knowledge and experiences accessible only to Indigenous peoples? This controversial question arose from time to time. Some people would just leave that flower alone. I believe that anyone can employ a wholistic methodology. I also see that specific to Indigenous methodologies are Indigenous peoples' worldviews, lens, location and experiences. Dawn M and I talked about this issue, and she said:

> Doing Indigenous methodologies has to be from ones' Indigenous knowing. The other thing is people said, "Oh, well, can anyone use this Wampum Research Model?" And I'm still unresolved about that in myself, because there's the whole — I've seen so many Indigenous ways and things taken out of context, disconnected, just like the stories. They lose meaning and they lose like the

whole embeddedness in the sacred. And so there's a very real danger of non-Indigenous people doing Indigenous re-search. But at the same time, I think non-Indigenous people can adopt Indigenous methodologies if they're doing it in a good way, in good relationships with the people they're doing it with and with full recognition, acknowledgement of the genealogy of that knowledge.

Like I'm finding more and more Indigenous ways being referenced without actually naming them as Indigenous. In the one sense, like Indigenous people don't own all these ways. You know, these are the ways of good life, the ways to live a good life. And a lot of the values, especially, are embedded within all kinds of different doctrines across the world. So if someone were to take the Wampum Research Model and use it in a totally non-Indigenous setting, I would say that was inappropriate. So it's about making appropriate choices for appropriate settings and appropriate groups of people.

Indigenous methodologies require situational appropriateness, which means that they can only be actualized when the whole context is relevant. The whole petal flower and its environment create the context for Indigenous re-search methodologies. Non-Indigenous people can employ some shared elements, such as respect, community benefit, relationship building and so on, but might not locate from similar cultural, spiritual, historical, personal or political experiences as an Indigenous methodology would entail. Situational appropriateness then asks the questions: Do you have an Indigenous worldview, history and experiences? Can you position your process in an Indigenous worldview and framework? If you can answer yes to these questions, then perhaps there is situational appropriateness and it is okay to employ Indigenous methodologies. If the answers are no, then perhaps a more general wholistic methodology is in order. It is important for us to be as specific as we can about our methodologies so that others who are travelling academic corridors and searching in the methodological maze may see Indigenous landmarks and not get lost. We need to leave our footprints as clearly as we can. We need to articulate and share as much as we can about how we went about searching for the knowledge we gather.

Without critical knowledge, searchers could be trapped by the academic requirement of confidentiality. Sometimes, confidentiality goes against culturally appropriate ways of acknowledging the genealogy of knowledge. In oral traditions, people often spend time acknowledging who and where they received their teachings and knowledge from. Acknowledging the people, animals or other realms as sources maintains the wholistic and respectful nature of knowledge production. In some cases, however, confidentiality is important, for example, where personal or emotionally sensitive information is being gathered. Indigenous re-searchers must decide on the appropriateness of confidentiality in relation to the context. I was really pleased to find an article that debunked myths related to the ethics of doing research in the academy. "Myths about Qualitative Research and the Tri-Council Policy

Statement" is a good reference tool, as Carolyn Ells and Shawna Gutfreud debunk eight myths related to ethics and qualitative research. The first myth was that anonymity must be guaranteed and sources kept confidential. "Yet contrary to this 'requirement,' qualitative researchers are aware that some research participants wish to be identified. Participants may have an additional motive in participating in the research that requires their identity to be disclosed" (2006: 364). This article also recognizes that written consent forms may be culturally inappropriate and incompatible with certain methodologies, that the format of consent can vary and that all risks and benefits need not be known in advance.

Finally, there are some flowers that just look different so people leave them alone. Because I reviewed search projects in the humanities, quantitative methodologies were not used by the searchers and came up only once, in a discussion with Raven. We are just beginning to articulate the issues of Indigenous methodologies for quantitative re-search. The use of Indigenous methodologies in quantitative studies is an area for further thinking and discussion. Certainly, Indigenous searchers would benefit from learning about statistical research and its application to particular fields. Indigenous health is an example of a search field where quantitative methodologies could be important. Raven mentioned that we will likely see more application of Indigenous search ethics in quantitative research in the health sciences as the Indigenous Peoples Health Research Centre in Saskatchewan,[2] for example, progresses, especially in the context of controversial research relating to blood and DNA sampling.

This book highlights the work of Indigenous graduate researchers who have completed and are completing the arduous journeys of conscious Indigenous re-search. Having such role models provides inspiration, hope and encouragement that we are growing in our discourse and presence. The leadership of other Indigenous academics and scholars has made our paths less rugged, and we are encouraged to continue. They have shared their stories about their searches and have helped us along, supporting us generously. Each time I hear of another Indigenous re-searcher completing their search using their methodologies, I know that change is happening.

Notes

1. Strategic decisions of committee can be based on cultural congruity; cultural competency, critical consciousness and whether potential members will be supportive or not. The committee experience can make or break our success and thinking strategically guided these re-searchers toward success.
2. The Indigenous Peoples Health Research Centre is a joint initiative of the University of Saskatchewan, the University of Regina and the First Nations University of Canada. Its website is <www.iphrc.ca>.

Chapter Eleven

Winding Down the Search

What is there to conclude?
The search continues…
There are still stories to be shared
Knowledge to learn
Methodologies to articulate
We are not finished
The journey continues…
How we come to know is our journey…
Our search for knowledge… survival
Searches and travellers continue…
I am one of them… so are you…
Beginnings and endings do not exist
Kaandoosiwin… how we come to know continues…
(Minogiizhigokwe)

When I started my doctoral journey in 2003, like other searchers, I was tired of the imposition of eurowestern methods of searching into Indigenous searchers. It is time to assert how we come to know. By unveiling a sampling of Indigenous methods of knowledge production, we legitimize our presence, and the academy can no longer deny, ignore, negate or dismiss us. There are many lessons to be taken from this work, and each reader will claim their own based on their context and needs. My hope is that this collective knowledge bundle inspires Indigenous re-searchers in their searches and fuels change within the academy and other arenas regarding the presence of Indigenous re-search methodologies. From my search journal, I share my own thoughts on the hard work ethic and fun of searching for berries with my mom. These experiences are close to my heart and helped me remember the hard work in how we search.

Gathering was hard work and as a kid we learned that searching meant work. I remember when my mom would make us go with her black current picking. The day was usually a hot summer day with the summer bugs buzzin at their peak. "Those bugs," she said, "were singing for the berries to ripen." The heat rays vibrated off the railway tracks and the stagnant swamp was abuzz with water insects. On really hot days my sisters and brother and I would just swim in the swamp — out of shear despair to cool down. On berry picking days, we had to walk down the railway tracks to the bushes where the black currents were. We entered the swamp where it wasn't too wet. That's where the black currents were. The bulrushes were so thick. This of course would instigate a bulrush fight where we'd smash them on each other to make them break and the fluff would be all over. That was fun. Searching wasn't all work. The bush was thick and picky and I didn't like the picky bushes scratching me. Worst of all were the bugs and mosquitos. We had to wear long pants and long sleeve blouses to protect our skin from the picky branches and bugs, and we were so hot. Our arms got sore because pickin' blackcurrents meant elevating your arms to reach. Being a kid meant elevating your arms a lot! Searching and picking was hart work but we just did it. (Minogiizhigokwe)

We have to find our way home to our own knowledge sources and make those pathways visible for others. I know that the pathway to emancipation is in reclaiming our own ways of knowing, being and doing and that we need to begin with who we are, what we know and where we come from. To get out of the consuming trap of being reactive to colonialism and dominance, Indigenous worldviews ought to be central in Indigenous search processes. The choice then becomes to move from a path of oppression and dominance to a path of self-determination and liberation. Our emancipation won't come if we use the colonizing tools of knowledge production. We make our knowledge and methodologies central to our searches and lift them as valid choices. The evidence is here. I say just do it!

Clearly, Indigenous methodologies *are* wholistic and relational and *are* built from an accumulation and genealogy of knowledge. The ways of searching for conscious Indigenous re-searchers who employ wholistic Indigenous methodologies are represented by the petal flower and include the following key elements:

Roots: Worldview
- Prioritize Indigenous knowledge, worldviews and principles in the research.
- Position Indigenous ways at the centre and refuse to see them in relation to western/dominant ways of knowing.

Flower Centre: Self
- Place yourself as the central presence in the research.
- Know your location: who you are, what you know and where you are from.
- Commit to re-searching relationships, Indigenous peoples and communities.
- Dedicate to recovering humanity and rehumanizing knowledge production.
- Remember your motives and re-member your relations.

Leaves: The Journey
- Embark on processes and travel on search journeys that are emergent, transformative, learning and healing.
- Attune to process.

Stem: Critical Consciousness and Supports
- Have a strong backbone: a confrontation of colonial history with socio-political honesty.
- Integrate Indigenous knowledge and decolonizing ideologies, thoughts, feelings, frameworks and models of practice.
- Acknowledge the supports of ancestors, family, community, Elders and Creation.
- Capitalize on our strengths and supports throughout.

Petals: Diversity in Methods
- Accept diverse, eclectic and varied Indigenous approaches as essential and useful for Indigenous scholars' research.
- Use a wholistic and cyclical approach that attends to Spirit, heart, mind and body.
- Use methods that are culturally relative and rooted in doing and being. Methodologies rooted in oral traditions involve ceremony, song, stories, teachings and knowledge that are creative, diverse, visual, oral, experiential and sensory based.

Environmental Contexts
- Make strategic decisions related to coping with obstacles and gatekeepers, the committee and writing oral traditions.
- Negotiate and deal with the clash of academic and Indigenous theories, methods and expectations to create change.

These wholistic methodologies move theory into practice, rhetoric into action and visions into reality. They are examples of walking the talk. Their very application brings traditional knowledge into contemporary contexts, thereby fuelling transformation, transcendence and translation of the old into the new. Indigenous re-search methods embody resistance, survival and renewal.

Gradually, Indigenous searchers are uncovering and realizing the appropriate use of Indigenous methodologies and knowledge in research. As search projects and their methodologies are disseminated, shared and talked about, doorways open up, permitting and legitimizing the presence and application of Indigenous ways of doing research. The academy is being pressured to create space for Indigenous forms of knowledge production, and change is occurring. I encourage Indigenous scholars to continue to have conversations and gatherings toward the ongoing articulation of Indigenous methodologies in search for knowledge. I am thankful for the Shawane Dagosiwin conferences on Indigenous re-search. Without a doubt we continue to establish channels to have an impact on making Indigenous ways of knowing, being and doing a solid methodological choice within the academy. Integral to the ongoing conversations is the explicit need to create "methodological space" in the academy for Indigenous searchers and scholars to actualize Indigenous knowledge. Academies need to support such gatherings and assist in creating space for collective minds to congregate, explore and learn from one another. Such spaces contribute to the development and articulation of Indigenous re-search, as this book does by providing a collective overview. We need space to be, to think and to do. Space is required to search for congruency and to explore methodological options.

The precedent has been set. This examination of Indigenous search methodologies and experiences by Indigenous scholars provides a sample of realistic possibilities. They are completed theses whereby the Indigenous scholars successfully fulfilled their academic requirements. We can meet both academic and community standards and do work which is relevant to our nations and peoples while making an academic contribution to the development of Indigenous knowledge libraries.

I hope the next precedent we set is to challenge the isolation factor of having to do our searches alone. Working in isolation contradicts Indigenous methodologies and perpetuates the duality Indigenous searchers experience. It counters our way of being and disconnects us from each other. A central tendency in all the searchers' methods was location and situating ourselves in our work. Why? Because we need to reconnect to our collective histories, memories, experiences, communities and relations. We are countering a history that severed us from our language, culture, parents, siblings, family, land, relatives and communities. Although Indigenous searchers evidence a variety of means of maintaining connections and relationships, joint dissertations would help reinforce, reconnect and re-member us, as opposed to dismembering and alienating us. Through the process of re-membering us to each other, joint graduate searches would and aid in rebuilding communities where knowledge production is once again a collective process. If we remain isolated in the academy, our searches are still alienated, thus separating us from each other and from what our searches are about — community relationships and survival. Perhaps our next leap will be to create Indigenous spaces for Indigenous forms of knowledge production. One step would be for the academy to create space for Indigenous searches to do joint dissertations.

One of the empowering lessons I now carry is that in all of the re-search projects there are personal connections and personal reasons why someone is doing the particular research that they're doing. We are inherently connected to our re-search. And I think this is true of every Indigenous person's re-search that I've read or looked at. Nobody's doing "scientifically" detached research because we are emotionally connected. And I believe that to be an important element. Moreover, Indigenous re-searchers have a motive that's connected to their community, personal life, history and experiences. We all somehow want to make life better and we want to improve the "Indian situation" in Canada. The topics in the theses I've read are wide ranging, but the motives are closely related. The meaning that we receive from our searches is related to our identity and community, improving conditions and ensuring survival.

Finding the words to conclude my search is like searching for the sky to end. What I mean is that for a process that must continue, no real conclusion exists. I cannot conclude a journey that I myself am still on. I continue to have conversations and search for methodologies of searching. There are many varieties of petal flowers out there. There is still much space for work in this area. I wish to encourage others to join the circle of Indigenous scholars in actualizing and articulating Indigenous ways of knowing into Indigenous ways of searching for knowledge. *Kaandossiwin*, this is how we come to know: we prepare, we do ceremony, we journey, we search, we converse, we process, we gather, we harvest, we make meaning, we do, we create, we transform, and we share what we know. Our Spirit walks with us on these journeys. Our ancestors accompany us. Our communities support us and our families hold us up. Last, but definitely not least, we come to know because we have to survive in a world that erodes and encroaches upon us. Our history has shown us that. We come to know because of a deep and profound love for our land, ancestors and Spirit. My search has taken me across the landscapes of unpublished dissertations where there is a wealth of knowledge. Conversations with other searchers helped to keep me grounded and attuned to our passions and our truths. A circle gathering helped us all believe that what we know is worth fighting for. How we come to know is both simple and complex; it is both fluid and concrete; it is both subjective and objective; and it is both rigorous and adaptable. How we come to know contains the traditions of a people's knowledge, whose life depended on searching, gathering and sharing. Today is no different; maybe the contexts have changed, yet we still have the knowledge and methodologies on how we come to know. Within the academy, graduate Indigenous re-searchers are successfully utilizing Indigenous methodologies and achieving academic acceptance. Change is no longer near. Change is here! *Kaandossiwin*, this is how we come to know!

References

Absolon, K. 1993. "Healing as Practice: Teachings from the Medicine Wheel." Unpublished paper prepared for the Wunska Network.

Absolon, K., and C. Willett. 2004 "Aboriginal Research: Berry Picking and Hunting in the 21st Century." *First Peoples Child and Family Review* 1, 1: 5–18.

---. 2005. "Putting Ourselves Forward: Location in Aboriginal Research Methodology." In L. Brown and S. Strega (eds.), *Research as Resistance: Critical Indigenous and Anti-Oppressive Research Approaches.* Torontom ON: Canadian Scholars Press.

Alfred, T. 2005. *Wasase: Indigenous Pathways of Action and Freedom.* Peterborough, ON: Broadview Press.

---. 2007. "Indigenizing the Academy? An Argument Against." *Journal of Higher Education. Academic Matters* 22–23.

Allen, P.G. 1986. *The Sacred Hoop: Recovering the Feminine in American Indian Traditions.* Boston: Beacon.

---. 1998. *Off the Reservation: Reflections on the Boundary-Busting, Border Crossing Loose Cannons.* Boston: Beacon Press.

Archibald, J. 1993. "Researching with Mutual Respect." *Canadian Journal of Native Education* 20, 2: 189–92.

---. 1997. "Coyote Learns to Make a Storybasket: The Place of First Nations Stories in Education." Unpublished doctoral dissertation, Simon Fraser University, Vancouver, BC.

---. 2008. *Indigenous Storywork. Educating the Heart, Mind, Body, and Spirit.* Vancouver: UBC Press.

Battiste, M. 2000a. "Maintaining Aboriginal Identity, Language, and Culture in Modern Society." In M. Battiste (ed.), *Reclaiming Indigenous Voice and Vision.* Vancouver, BC: UBC Press.

---. 2000b. *Reclaiming Indigenous Voice and Vision.* Vancouver, British Columbia, Canada: UBC Press.

Battiste, M., and J. Youngblood Henderson. 2000a. "Ethical Issues in Research." In *Protecting Indigenous Knowledge and Heritage.* Saskatoon, SK: Purich Publishing.

---. 2000b. *Protecting Indigenous Knowledge and Heritage: A Global Challenge.* Saskatoon, SK: Purich Publishing.

Benston, M. 1989. "Feminism and the Critique of Scientific Method." In A.R. Miles and G. Finn (eds.), *Feminism: From Pressure to Politics.* New York: Black Rose Books.

Benton-Banai, E. 1988. *The Mishomis Book.* Hayward, WI: Indian Country Communications.

Berkhofer, R.F. 1979. *The White Man's Indian: Images of the American Indian from Columbus to the Present.* New York: Vintage Books.

Bishop, R. 1998a. "Examples of Culturally Specific Research Practices: A Response to Tillman and Lopez." *Qualitative Studies in Education* 11, 3: 419–34.

---. 1998b. "Freeing Ourselves from Neo-Colonial Domination In Research: A Maori Approach to Creating Knowledge." *Qualitative Studies in Education* 11, 2: 199–219.

Brant Castellano, M. 2000. "Updating Aboriginal Traditions of Knowledge." In G.J.S. Dei, B.L. Hall and D.G. Rosebery (eds.), *Indigenous Knowledges in Global Contexts: Multiple Readings of Our World*. Toronto, ON: University of Toronto.

Brown, L., and S. Strega (eds.). 2005. *Research as Resistance: Critical, Indigenous, and Anti-Oppressive Approaches*. Toronto, ON: Canadian Scholar's Press.

Cajete, G. 1994. *Look to the Mountain: An Ecology of Indigenous Education* first edition. Durango, CO: Kivaki Press.

---. 2000. "Indigenous Knowledge: The Pueblo Metaphor of Indigenous Education." In M. Battiste (ed.), *Reclaiming Indigenous Voice and Vision*. Vancouver: British Columbia Press.

Calliou, S. 2001. "Decolonizing the Mind: A Non-Empirical Reflection of Some First Nations Scholarship." In K.P. Binda and S. Calliou (eds.), *Aboriginal Education in Canada: A Study in Decolonization*. Mississauga, ON: Canadian Educator's Press.

Cardinal, L. 2001. "What Is an Indigenous Perspective?" *Canadian Journal of Native Education* 25, 2: 180–82.

Churchill, W. 1992. *Fantasies of the Master Race: Literature, Cinema and the Colonization of American Indians*. Monroe, ME: Common Courage Press.

Cole, P. 2000. "First Peoples Knowings as Legitimate Discourse in Education: Coming Home to the Village." Unpublished doctoral dissertation. Vancouver, BC: Simon Fraser University.

---. 2002. "Aboriginalizing Methodology: Considering the Canoe." *International Journal of Qualitative Studies in Education* 15, 4: 447–60.

---. 2006. *Coyote Raven Go Canoeing. Coming Home to the Village*. Montreal and Kingston: McGill-Queen's University Press.

Colorado, P. 1988. "Bridging Native and Western Science." *Convergence* XXI, 2 (3): 49–68.

Colorado, P., and D. Collins. 1987. "Western Scientific Colonialism and the Re-Emergence of Native Science." *Practice: The Journal of Politics, Economics, Psychology, Sociology, and Culture* Winter: 51–65.

Dankoski, M.E. 2000. "What Makes Feminist Research?" *Journal of Feminist Family Therapy* 12,1.

Day, P., E. Blue, and M. Peake Raymond. 1998. "Conducting Research with an Urban American Indian Community: A Collaborative Approach." *Journal of American Indigan Education* 37, 2 (Winter): 21–33. <jaie.asu.edu/v37/V37S2con.htm>

Dei, G.J.S., and G.S. Johal (eds.). 2005. *Critical Issues in Anti-Racist Research Methodologies*. New York: Peter Lang Publishing.

Deloria, V.J. 1996. *Red Earth, White Lies: Native Americans and the Myth of Scientific Fact*. New York: Scribner.

---. 1998. "Comfortable Fictions and the Struggle for Turf: An Essay Review of 'The Invented Indian: Cultural Fictions and Government Policies.'" In D.A. Mihesuah (ed.), *Natives and Academics: Researching and Writing about American Indians*. Lincoln, NE: University of Nebraska Press.

---. 2002. *Evolution, Creationism, and Other Modern Myths: A Critical Inquiry*. Golden, CO: Fulcrum.

Denzin, N.K., and Y.S. Lincoln. (eds.) 2003. *Strategies of Qualitative Inquiry* Second edition. Thousand Oaks, CA: Sage Publications.

---. 2005. "Introduction: The Discipline and Practice of Qualitative Research." In

N.K. Denzin and Y.S. Lincoln (eds.), *The Sage Handbook of Qualitative Research* third edition. Thousand Oaks, CA: Sage Publications.

Duran, B., and E. Duran. 2000. "Applied Postcolonial Clinical and Research Strategies." In M. Battiste (ed.), *Reclaiming Indigenous Voice and Vision.* Vancouver, BC: UBC Press.

Dyck, L. 2001. "A Personal Journey into Science, Feminist Science, and Aboriginal Science." In K. James (ed.), *Science and Native American Communities: Legacies of Pain, Visions of Promise.* Lincoln and London: University of Nebraska Press.

Ells, C., and S. Gutfreund. 2006. "Myths about Qualitative Research and the Tri-Council Policy Statement." *The Canadian Journal of Sociology* 31, 3: 361–73.

Ermine, W. 1995. "Aboriginal Epistemology." In M. Battiste and J. Barman (eds.), *First Nations Education in Canada: The Circle Unfolds.* Vancouver, BC: UBC Press.

---. 2000. "A Critical Examination of the Ethics in Research Involving Indigenous Peoples." Unpublished master's thesis. Saskatoon, SK: University of Saskatchewan.

Faye, J. 2001. "Subverting the Captor's Language: Teaching Native Science to Students of Western Science." *American Indian Quarterly* 25, 2: 270–73.

Fitznor, D.L. 1998. "Ethics and Responsibilities in Writing American Indian history." In D.A. Mihesuah (ed), *Natives and Academics: Researching and Writing about American Indians.* Lincoln, NE: University of Nebraska Press.

Fitznor, L. 1998. "The Circle of Life: Affirming Aboriginal Philosophies in Everyday Living." In D.C. McCance (ed.), *Life Ethics in World Religions.* Atlanta, GA: Scholars Press.

---. 2002. *Aboriginal Educators' Stories: Rekindling Aboriginal Worldviews.* Toronto: Ontario Institute for Studies in Education of the University of Toronto.

Fonow, M.M., and J.A. Cook (eds.). 1991. *Beyond Methodology, Feminist Scholarship as Lived Research.* Indianapolis, IN: Indiana University Press.

Francis, D. 1992. "The Imaginary Indian: The Image of the Indian in Canadian Culture." Vancouver, BC: Arsenal Pulp Press.

Freire, D. 1996. *Pedagogy of the Oppressed* twentieth anniversary edition. New York: Continuum.

Gilchrist, L. 1995. "Kapitipis E-pimohteyahk: Aboriginal Street Youth in Vancouver, Winnipeg, and Montreal." Unpublished doctoral dissertation, Vancouver, BC: University of BC.

---. 1997. "Aboriginal Communities and Social Science Research: Voyeurism in Transition." *Native Social Work Journal* 1, 1: 6985.

Glaser, B., and A. Strauss. 1967. *The Discovery of Grounded Theory: Strategies for Qualitative Research.* New York: Aldine de Gruyter.

Graveline, F.J. 1998. *Circle Works: Transforming Eurocentric Consciousness.* Halifax, NS: Fernwood Publishing.

---. 2000. "Circle as Methodology: Enacting an Aboriginal Paradigm." *Qualitative Studies in Education* 13, 4: 361–70.

---. 2004. *Healing Wounded Hearts.* Halifax, NS: Fernwood Publishing.

Gross, L.W. 2002. "Bimaadiziwin, or the Good Life, as a Unifying Concept of Anishinabe Religion." *American Indian Culture and Research Journal* 21, 1: 15–32.

Gunn Allen, P. 1991. *Grandmothers of the Light. A Medicine Woman's Source Book.* Boston: Beacon Press.

Hampton, E. 1995a. "Memory Comes Before Knowledge: Research May Improve if Researchers Remember Their Motives." *Canadian Journal of Native Education* 21: 46–54.

---. 1995b. "Towards a Redefinition of Indian Education." In M. Battiste and J. Barman (eds.), *First Nations Education in Canada: The Circle Unfolds.* Vancouver, BC: UBC Press.

Hart, M.A. 1996. "Sharing Circles: Utilizing Traditional Practice Methods for Teaching, Helping and Supporting." In S. O'Meara and D. Wes (eds.), *From Our Eyes: Learning from Indigenous Peoples.* Toronto, ON: Garamond Press.

---. 1997. "An Ethnographic Study of Sharing Circles as a Culturally Appropriate Practice Approach with Aboriginal People." Unpublished master's thesis. Winnipeg, MB: University of Manitoba.

---. 2002. *Seeking Mino-Pimatisiwin.* Halifax, NS: Fernwood Publishing.

---. 2009. "For Indigenous People, by Indigenous People, with Indigenous People." In R. Sinclair, M.A. Hart and G. Bruyere (eds.), *Wicihitowin Aboriginal Social Work in Canada.* Winnipeg: Fernwood Publishing.

Henderson, J.Y. 2000a. "Ayukpachi: Empowering Aboriginal Thought." In M. Battiste (ed.), *Reclaiming Indigenous Voice and Vision.* Vancouver, BC: UBC Press.

---. 2000b. "Challenges of Respecting Indigenous World Views in Eurocentric Education." In R. Neil (ed.), *Voice of the Drum: Indigenous Education and Culture.* Brandon, MB: Kingfisher Publications.

Hermes, M. 1998. "Research Methods as a Situated Response: Towards a First Nations' mMethodology." *Qualitative Studies in Education* 11, 1: 155–68.

Hill Collins, P. 1991. "Learning from the Outsider Within: The Sociological Significance of Black Feminist Thought." In M.M. Fonow and J.A. Cook (eds.), *Beyond Methodology: Feminist Scholarship as Lived Research.* Indianapolis, IN: Indiana University Press.

Hill, D.J. 1995. "Lubicon Lake Nation: Spirit of Resistance." Unpublished doctoral dissertation. Hamilton, ON: McMaster University.

Holmes, L. 2000. "Heart Knowledge, Blood Memory, and the Voice of the Land: Implications of Research among Hawaiian Elders." In G.J.S. Dei and B.L. Hall (eds.), *Indigenous Knowledges in Global Contexts.* Toronto, ON: University of Toronto Press.

hooks, b. 1981. *Ain't I a Woman: Black Woman and Feminism.* Boston: South End Press.

---. 1990. *Yearning: Race, Gender, and Cultural Politics.* Boston: South End Press.

---. 1992. *Black Looks: Race and Representation.* Toronto, ON: Between the Lines.

---. 1993. *Sisters of the Yam: Black Woman and Self-Recovery.* Toronto, ON: Between the Lines.

---. 1994. "Outlaw Culture: Resisting Representations." New York: Routledge.

Janesick, V.J. 2003. "The Choreography of Qualitative Research Design." In N.K. Denzin and Y.S. Lincoln (eds.), *Strategies of Qualitative Inquiry.* Thousand Oaks, CA: Sage Publications.

Jupp, V. (ed.). 2006. *The Sage Dictionary of Social Research Methods.* Thousand Oaks, CA: Sage Publications.

Kenny, C. 2000. "A Sense of Place: Aboriginal Research as Ritual Practice." In R. Neil (ed.), *Voices of the Drum: Indigenous Education and Culture.* Brandon, MB:

Kingfisher Publications.

Kincheloe, J.L., and L.M. Semali (eds.). 1999. *What Is Indigenous Knowledge? Voices from the Academy.* New York: Falmer Press.

Kirby, S., and K. McKenna. 1989. *Experience Research Social Change: Methods from the Margins.* Toronto, ON: Garamond Press.

Kovach, M. 2005. "Emerging from the Margins: Indigenous Methodologies." In L. Brown and S. Strega (eds.) *Research as Resistance: Critical Indigenous and Anti-Oppressive Approaches.* Toronto, ON: Canadian Scholars Press.

---. 2009. *Indigenous Methodologies: Characteristics, Conversations, and Contexts.* Toronto: University of Toronto Press.

Lather, P. 1991. *Getting Smart: Feminist Research and Pedagogy with/in the Postmodern.* New York: Routledge.

Lischke, U., and D.T. McNab (eds.) 2005. *Walking a Tightrope: Aboriginal People and Their Representations.* Waterloo, ON: Wilfred Laurier Press.

Little Bear, L. 2000. "Jagged Worldviews Colliding." In M. Battiste (ed.), *Reclaiming Indigenous Voice and Vision.* Vancouver, BC: UBC Press.

Lopes, A. 2006. "Participatory Action Research." In V. Jupp (ed.), *Sage Dictionary of Social Research Methods.* Thousand Oaks, CA: Sage Publications.

Maina, F. 2003. "Indigenous Insider Academics: Educational Research or Advocacy?" *Canadian Journal of Native Studies* XXIII, 2: 207–26.

Marker, M. 2004. "Theories and Discipline as Sites of Struggle: The Reproduction of Colonial Dominance through the Controlling of Knowledge in the Academy." *Canadian Journal of Native Education* 28, 1/2: 102–10.

Marsden, D. 2005. "Indigenous Wholistic Theory for Health: Enhancing Traditional-Based Indigenous Health Services in Vancouver." Unpublished doctoral dissertation. Vancouver, BC: University of British Columbia.

Martin, K. 2002. "Ways of Knowing, Ways of Being and Ways of Doing: Developing a Theoretical Framework and Methods for Indigenous Re-Search and Indigenist Research." Unpublished manuscript. James Cook University, Queensland, Australia.

Martin-Hill, D. 2008. *The Lubicon Lake Nation, Indigenous Knowledge and Power.* Toronto: University of Toronto Press.

Martinez, A., and M. Stuart (eds.). 2003. *Out of the Ivory Tower: Feminist Research for Social Change.* Toronto, ON: Sumach Press.

Max, K. 2005. "Anti-Colonial Research, Working as an Ally with Aboriginal Peoples." In G.J.S. Dei and G.S. Johal (eds.), *Critical Issues in Anti-Racist Research Methodologies.* New York: Peter Lang Publishign.

McGuire, P. 2003. "Worldview in Transition: The Changing Nature of the Lake Nipigon Anishinabek Metis." Unpublished master's thesis. Thunder Bay, ON: Lakehead University.

McLeod, N. 2005. "Exploring Cree Narrative Memory." Unpublished doctoral dissertation. Regina ,SK, University of Regina.

McPherson, D.H., and J.D. Rabb. 2001. "Indigeneity in Canada: Spirituality, the Sacred and Survival." *International Journal of Canadian Studies* 23, Spring: 57–79.

---. 2003. Restoring the Interpretive Circle: Community-Based Research and Education. *International Journal of Canadian Studies* 28 (Fall), 133–61.

Menzies, C. 2004. "Putting Words Into Action: Negotiating Collaborative Research in Gitxaala." *Canadian Journal of Native Education* 28,1/2: 15–32.

Michell, H. 1999. "Pakitinasowin: Tobacco Offerings in Exchange for Stories and the Ethic of Reciprocity in First Nations Research." *Journal of Indigenous Thought* 2, 2.

Mihesuah, D.A. 1998a. "Introduction." In D.A. Mihesuah (ed.) *Natives and Academics: Researching and Writing about American Indians.* Lincoln, NE: University of Nebraska Press.

---. (ed.). 1998b. *Natives and Academics: Researching and Writing about American Indians.* Lincoln, NE: University of Nebraska Press.

Miles, R. 1989. *Racism.* New York: Routledge.

Money, M.A. 1997. "Broken Arrows: Images of Native Americans in the Popular Western." In D. Morrison (ed.), *American Indian Studies: An Interdisciplinary Approach to Contemporary Issues.* New York: Peter Lang.

Monture-Angus, P.A. 1995. *Thunder in my Soul: A Mohawk Woman Speaks.* Halifax, NS: Fernwood Publishing.

Nabigon, H. 2006. *The Hollow Tree. Fighting Addiction with Traditional Native Healing.* Montreal and Kingston: McGill-Queen's University Press.

Nabigon, H., R. Hagey, S. Webster and R. MacKay. 1998. The Learning Circle as a Research Method: The Trickster and Windigo in Research. *Native Social Work Journal* 2 (1): 113–37.

Pinderhughes, E. 1989. *Understanding Race, Ethnicity, and Power: The Key to Efficacy in Clinical Practice.* Toronto: Maxwell Macmillan.

Potss, K., and L. Brown. 2005. "Becoming an Anti-Oppressive Researcher." In L. Brown and S. Strega (eds.), *Research as Resistance: Critical, Indigenous, and Anti-Oppressive Approaches.* Toronto: Canadian Scholars' Press.

Reason, P., and H. Bradbury (eds.). 2006. *Handbook of Action Research: The Concise Paperback Edition.* London: Sage Publications.

Rice, B. 2003. "A Methodology Based on Rotinoshonni Traditions." In J. Oakes, R. Riewe, K. Wilde, A. Edmunds and A. Dubois (eds.), *Native Voices in Research.* Winnipeg, MB: Aboriginal Issues Press.

Rigney, L. 1999. "Internalization of an Indigenous Anticolonial Cultural Critique of Research Methodologies: A Guide to Indigenist Research Methodology and Its Principles." *Wicazo SA Review: A Journal of Native American Studies Review* 14, 2: 109–21.

Ross, L. 2005. "Personalizing Methodology: Narratives of Imprisonment." In I. Hernandez-Avila (ed.), *Reading Native American Women: Critical/Creative Representations.* New York: Altamira Press.

Royal Commission on Aboriginal Peoples. 1996. *Report of the Royal Commission on Aboriginal Peoples.* Ottawa: Queens Printer.

Simpson, L. 1999. "The Construction of Traditional Ecological Knowledge: Issues, Implications and Insights." Unpublished doctoral dissertation. Winnipeg, MB: University of Manitoba.

---. 2001. "Aboriginal Peoples and Knowledge: Decolonizing Our Process." *Canadian Journal of Native Studies* XXI, 1: 137–48.

Smith, G.H. 2000. "Protecting and Respecting Indigenous Knowledge." In M. Battiste (ed.), *Reclaiming Indigenous Voice and Vision.* Vancouver, BC: UBC Press.

Sinclair, R. 2003. "Indigenous Research in Social Work: The Challenges of Operationalizing Worldview." *Native Social Work Journal* 5: 117–39.

Smith, L.T. 1999. *Decolonizing Methodologies: Research and Indigenous Peoples.* New York, NY: Zed Books.

---. 2000. "Kaupapa Maori Research." In M. Battiste (ed.), *Reclaiming Indigenous Voice and Vision.* Vancouver, BC: UBC Press.

---. 2005. "On Tricky Ground: Researching the Native in the Age of Uncertainty." In N.K. Denzin, and Y.S. Lincoln (eds.), *The Sage Handbook of Qualitative Research* third edition. Thousand Oaks, CA: Sage Publications.

---. 2006. "Introduction." *International Journal of Qualitative Studies in Education* 195: 549–552.

St. Denis, V. 1992. "Community-Based Participatory Research: Aspects of the Concept Relevant for Practice." *Native Studies Review* 8, 2: 51–74.

Steinhauser, E. 2002. "Thoughts on an Indigenous Research Methodology." *Canadian Journal of Native Education* 26, 2: 69–81.

Steinhauser, P. 2001. "Situating Myself in Research." *Canadian Journal of Native Education* 25, 2: 183–87.

Stevenson, W. 2000. "Decolonizing Tribal Histories." Unpublished doctoral dissertation. Berkeley, CA: University of California,.

Stiffarm, L.A. (ed.). 1998. *As We See.... Aboriginal Pedagogy.* Saskatoon, SK: University of Saskatchewan Extension Press.

Stringer, E.T. 1999. *Action Research* second edition. London: Sage Publications.

Talbot, S. 2002. "Academic Indianismo: Social Scientific Research in American Indian Studies." *American Indian Culture and Research Journal* 26, 4: 67–96.

Tang, Y., and C. Joiner (eds.). 2006. *Synergic Inquiry: A Collaborative Action Methodology.* Thousand Oakes, CA: Sage Publications.

TeHennepe, S. 1997. "Respectful Research: This Is What My People Say, You Learn it From the Story." In S. De Castell and M. Bryson (eds.), *Radical In<ter>ventions: Identity, Politics, and Difference/s in Educational Praxis.* New York: State University of New York Press.

Thomas, R.A. 2005. "Honouring the Oral Traditions of My Ancestors Through Storytelling." In L. Brown and S. Strega (eds.), *Research as Resistance: Critical Indigenous, and Anti-Oppressive Approaches.* Toronto, ON: Canadian Scholars' Press.

Voyageur, C.J. 2000. "Contemporary Aboriginal Women in Canada." In D. Long and O.P. Dickason (eds.), *Vision of the Heart: Canadian Aboriginal Issues.* Toronto, ON: Harcourt.

---. 2003. "The Community Owns You: Experiences of Female Chiefs in Canada." In A. Martinez and M. Stuart (eds.), *Out of the Ivory Tower: Feminist Research for Social Change.* Toronto, ON: Sumach Press.

Wa Thiong'o, N. 1986. *Decolonising the Mind: The Politics of Language in African Literature.* Oxford, UK: James Currey/Heinemann.

Weber-Pillwax, C. 1999. "Indigenous Research Methodology: Exploratory Discussion of an Elusive Subject." *Journal of Educational Thought* 33, 1: 31–45.

---. 2001. 'What Is Indigenous research?' *Canadian Journal of Native Education* 25, 2: 166–74.

Weenie, A. 1998. "Aboriginal Pedagogy: The Sacred Circle Concept." In L.A.

Stiffarm (ed.), *As We See... Aboriginal Pedagogy*. Saskatoon, SK: University of Saskatchewan University Extension Press.

Wilson, S. 2001. "What Is an Indigenous Research Methodology?" *Canadian Journal of Native Education* 25, 2: 175–79.

---. 2003. "Progressing Toward an Indigenous Research Paradigm in Canada and Australia." *Canadian Journal of Native Education* 27, 2: 161–78.

---. 2008. *Research Is Ceremony: Indigenous Research Methods*. Halifax, NS: Fernwood Publishing.

Young, M. 2003. "Anishinabemowin: A Way of Seeing the World Reclaiming My Identity." *Canadian Journal of Native Education* 27, 1: 101–107.